Message from
MOSCOW

Message from
MOSCOW

BY AN OBSERVER

JONATHAN CAPE
THIRTY BEDFORD SQUARE
LONDON

FIRST PUBLISHED 1969
© 1969 JONATHAN CAPE LTD

JONATHAN CAPE LTD
30 BEDFORD SQUARE, LONDON WCI

SBN 224 61791 5

PRINTED AND BOUND BY
BUTLER AND TANNER LTD, FROME AND LONDON

CONTENTS

1 INTRODUCTION

A REPORT about a nation's mood is so delicate an undertaking that, as I begin this one, I find myself thinking of the traditional disclaimers and prefatory apologies that have always made me impatient in the books of others. 'I can only report what I saw ... ' 'My observations and experiences were, of course, limited ... ' 'The human psyche is so complex and contradictory that it is extremely difficult to generalize intelligently about a single person, not to speak of two hundred million-odd of them ... '

These truisms, which apply, of course, to any attempt to describe any country, might well be taken for granted. But at the risk of labouring the obvious, I want to call attention to a few of the special hazards of reporting about Russia. This extraordinary country's vastness and 'inscrutability' (which can be taken to mean her variations from European habits) are well known. Besides, there is the great store of secrets—Russia's special history, pressures and reactions; and the accumulation of folk wisdom, sayings and attitudes that are difficult for a foreigner, living principally in the major cities, to grasp. Although I am freer to travel and mix with people than the vast majority of foreign residents here, it is unthinkable that I could settle for a time in a town or village on, say, the far bank of the Volga and enlighten myself there on local customs and attitudes, which may be more typical than those I encounter in Moscow and Leningrad.

And this leads naturally to another kind of Russian

secret: the governmental, or state variety. It is difficult to over-emphasize the penchant for secrecy of Russia's leaders. Except for assiduously rehearsed public appearances, they are almost totally hidden from ordinary Russians. They live behind high, guarded fences and ride in curtained limousines. They work in their villas on Lenin Hills and Kremlin offices in almost total seclusion, and their personal lives are never mentioned in print. They move through the city silently, as if (like the pre-war Japanese emperors) their mortal existences and activities were incompatible with their roles as Leaders of the Party—that is, public servants and anointed gods.

This is not altogether unpleasant by contrast with the often vulgar publicity surrounding every move, however private, of the leaders of many Western countries. But since the Russian oligarchs exercise vast power—since their prerogatives extend to every sphere of public life, including many matters that are regarded as wholly private in other countries—their obsessive secrecy contributes abundantly to the mysteriousness of Russian life. It is not only that one knows nothing (except what is rumoured) about, say, President Podgorny's wife, relaxations and tastes—or even about the health and whereabouts of M. Podgorny himself for considerable periods of time. More important, one knows almost nothing (except what is reported in the form of the usual slogans) about whom the President (actually Chairman of the Praesidium of the Supreme Soviet) is seeing and what he is saying in his office. In other words, the way decisions are reached—ranging from what films can be shown, to what divisions have been sent to the Chinese border—is also hidden. In fact, many of the most important decisions and facts are denied altogether, or their meaning and intention elaborately camouflaged or distorted. Therefore, the clues to national life and mood which in Western countries can ordinarily be found in open debate and reporting are missing here.

In addition, there are the contrasts. What is true in Moscow is not necessarily true in Leningrad—certainly not in Saratov, Yalta, Vilnius or a bleak little northern village. Nor is it even true everywhere in Moscow. For every dozen stories about, say, police brutality in the capital, there are four or five about unusual consideration for and gentleness towards citizens—even drunk citizens—in distress.

And of course there are the glaring contrasts: between deeply cultured, educated men, and coarse muzhiks; between dazzling scientific creativity and technological achievements, and drinking-water hand-drawn from wells and housewives doing their washing on river-banks.

'However long you live in Russia,' wrote Konstantin Paustovsky (one of the few widely published authors of recent years who is universally respected by people who care about literature), 'it never ceases to astonish you by its contrasts.' This, naturally enough, makes Russia exciting to live in, but difficult to generalize about with any certainty or honesty.

Moreover, the difficulty increases in proportion to the time one spends here. It is a commonplace that a summer tourist can describe the people and attitudes of a country more easily than a resident of many years. The tourist has seen less of the complexity and contradiction; he has met fewer people who tell him conflicting facts. And, naturally, he has fewer doubts.

'I knew too much,' wrote a man recently who was trying to describe his own country to others. 'I could sometimes prove one thing or its contrary with equal ease. I was embarrassed by the exceptions.' I myself could have written much more about Russia—and written it much more quickly—after the summer of my first arrival. But at the time of writing this, I have spent three years here.

*   *   *

I should explain two 'procedural' points now. From time to time, I will quote comments and remarks of my Russian acquaintances and friends. These are not verbatim quotations. Naturally, I do not go to flats, parks, and theatres with a tape recorder; that would be silly and embarrassing—as well as dangerous, if the tapes were to fall into the wrong hands. For this reason, too—to protect my friends—I have disguised many of them. Their real identities, like mine, must be camouflaged. This subterfuge is distasteful, but it is by far the lesser of two evils. In fact, I should be suspicious of any writing from inside Russia now that was *not* published under a pen name. Anyone writing under his own name has either learnt so little about the country that his report will not anger the authorities, or does not care about the fate of his friends who told him the important—and unpleasant— things he knows.

However, I do take notes after interesting conversations, and they are kept in a safe place by a friend. The quotations I have used in this book are based on these notes, and on the comments that ring in my ears after many repetitions, and do not need recording.

They are the kind of things these people say every day— and as close as I can make them to the way they are said. The fact that this or that statement was made by a doctor and not a translator, or a woman born in Kiev and not Kharkov, makes, I think, little difference to the substance or implication of the remarks themselves. I have tried to make no changes that would mislead a reader about anything important.

The second 'procedural' matter concerns the use, or mis-use, of 'Russian' and 'Soviet'. Russia, of course, is but one of the fifteen republics that comprise the Union of Soviet Socialist Republics. Technically speaking, therefore, 'Soviet' or the 'Soviet Union' should be used in many places where I write 'Russian' or 'Russia'. Certainly this is true when I refer to the central government in Moscow, central institutions, and the 'system' or 'regime'.

However, I prefer to use the traditional 'Russian' where I can, when it will not create excessive confusion. For although all fifteen republics are equal under the constitution and the law, the Russian republic is far more equal than the others. Its territory comprises nearly three-fourths of the Soviet Union, and its influence is perhaps equally preponderant. Russia is the centre, inspiration and driving force of the great majority of plans, projects and controls, not only inside the lopsidedly large Russian Republic but everywhere in the Soviet Union.

Moreover, there is a personal bias for my use of 'Russian' rather than 'Soviet'. Except for brief holidays in Central Asia, Georgia, the Ukraine and the resorts of the Baltic and Black Seas, I have travelled little outside the area that is traditionally known as Russia. Obviously my comments must not be taken to apply equally to all the various nationalities of the Soviet Union with their distinctly different histories and cultures. I myself feel, though not everybody agrees, that the best way to understand the 'Soviet experience' is through the study of Russian history. At any rate, the Russians and the Russian experience are what chiefly interest me, and I have restricted my observation primarily to them.

*　　*　　*

And now two words, as the Russians say, about myself. Anyone writing about a subject so emotionally charged as that of Russia should, I think, lay his cards on the table at the outset. But this, too—my own attitude towards Russia— is contradictory and confusing.

Before I lived in Russia, nothing angered me more than the dogmatism, self-righteousness and anti-humanism of Western professional anti-Communists. Yet now, I find myself agreeing with some of their analyses of Soviet rule, if not the premises on which they are based or the social goals they are meant to serve. I strongly regret this turn of affairs, and still disrelish 'anti-Communism'. 'In fighting the Communists,' as Koestler remarked, 'one is always embarrassed by one's allies.'

There are moments when I love this country much more, and much more intensely, than any other I've known, including my own; and other moments when I hate it just as intensely—when I nearly choke with the need to leave on the next plane, despite the sacrifices of my studies and career that would entail. I am not a Communist or 'Communist-sympathizer' in the narrow sense of that term, but there are moments when, in spite of myself, I am deeply moved by Communism's message and appeal: I feel like joining the triumphant march to a better world, instead of standing on the sidelines, scoffing at the waste of energy. And there are other moments when the Communist Party, Marxism–Leninism, everything specifically 'Soviet' in the Soviet system, seem a gigantic, vicious, maddening fraud. No doubt my reportage and commentary will reflect this ambivalence. I hope they do. An attempt to be consistent in attitude, to maintain an even tone on all days about all things, would be quite out of keeping with what life here is like.

At the moment, however, my 'balance of attitudes' has shifted towards the negative. The failures of Soviet life are what I notice most often this winter, and what I want to describe now. Why? Because of the 'events' in Czechoslovakia—the immediate stimulus for this book. And the monstrous lies preached about them here, a thousand times a day. And the knouting of the one Russian in a million who dares to announce that he disagrees. Perhaps it is because of my own disillusionment. I am a socialist by inclination, and used to feel that the Motherland of socialism, despite its hard history, its terrible errors and terrible misfortunes, nevertheless had much to teach the world about running a civilized, twentieth-century state. It was a fond hope, indulged from afar; from the inside, I am more and more convinced it was a sad mistake. The behaviour of the Russian government in Czechoslovakia, where they are exposed to the world press and measured against European standards, is bad enough; they run their own country, having protected themselves with compulsive zeal against outside scrutiny, correspondingly worse.

And this takes me to another point. The failures that catch my eye, these astounding departures from civilized standards (civilized in the broadest sense of the word), are almost unknown outside Russia. Every intelligent Russian knows them, lives with them, has learnt to take them for granted; often he no longer recognizes them—or, if he does, merely shrugs his shoulders. In other countries, they would be the subject of outraged exposés by the press, of parliamentary questions and investigating commissions. Here, they are not only ignored, but elaborately concealed and officially denied.

And this itself is one of the most depressing defects. These failures are not reported in Russian newspapers, for Russian newspapers are slogan-level advertisements for the Party, government, army and Motherland, and pretend to little else. Nor, indeed, do they often appear in the Western press. For most Western correspondents here live in the ghetto of the Western colony: isolated, watched, afraid for themselves and their Russian informants, if they have them. They are followed often and conspicuously enough to make them assume, as the security police want them to, that the surveillance is constant. It is taken for granted their telephones are tapped and flats and offices equipped with listening and recording devices. No Russian official may be interviewed about any subject without permission from the foreign press department, and the conditions are such that unauthorized conversations with non-official Russians are risky for both parties if the matters discussed are in any way sensitive.

And beyond these severe limitations imposed by the Soviet authorities, many correspondents impose additional restrictions on themselves. Those who speak almost no Russian — still a considerable percentage — cannot hope to break out of the isolation, even for an afternoon. And many others who know the language are too afraid to converse with Russians, even in a cinema or football stadium — not to speak of inviting a Russian girl or couple to spend an evening with them. Moreover, they do not enjoy Russian films or football matches; they prefer Western-colony parties and films shown in foreign embassies. A powerful — and understandable — paranoia overcomes even the most resolute new correspondents after several months in Moscow, and they tend to seek out each other's company for relaxation, commiseration over the difficulty of reporting real news, and escape from the steady, exhausting pressures of their hostile environment. It is unfortunate, but again understandable, that many of these correspondents spend some ninety-five per cent of their time within the foreign colony and with their officially assigned interpreters and other native 'assistants', who, of course, report on their activities. They have lost the habit even of taking a stroll through the side streets of Moscow, and buying a jar of pickles there instead of in the special foreign-currency stores or embassy canteens. In other words, the isolation imposed on them by Soviet conditions encourages them to isolate themselves still more.

There are, by contrast, a handful of Western correspondents who have lived here for decades, and know Russia and many Russians intimately. They are superbly knowledgable, and in other countries would make excellent interpretative reporters. But the members of this tiny group are even more careful about what they write than the correspondents who are serving their two- or three-year assignments. They more than anyone must take pains to protect their close and trusted Russian friends, as well as their settled (and extremely comfortable) way of life in Moscow. They are never free of the fear of expulsion, still a frequent occurrence in this country. The fear manifests itself most obviously in the contrast between what they say in private conversation and what they file for their newspapers. The blackmail of deportation is implicit in all the conditions of a foreigner's life here—and sometimes made explicit as well: correspondents' copy is scrutinized, and they are told in so many words by Foreign Ministry officials that their continued presence in Russia depends directly on what they write about the country.

So the people who have the greatest knowledge about 'inside' Russia are those who have most to lose by sharing it. The paradox was put to me soon after my arrival by a veteran Danish correspondent: 'The more you know about this country, the less you're able to write. Because the unofficial things are always the dangerous ones, and you've learnt them from some Russian who trusts you and whom you must protect. That's why the important stories about Russia are as secret as ever.'

More secret, in fact, than even a few years ago. The Danish correspondent lives in one of the special buildings for foreign diplomats and journalists on the new Kutuzovsky Prospekt. I visited him recently, and noticed something new: a ten-foot wire fence round the building, visibly and very crudely isolating it from the neighbouring courtyards, from the city, from ordinary Russian life. The fence is more a symbolic than a physical barrier, for there has always been a K.G.B. guard (posing as ordinary policemen) at these buildings, inspecting all cars and visitors. But it is meant to warn all Russians once again of the dangers of acquaintance with a foreign correspondent. And although the Danish correspondent continues to see his Russian friends in back-street cafés and for walks, none now visit his flat.

He has told me the pressure to write copy acceptable to these press officials is now stronger than it has been for years. 'Now "neutral" stories are considered unacceptable,' he said. 'You have to say favourable things about the country. They're now operating under the theory, "If you're not with us, you're against us." ' This pressure has caused him to write fewer and fewer articles. 'If I want to do a story about, say, new cars, I can't do it honestly without describing the tremendous shortage, the black market servicing, and so on. But this is considered "anti-Soviet". It's very hard to find a story you can tell with a clear conscience — without leaving so many important things unsaid you feel you're actually lying.'

Pressure of another kind is now being exerted in the case of an English correspondent whose tour in Moscow recently ended. Dissatisfied with his paper's attitude towards the Soviet Union, the press department has refused for months to issue a visa for the man selected to replace him. Instead of publishing this story, the newspaper—one of the three or four most influential and respected in the world, whose name is a symbol for excellence in journalism—has kept entirely silent about it, for fear of provoking the Soviet authorities into closing its Moscow bureau indefinitely. This kind of blackmail is a matter of course here, and every foreigner, even the most mighty, submits to it to a greater or lesser degree.

* * *

But I am ahead of myself. At this point I wanted to say simply that I understand as well as anyone that a report about a country's mood must, in the nature of things, be severely selective. To tell the 'whole truth' is of course impossible, and I make no such claim—indeed, I had no such goal when writing this book. I have tried only to describe a few characteristic aspects of the Russian scene—to suggest its flavour —on and around that day of days when Czechoslovakia was invaded and I was jolted and disappointed enough to reflect on the place of that event in the pattern of daily Russian life.

B

2 AUGUST THE TWENTY-FIRST

On the morning of August 21st, I woke up soon after ten o'clock and lay in bed for perhaps another half an hour, dozing and dreaming, hearing a fly buzzing lustily from the oilcloth of the night table to the window, but being soothed rather than irritated by him: somehow he helped swell the feeling of summer peace that pervaded the room. I lay there as long as I liked, luxuriating with a clear conscience: I had finished the few projects I'd undertaken during the holidays and had nothing important to do until the new term began in September. My bed, called a 'cot' in student jargon, was narrow, noisy, made of bare metal tubing, and much too soft in the springs. But I'd grown fond of it, like all previous beds I'd had in my life. Besides, I was one of the lucky ones: I was in a room for two, instead of four, eight or ten; and my room-mate had been away for almost three weeks, visiting his parents in a village near Volgograd. Having a room of one's own in a Russian student hostel is a rare and enchanting luxury — almost a holiday in itself.

I was lucky, too, because my building is near the very centre of the city and not, like the university hostels, in the stark, newly built outskirts. We are a ten-minute walk from Red Square (which I hardly visit now, except to rush in and out of G.U.M. and meet a girl who lives close by). The hostel is attached to the B——Institute, one of the country's better-known institutions of higher education. It's academic standards were established during the last decades of tsarist

Pravda displayed for public consumption—for people who do not want to spend two kopecks (worth roughly a penny) on their own copy. Everywhere in the city, national and Moscow newspapers are displayed in special glass cases with weatherbeaten wooden frames. This one was nailed to a sagging fence screening the courtyard of a block of flats. I scarcely glanced at it, expecting nothing newsworthy, and seeing apparent confirmation of this in that only two or three people out of the crowd of pedestrians had stopped to look. By early afternoon, however, I had learned that it was this issue of *Pravda* that had announced the invasion of Czechoslovakia, and I bought a copy and read it carefully— an arduous task; the content is so turgid and tedious, so ploddingly repetitive, that merely scanning the pages and glimpsing the ritual phrases provokes a faint headache. But this was an important edition, and since it helps convey the atmosphere of Russia on August 21st, I want to analyse the material on the first page. (A complete translation of this first page appears in Appendix I, page 248 ff.)

The now famous Tass announcement was in the left-hand corner:

> Tass is authorized to announce that Party and state leaders of the Czechoslovak Socialist Republic have appealed to the Soviet Union and other allied states to provide urgent help to the fraternal Czechoslovak people, including help by their armed forces ... The fraternal countries firmly and resolutely oppose any outside threat whatsoever to their unshakable solidarity. No one will ever be allowed to wrest a single link from the community of socialist states.

It was a short statement under a solid but undramatic headline—articles dealing with subjects like a new

educational reform are often given more prominent type. It was also the only unusual article among the sixteen on the page. The others were entirely representative of a normal day's news.

The foreign news, in addition to the Tass announcement, consisted of six items: (1) renewed attacks by the N.L.F. in South Vietnam, in which heavy losses were inflicted on American forces; (2) protest demonstrations by Uruguayan workers and students; (3) projected reforms of local government in Syria; (4) renewed violations of the cease-fire agreement by Israeli 'aggressors' in Jordan; (5) the spectacular success of a Soviet trade fair in London that was dazzling English people with the marvels of Soviet life and achievements; and (6) a press conference held by the Finnish Communist Party on celebrations for its forthcoming fiftieth anniversary.

The last item was as typical as any of the six in terms of style, depth of reporting and interest to the Russian people. Surely no other major newspaper in the world, save perhaps in Finland itself, paid any attention at all to the utterly routine press conference in Helsinki. But *Pravda — on the day of the invasion —* selected it from all the events in the world and gave it prominence on the front page, under the headline, 'A Glorious Date':

Helsinki, 20th (Tass) In connection with the forthcoming celebrations on the occasion of the fiftieth anniversary of the Communist Party of Finland, a press conference was held today in the C.C. [Central Committee] of the C.P.F. [Communist Party of Finland].

The General Secretary of the Party, Ville Pessi, the Chairman, Aarne Saarinen, and the Chairman of the Organizational Committee arranging the anniversary celebrations, Anna-Lisa Huvonen, told Finnish and

foreign journalists about the forthcoming festivities, which will take place on August 23rd–25th, and answered questions.

In connection with the anniversary, an exhibition devoted to the history of the C.P.F. will open in the Finnish capital's House of Culture. On August 24th, a seminar will start work on the subject 'C.P.F.–Revolution–Youth'. The principal report at the jubilee plenum of the C.C. C.P.F., which is also scheduled for August 24th, will be given by the General Secretary of the Party, Ville Pessi ...

The domestic news, as always, seemed even more carefully written to ensure no one would actually read it. It was the kind of copy churned out day after day, surely in the knowledge that it cannot possibly mean anything to anyone except, perhaps, to the people named in the articles. That copy is written in this style is a deliberate decision; it is an essential part of the ritual of Soviet rule.

There were reports, on the domestic 'front', about: (1) the opening in Chardzhou of an exhibition entitled, 'V. I. Lenin and Technical Progress' (... 'Collections of articles, brochures and magazines about technical progress in the U.S.S.R. and the Leninist plan for the scientific-technical rearming of industry are displayed on the stands ... '); (2) the opening of fifty exhibitions devoted to Lenin in the cities, towns and villages of the western Ukraine ('The staff of the Lvov branch of the V. I. Lenin Central Museum is helping collective farms, enterprises and educational institutions of the western regions of the Ukraine to organize Leninist halls and rooms ... '); (3) the opening of a congress of the World Energy Conference in Moscow (' ... in the name of the Praesidium of the Supreme Soviet of the

U.S.S.R. and the Soviet government, the congress's delegates and guests were greeted by the Vice-Chairman of
the Praesidium of the U.S.S.R. Supreme Soviet, Ya. E.
Kalnberzin.')

Then followed news of the campaign for the harvest on
the farms. Today it came from Saratovsky region, whose
capital is Saratov, on the Volga:

> The left-bank Volga steppe stretched out over hun-
> dreds of kilometres. Sixteen of the most important
> corn-growing districts of Saratovsky region are situated
> here. At this time, the sounds of the harvest never cease
> on the boundless steppe.
>
> It was last winter that the Maxim Gorky collective
> farm of Dergachevsky district inaugurated its campaign
> for improving the quality of its produce and for growing
> top-quality corn. Based on the example of Saratov's
> leading factories, the agricultural experts worked out
> a system of procedures to eliminate defects in the collec-
> tive's work.
>
> 'The first commandment of every combine operator,
> every collective farmer,' recounts the Chairman of the
> collective, N. Melnikov, and the Secretary of the part-
> com [Party committee], R. Barzhanov, 'has become the
> maxim: check the quality of your own work yourself,
> before handing it in to the brigade leader or control
> supervisor. If you see a defect somewhere — correct it ... '

There was the usual collection of articles devoted to
factory news. One plant in Vilnius had overfulfilled its
production of linoleum by ten per cent. Another article
announced the completion 'a few days ago' (apparently
there's no haste in reporting these things) of an oxygen-
converting complex in a distant steel plant. And a third,

rather lengthy report described the campaign for improving production in an electric locomotive plant.

> The work of the thousands of men building electric locomotives is going forward with great intensity. In the various departments, new methods of improving the reliability of locomotives and of implementing all the new ideas introduced into the life of the enterprise by the economic reform are being worked out.

Finally, in the top right-hand corner — the most prominent position on the page — there was a photo-story about the construction of a dam beyond the Caucasus. The photographs (the only ones on the page) were, inevitably, of massive construction machinery and a radiant worker.

> The scope of construction in our country is unparalleled ... The clamour of excavators, scrapers and bulldozers carries deep into the steppe ... In the photograph below: bulldozer-driver Valdimir Shustov. He has been awarded the title, 'Best Skilled Worker on the Construction Site.'

Looking at the *Pravda* page now and trying to imagine its impression on people not accustomed to reading the newspaper, I am afraid my point may be lost. It may seem a quaint, perhaps an interesting approach to news — I myself was fascinated by it for a short time after my first arrival. But the copy has barely changed since then: the identical phrases and slogans, the 'Sovietese' style, the self-congratulatory, yet whining-and-exhorting sermons — it seems as if the only new element consists in the names of the different tractor drivers, factories and construction sites which are substituted for the old names each morning. And every day, a hundred times a day, the story of the Revolution is retold, in a tone appropriate to the Second Coming, so that everyone will be properly grateful to the Party that gave him his glorious new life. And every day, in every conceivable way, thanks are chanted to Lenin. (On the first page of this issue of *Pravda* alone, his name appeared eleven times. On the inside pages, the frequency was greater; I stopped counting at fifty mentions.)

This, of course, is one issue of one newspaper. The accumulation of a thousand virtually identical to it drives one sometimes to the edge of despair. And it is not only the newspapers: 'news' stories and editorials exactly like these are broadcast between ten and twenty times a day on Moscow radio. Indeed, *Pravda* itself is read aloud, in tones even more melodramatic and quiveringly religious than that of the copy itself. Moreover, the same material pours forth, day in and day out, from every magazine, journal, government and Party office, and a mountain of tracts and brochures.

All this is so much a part of Russian life that one is hardly aware of it except at those brief moments when there is a shift in the 'line' or when something particularly grating or fatuous calls attention to itself and pierces the customary immunity. Normally, the propaganda is like a steady but faint static somewhere in the background of daily life and consciousness. In this sense the presentation of the present version of the Marxist–Leninist message can be compared to advertising in America. That is to say, if all the most insistent and obnoxious advertisements for deodorants and detergents, motor cars and headache remedies were imagined to be emanating from the 'creative departments' of a single corporation, and that corporation had a monopoly of insight, virtue and the qualities necessary to achieve happiness and the 'American way of life', one might get an idea of the effect of the Party's incessant message. Even this unpleasant hallucination, however, probably underestimates the uniformity, staleness and above all the intensity of the Marxist–Leninist ideological 'advertising'; for it is repeated on every radio station, in every newspaper and in the ceremonial introduction to every amateur evening, public birthday celebration and television spectacular.

And in substance, advertising in America, however vulgar and stupefying, is innocuous compared to Party propaganda. If large sections of America resemble a giant supermarket for the hawking and selling of goods, all Russia is an even larger revival meeting where the mind and soul, damnation and salvation, are the issues. Here it is not mere goods and services that are being hawked, but nothing less than cosmic goals and a total explanation of man, society and history — together with the Party's advertisement for itself as the sole interpreter of these matters, and therefore the sole source of wisdom, truth and happiness. For this reason, the Marxist–Leninist message is much more mesmerizing than American advertising, and it is correspondingly more important to shut oneself off from its bombardments in order to lead a sane, peaceful life.

This is why I didn't stop to read the issue of *Pravda* on display that morning. Most of my friends do not bother to look at the national newspapers for weeks in succession. Among liberal students, in fact, the measure of a man is often taken by his newspaper-reading habits: if he reads *Pravda* or *Izvestiya* for anything but their unconscious humour, they know they will have nothing in common with him.

* * *

I walked on slowly towards the café, stopping to buy a pair of shoe-laces from an old legless ex-soldier, then stopping again to watch a housewife arguing shrilly with a rough-looking lorry driver who was apparently delivering a new sink. A group of schoolboys, sensing I was a foreigner, asked me the time. (Telling the time requires unusual grammatical constructions in Russian, and is usually a reliable method of identifying a foreigner.) Waiting for a traffic light to change, I overheard two well-dressed middle-aged men, evidently officials, discussing the question, always crucial at this time of year, of the prospects for the mushroom season.

I arrived at the café just as a battered lorry delivering bread was departing. It is a one-storey brick-and-glass building in the contemporary Soviet style. Hundreds of structures are being built on this precise pattern and equipped as cafeterias, snack bars and small specialist restaurants. They are both stark and shoddy, and their outer walls are finished in a way more befitting a warehouse than a restaurant; but they testify to the city fathers' appreciation of the need for small local consumer facilities to relieve Moscow's atmosphere of impersonal austerity, and to provide the throngs of weary shoppers with a place for coffee and a moment's rest. The tables and chairs are also in the contemporary Soviet style, and are splintering and warping after less than a year's service. They look like an imitation of Woolworth's imitation of Scandinavian modern, and are standard equipment in literally a thousand new and redecorated establishments from Murmansk to Baku. But this particular café offers the luxury of relative peace and a refuge from the crowds: one can actually find a table and sit down when one has the time.

A tall young brunette called Galya was behind the counter, simultaneously scowling, battling with the Hungarian espresso machine, and carrying on the churlish exchange of words with the people in the short queue that in Moscow is virtually *de rigueur* between sales staff and customers. Galya is twenty years old, and when not at work (or not in a queue herself) she is as carefree, good-humoured and complaisant as most Russian girls of that age. But the tradition of service in the major Soviet cities seems to require shop assistants to be as uncooperative and antagonistic as possible. Even when not besieged at their counters, even when stocks have not been exhausted, even when not provoked by a customer who wants to score the first insult, Moscow sales staff seem under some compulsion to be rude. When they spy someone they know, however, they instantly abandon their official surliness and revert to their own naturally warm and friendly personalities. Galya smiled when she saw me, then giggled and blushed like a country girl asked to dance at a village party.

'You again.'

'Good morning.'

'Morning! Lazy, good-for-nothings you are, you students. I don't like your hair-cut.'

She served me a pair of frankfurters with bread and mustard and a double espresso (the gritty, murky liquid with the ersatz taste that passes for coffee in Moscow), then set her face in a scowl for the next customer. I found a free stand-up table near the counter, cleared away the dirty dishes to make room for my own, and started on my breakfast. Traditional balalaika music and folk songs, part of the heavy daily ration, were playing on someone's transistor radio.

Through the large plate-glass window with the chipped edges and cracking putty, I watched a young boy playing delightedly with his floppy brown and white mongrel puppy, whose lead was a length of old clothesline. Soon, a small crowd of excited children had gathered to admire the dog, and a pensioner with a full white beard, and wearing the traditional tunic, stopped to watch, his ancient, battered chess set—with which he passes the summer days in the park —tucked carefully under his arm.

It was a fairly typical back-street scene, and illustrates the slow change in Moscow's living standards and styles.

When I first arrived in the city, months passed without my seeing a dog, and this striking 'petlessness' contributed considerably to the Spartan and sombre atmosphere. Perhaps they had disappeared during the war: in Leningrad, of course, the entire pet population was devoured during the early months of the nine-hundred-day siege. Or perhaps Muscovites simply could not afford them: keeping a pet is a luxury when a skilled worker's wages barely feed a family of four. Certainly, they could not afford the living space: with two or three people jammed into each room of most communal flats, there was hardly room for an extra suitcase or saucepan, let alone a dog. As Moscow has become richer in recent years, however, the number of pets has increased. They are still few and far between, still novelties that attract fuss and attention from passers-by, but they have returned, have become a kind of status symbol for 'upper middle-class' couples, and have added one more touch of normality to the city streets.

The boy and his puppy moved off, still surrounded by the crowd of admiring children. A short, pudgy army officer in a crumpled uniform passed, head down and seemingly resigned to the steady berating of his short, pudgy wife. Inside the café, the tables were filling up and the queue at the counter was growing longer: the vanguard of the lunch-time rush. A rough-looking man in the old-fashioned two-foot-wide trousers—probably a minor provincial official or factory executive come to the city for his annual spree—was shouting angrily because the café did not serve champagne.

Several youngish men and women entered, dressed and groomed almost as smartly as their counterparts in Eastern Europe: they worked in the editorial department of a well-known magazine with offices near by. The old cleaning woman—the one responsible for clearing the dirty dishes and wiping the tables with her vile-looking rag—fell into an argument with one of the customers, and the manager of the café, an enormous lady with a startlingly pink rayon blouse underneath the unbuttoned white smock, came to her defence, screaming at the customer about the difficulties of cleaning, of running the café, of life in general. Soon after, Galya's espresso machine seemed to explode in a cloud of hissing steam, and she announced triumphantly that there would be no more coffee today.

None of this was in any way unusual or exciting—which is the point I want to make. On this day of supreme importance for the Soviet Union and the world Communist movement, Moscow life continued in its usual patterns—'onward along the Leninist path' as my friends say ironically, mocking the ubiquitous slogan. The radio, I learned later, had been reporting news of the invasion (described, of course, as a fraternal accession to Czechoslovakia's request for help) since early morning. Frequent broadcasts of the Tass statement had been made, together with the reading of a long text by Yuri Zhukov, a highly authoritative *Pravda* commentator, lauding the action. Galya, the café manager, the customers, the army officer—everyone had certainly heard the news; but it was impossible to guess that from their demeanour. They evinced no surprise, or even interest. Nothing I had seen during the entire morning suggested shock or curiosity; in fact there was no reaction of any kind.

*   *   *

I first heard the news from a friend I visited in hopes of persuading him to go bathing in a reservoir north of the city. Edik (as I'll call him) lives with his wife in a small gloomy room—one of three or four families in a communal apartment—in an old building not far from Pushkinskaya Street. He is a slight, pixyish, interior designer, one of a new breed in Russia, whose crew-cut makes him look even younger than he is. After letting me in, he dashed back to his room with uncharacteristic lack of hospitality, and I found him there, hunched over his radio. He was having difficulty understanding the news commentary to which he was tuned, a West German short-wave broadcast, because elementary written German is his only foreign language. Jamming had already begun on Russian language broadcasts whenever mention of Czechoslovakia was made—which meant almost continuously. This had started early that morning—the first time for years on most foreign stations. The jamming was surprisingly ineffective, however (probably as Edik and his friend later speculated, because the jamming equipment was in poor condition or the technicians out of practice), and we were able to hear occasional snatches of broadcasts in Russian as well as in the European languages I understood. Several B.B.C. wavelengths were quite clear.

The news itself was as dramatic as any I have heard, and the setting—that small, shabby room in the heart of Moscow—gave it a special, eerie quality. There were shocking, tragic reports from Prague, Bratislava and Brno about the disposition of Russian troops and tanks; the reactions of Czechs and Slovaks in the streets; sporadic firing and agonized verbal exchanges with Russian soldiers; speculation about the fate of the Czechoslovak leaders; and the extraordinary feat of Czechoslovak radio and television in continuing to broadcast, supplying the world as well as Czechoslovak citizens, with a vivid chronicle of the invasion. The news was fragmented, highly emotional and full of gaps and hypotheses—it was only mid-morning in central Europe—but the scale of the invasion, its implications, and above all the dimensions of the injustice and tragedy, were already clear.

Edik's reaction was a mixture of anxiety and resentment. He was almost incredulous, and visibly shocked by the invasion, and yet insisted with a kind of fatalism that he had expected it for months. 'Our bastards [the Soviet leadership] just couldn't let the Czechs go on like that, making something civilized out of socialism.' (Edik was whispering, for no apparent reason; there was surely no microphone in *his* room.) Yet the fact that the Soviet leadership had permitted Czechoslovakia's remarkable democratic renaissance to gather momentum for almost eight months had led him to believe—or hope—that the Russian leaders had sanctioned the Czechoslovak reforms beforehand, and, except for occasional verbal threats to slow their execution, would leave well alone.

Like many Russians in creative professions, Edik often works at home, an arrangement that suits both him and his supervisors, who are eager to save precious office space. He was to have reported at his office early that afternoon for meetings but, as the time approached, decided he would not go. We remained in his musty room, with its worn linoleum, switching from wavelength to wavelength and station to station on the radio. (Later it struck me that he never so much as thought of tuning in to Radio Moscow for the official Soviet version of the news.) A grumpy, dishevelled woman in bedroom slippers, one of Edik's neighbours in an adjoining room, came to complain about something he had or hadn't done in the communal bathroom. Several of his

c

friends telephoned to ask, Had he heard the news? Could he believe it? What would happen now? (Only those friends telephoned who were at home or had access to a private line. Edik's wife, who teaches algebra in a technical college for draughtsmen, said later she did not want to risk telephoning from the teacher's room where she might be overheard.) As new radio reports enlarged the scope of the tragedy, we sat silently at the table, feeling both excited and deeply depressed. Above all, we felt very small and weak— not very different, I imagine, from the people gathered round radio sets everywhere in the West at that very moment.

Sometime after noon, several short-wave stations broadcast speculation that the Prime Minister, Mr Kosygin, and Marshal Grechko, the Minister of Defence, had resigned. Shortly thereafter, the jamming became more effective, and it was difficult to follow the reports without switching furiously from one station to another. By this time, in any case, Edik and I felt we could absorb no more news. We left his room and set out on an aimless walk through the centre of the city.

*   *   *

Several things stand out about that afternoon:

A caravan of Chaika limousines transporting an Arab delegation down Gorky Street, evidently from the airport to the Kremlin, its motor-cycle escort waving traffic to stop on both sides of the broad avenue, like Cossacks pushing their way through a crowd of Jews.

An enormous queue—three abreast and perhaps a hundred yards long—on a busy shopping street called Petrovka outside a small shop specializing in women's clothing from Poland. I often push my way through to find out what has caused this sort of excitement, but this time, Edik and I walked by without stopping.

A small knot of people who had stopped to read a news-paper displayed under glass on the wall of a block of flats. (This was several hours later, in the lingering light of early evening.) The paper was *Izvestiya,* and it was not the Tass announcement — published on the first page, as in *Pravda* — that had attracted their attention, but an article about the Russian *byt* (the reality of daily life) that dealt with matters of real interest to most Russians: bazaars where second-hand and 'deficit' — i.e. scarce — goods are traded, shortages, speculators and the black-market sale of goods smuggled by workers from state enterprises. (See Chapter 4, p. 156.)

A vigorous old man selling lottery tickets in a pedestrian subway, whose amusing chatter, like a fairground tout's, attracted a crowd and provoked smiles from the ordinarily harried shoppers.

The maître d'hôtel of a large restaurant we entered late in the afternoon, who was so unbearably rude — barking that there was no room to serve us, although there were several empty tables — that Edik, in contrast to his usual resignation about such treatment, demanded the man's name in order to write a complaint.

Russian and foreign tourists strolling unhurriedly through the Kremlin (where Marshal Grechko and the Prime Minister, Kosygin, had supposedly just resigned, and crucial decisions were being taken), posing for snapshots in front of the Tsar Cannon and other monuments, and talking about whether to continue sightseeing or stop for dinner.

A dozen men and women, obviously visitors from the provinces, stopping us to ask directions to G.U.M., Children's World, and other prominent department stores. A man whom we believed was Mstislav Rostropovich sitting with a woman in her thirties on a park bench opposite the one where we were resting ...

*   *   *

But what was most extraordinary about the city that afternoon was its utter ordinariness. Under the circumstances, the tranquillity seemed almost to scream. There was not only no panic, outrage or manifestation of popular support; there appeared to be no *interest*. On the surface, at least, the daily routine of Moscow life — the struggling shoppers, the calm islands of leafy, dusty parks, the queues of people at ice-cream and soft-drink stands — went on with absolutely no visible change; it could have been any pleasant summer day. This seemed to disturb Edik as much as the invasion itself.

'Just look at it,' he said, after we emerged from old Arbat Street, its hordes of shoppers pushing in and out of the small shops, and came to Arbatskaya Square, where large crowds were waiting for tickets to the re-modelled, wide-screen cinema. 'Look at it: at this moment we are consummating the invasion of a neighbouring country. Forget for the moment that it's a fraternal socialist country. Forget our action is a travesty of every socialist ideal. Just say it's an ordinary invasion. *And nobody gives a damn*! As long as we're the ones doing the invading, everything's fine. Lenin's smiling down at us, the Party's infallible, the socialist Motherland is getting stronger and richer — so why not smash the "counter-revolution" in Prague? Besides, it's not the affair of all these good people; they're busy buying kasha and thinking, what else do I need for supper?'

*   *   *

But it is not true that there was no concern at all, no surprise, doubt or curiosity. A few people told me later they had heard something important had happened, turned on their short-wave radios, heard the jamming, and understood from this that the Soviet Union was in trouble again—but knew it would be weeks before they could find out the facts. A few others said they would never again be able to look a Czechoslovak in the face. And late on that same afternoon, after Edik and I had parted, a middle-aged woman fairly thrust herself into my arms and begged me to accept an apology in the name of the Russian people.

'It's dreadful. I am so ashamed. You must believe me: this is not something my people would have done if they understood what it meant. There are people here—perhaps you won't meet them—who feel deeply humiliated by what we have done to you.' She had been standing in front of me in a bus queue and had assumed from my accent I was Czech; and she was hardly less apologetic after I had corrected the misapprehension. Nor did she hide her indignation from the others waiting in the queue. She was one of that type of Russian woman—face scrubbed, hair swept back into an uncompromising bun—who, in spite of their weight and dowdiness, remind one of the Lady Asquiths and Wottons. They work hard, live admirable professional and personal lives, and are incapable of even the thought of telling a lie.

'This is a black day for our country,' she said when her bus arrived. 'We have made mistakes before, but it was our own people who paid for them. Now we have done this to the Czechs, and I'm afraid to think of what this will mean for us all.'

Later, several less upper-crust people also expressed doubt, if not indignation. 'What do you think?' asked a taxi driver who was taking me back to the hostel late that night.

'You're a foreigner—what's *your* opinion? Did we do right?' Another man, who was staggering along near the hostel, was less unsure. He was an Estonian; his Russian was heavily accented, and his speech slurred, for he had obviously had a great deal to drink. 'Well, it was their turn today, wasn't it? They did it to us in 'thirty-nine, took over our country— now they do it to the Czechs. No, I'm not afraid to say it. I've already served time for saying what I think; served time more than once. I hate those damn Party bastards.'

During the day, Edik and I overheard several worried conversations. Would there be war? several people asked each other. How would the Americans react? Surely there had been an agreement beforehand with Washington. But could anyone be sure the Americans and West Germans would not retaliate?—*that there would not be another war*? And when, back in the hostel, I scanned the newspapers in the common room just before going to bed, I noticed a remark in *Evening Moscow* alongside the Tass announcement. 'Who invited us?' was pencilled in the margin.

But that terse question seemed to symbolize the limits of interest and protest. There was, it is true, a tiny but well publicized demonstration on Red Square the following Sunday. A handful of Moscow intellectuals, including Pavel Litvinov, grandson of the illustrious Soviet Foreign Minister, and Larisa Daniel, wife of the imprisoned writer Yuli Daniel, assembled in Red Square on August 25th with banners reading, 'Long Live Free and Independent Czechoslovakia' and 'Hands off Czechoslovakia'. They were arrested before they could unfurl the banners, and five of them were tried two months later for disturbing public order and defaming the Soviet Union. Mrs Daniel was exiled for four years to a village near the Siberian city of Irkutsk, where she is reportedly doing hard labour in a saw mill. Litvinov's exile was to an even more remote part of Siberia near Chita. But the Sunday demonstration on Red Square, like the small and isolated manifestations of concern and disapproval on August 21st, were the exceptions that proved the rule.

* * *

During the next few weeks, my close friends — those who were not away on their summer holidays — discussed that day in great detail. Most of them, like Edik, are junior members of the intelligentsia. They might be called Russia's 'angry young men', although their 'anger' is closer to despair, and kept very carefully to themselves. The events of August 21st deepened their gloom about Russia's future to its lowest point for years.

Like most educated people everywhere, they felt that the invasion violated every norm of civilized national behaviour and confirmed the extinction of the world socialist movement. The Czechoslovaks, they said, had been trying to save Marxist socialism by making it economically viable and politically and socially tolerable — something Russia, because of its economic, political and cultural backwardness, could not attempt until it was too late and the very notion of Marxist socialism discredited among advanced, industrialized peoples. However, the Politburo could not tolerate the experiment, for democratic socialism is anathema to Communist dictators. Democratic socialism means the end of dictatorship, and Communist dictators, like all others, have one overriding aim: to preserve their power. Once the Czechoslovak leaders demonstrated that they were serious about restoring political and personal freedom, there was no hope for their experiment.

In short, the invasion was a cynical, barbaric act, as well as a ghastly mistake. There was no justification for it;

nothing revealed more clearly the brute force behind the rhetoric about socialism and the liberation of mankind. And my friends had reasons more personal than these for lamenting the invasion. Like American intellectuals anguished by their country's destruction of Vietnam, these young Russians were deeply saddened that their own country had committed the evil.

Moreover, Czechoslovakia had meant something special to them: until the invasion, it was the freest and most exciting country they could visit as tourists—in its art and literature it virtually offered a look at the West itself. (A young artist I know was heartbroken when his scheduled trip to Prague had to be cancelled. He doubted that he would be able to visit Prague now for years—even supposing its artistic freedom was not destroyed by the Russian occupation.) And in spite of their fears for the future of the 'Czechoslovak spring' and 'socialism with a human face', they were nevertheless hoping that the Dubcek experiment might succeed, and play a crucial part in liberalizing the rest of Eastern Europe and, eventually, Russia itself.

Nevertheless it was less the invasion itself that appalled the intellectuals than the reaction to it inside Russia.

A graduate mathematician: 'I looked around all that day [August 21st] and I was dumbfounded. The reaction was extraordinary: there *was* no reaction. What other country in the world could take a step like that, commit a crime like that—and not one citizen in a thousand stops pushing his way into some shop long enough even to ask himself a question about it?'

A talented surgeon: 'A few women cried. And, oddly enough, a few old Stalinists—because they knew what was going to be done in Czechoslovakia, I suppose, and understood their guilt. But they were a tiny minority, just a handful. In general, nobody cared and nobody cares.'

A civil engineer: 'I happened to be in Kiev, Kharkov and Odessa that day. It was the same everywhere: almost total indifference, passivity, apathy.'

An undergraduate physics student: 'If you still had any hope for political progress in this country, you would have lost it that day. There was a flicker of interest among certain circles in the major cities; in the countryside, nothing, *nil*. Because we're a nation of political robots. We not only lack all the machinery for democratic government, but the instincts and the brains and the interest as well.'

How can one explain the non-reaction? It was a manifestation, I think, of the indifference of most Russians to foreign affairs—indeed, to politics of any kind, domestic or foreign. I shall try to examine the reasons for this monumental apathy later.

But I think there is another explanation for the otherwise bizarre tranquillity of August 21st. As far as the Russian people took any interest in the invasion, the great majority vaguely approved. There was no general anxiety, no shock or outrage, because most Russians felt that their country's foreign policy was in good hands, and the measures taken were certainly justified, and probably just.

In the absence of polls and questionnaires, it is extremely difficult to measure public opinion in Russia accurately. For a foreigner, whose contacts with blue- and white-collar workers—not to mention peasants—is usually passing, it is impossible. Moscow intellectuals feel that some eighty per cent of the Russian people, if forced to express an opinion, would have supported the invasion and its stated goals. That estimate is necessarily rough, and perhaps exaggerated. But during the weeks following August 21st, my conversations with taxi-drivers and cleaning women, cloakroom attendants and dustmen, and the comments I overheard in queues, trams and shopping crowds, seemed to confirm the intellectuals' estimate. When I heard anything at all, it was almost always condemnation of the Czechoslovaks.

'Those bastards, we freed them from the Germans, spilled our blood for their freedom — and now look: they're going behind our backs to the West Germans again.'

'I saw the newsreels. These long-haired youngsters painting swastikas on our tanks. Do you expect us to let Fascists like that get away with it after what we suffered in the war?'

'Our newspapers quoted from their own press. The Czechs were smearing mud on their own government, criticizing everything in their own system. All that work to build socialism, and they're ready to hand the country back to the capitalists, just like that.'

Occasionally there were more thoughtful comments. A few people recognized that the invasion was legally and morally indefensible — but felt, sadly, that it was strategically unavoidable: NATO could not be allowed to swing the balance against the Warsaw Pact, which it might do if Czechoslovakia withdrew from the latter alliance (something the Czechoslovak leaders promised specifically would never happen). Others thought it was justifiable in terms of Russia's absolute need to protect itself against the perpetual German threat. Several were pleased by the obvious stupidity of the invasion — they are delighted by all their government's mistakes — but unmoved by Czechoslovakia's fate. On the contrary, these people (and others) felt spite and jealousy for the Czechs and

Slovaks: they were a lesser breed of Slavs, and should not be allowed to raise themselves above the Russians.

Most of the comments, however, were simpler: Czechoslovakia had strayed from the socialist camp, was succumbing to counter-revolution and flirting with fascism, had forgotten her enormous debts to Russia (who had liberated and helped to feed, industrialize and protect her against NATO), and represented a serious threat not only to Russia but to European peace. The Czechs were behaving reprehensibly and had to be stopped. And besides, why should they, our subordinates, have it better than us? Why should we give them what we ourselves don't have? Everyone feels sorry for the Czechs — but what about we Russians, who are so much worse off?

This was the typical reaction of the typical Russian — and striking evidence, for anyone who still needed it, of how political reflexes here differ from the rest of Europe.

3 NEO-STALINISM

To the world traveller Russia can seem a normal country. Material conditions are poor, everything is dilapidated, eroded, hopelessly slovenly; but on the surface there is no evidence of the dark, hidden side of political life. I had lived here for a long time—completely dissociated from the foreign colony—before I was trusted enough to be told some of the secrets. The surface is calm; that is to say, disturbed only by the daily struggle for the warm pair of socks, the miraculously spied oranges, the small but precious luxuries that brighten the sombre material life. This outward normality makes the witch hunt seem all the more macabre.

Westerners who stay briefly here suspect nothing. It is infuriating, but understandable: not one Russian in ten thousand who has suffered in this new time of troubles would think of talking about it to a stranger, even supposing they chanced to meet. The tourists go home, therefore, with observations acquired on Intourist tours and in Intourist restaurants—and this superficial knowledge of Russia is particularly misleading.

Not long ago, my own longing for a hint of luxury led me to one of these Intourist restaurants. It is in a well-known Leningrad hotel, the brightest light in the little cluster of tourist facilities that try desperately to match Western standards. A party of Americans on a European tour were digging into their caviare: they had just been shown St Petersburg's architectural delights and a selection of massive

Soviet construction projects, and were discussing their happy discovery that the Russians are a great people, after all. (Incidentally, ordinary Russians have not been able to buy caviare for over a year; virtually the entire supply is sold to foreigners in the hard-currency shops and in the special shops for high Party, government, military and secret police officials.) It was fine, said one of the Americans, that President Nixon would be following them to Russia—when a decent interval had elapsed after the unfortunate Czechoslovak business—to talk things out with the Kremlin leaders. After all, didn't Washington and Moscow want the same things for their people?

But the point was made even more clearly by the two affable gentlemen at my table: they were not brassy tourists, but well-travelled British businessmen who spent several months a year in Moscow. After the meal, I accompanied them on a short walk. (We could not talk in the restaurant because many of its tables are 'bugged'. Visitors to Russia often don't believe this, but any off-duty waitress met at a party or dance will confirm it.) I tried to tell them what was happening in Russia—what my friends had been telling me, what I want to report now. But the businessmen were visibly embarrassed by my distress. 'Really, now, we've lived in Russia for some time. No one we know talks like you. Look around you—people are quite normal. Frankly, I think you're a bit under the weather.'

We parted. Nothing I could say would convince them of anything— except, perhaps, that I was a somewhat hysterical anti-Communist. Their Russia and mine rarely meet, and the most dismaying thing is that one can live here, on the surface, without being dismayed.

* * *

That afternoon, I kept a rendezvous with an old friend. We were to have met in a basement cafeteria not far from the Nevsky Prospekt. 'The usual place,' Volodya had said quickly, almost mumbling, and put down the receiver. But he wasn't in the sweat- and cabbage-smelling cafeteria, and I decided to leave; something told me not to be seen lingering there. Then the cloakroom attendant, a slow-moving old man with elephantiasis (we had tipped him well all these years), took my arm and whispered, 'It's Volodya you want? Not here. In the main waiting-room, Moscow station.'

I walked the length of the Nevsky Prospekt, shivering in the damp cold. The Moscow station was packed, like every railway station in every Russian city, day and night. A mass of sturdy Russians were queueing for tickets, eating hunks of bread and chicken, dozing, waiting to find room on trains — or seemingly simply waiting, as Russians do, for waiting's sake. In the main hall, amidst peasants with their countrified clothes and bundles, I saw Volodya adjusting his prized Belgian beret.

He motioned me not to join him. With head and eyes, he directed me to follow at a distance to an underground station. According to the standard arrangements, we kept fifteen metres apart and entered a carriage at separate ends. After two stations, we dashed out just before the doors slammed and boarded a train travelling in the opposite direction; then a trolley, a taxi, and another trolley to a shabby residential quarter of the city built some time after the war. At last, certain no one was following us on the long silent street, we made our way on foot to a communal bath-house and steam-room.

The banya is one of the delights of Russian cities — and also a good place to talk freely on days too raw for walking in the park. The one Volodya chose is more dilapidated and dirty than most in Leningrad, but almost empty in the early afternoon. I paid the few kopecks for our tickets and use of the birch besoms, towels and soap, and we went inside. (Volodya has no income since he was fired from his job, and is supported by his mistress and his friends.) In the seclusion of a corner of the steam-room Volodya unburdened himself of his fears.

'It's getting steadily worse, more threatening all the time. Leningrad's in a very bad way. The whole city's trembling.'

I didn't know how to answer him; I never do. And when he talked about his own circumstances—he had been warned again by the secret police since I had seen him last—I felt completely at a loss. How does one comfort the victim of his own government?

Volodya is a young chemical engineer. He is slight, stutters a little, and his great loves are the guitar, underground songs and unpublished poetry. Two years ago, when I made frequent trips to Leningrad, we used to spend evenings together in his small room. But I did not go there at all on my last trip; his visitors and movements are now watched by a neighbour in the communal flat, and he telephones only from public boxes because his own phone is tapped. The surveillance began after he had been summoned by the K.G.B.; he was bullied, threatened with three years of mixing cement at a Siberian construction site, and then discharged from his job in a factory laboratory. His transgression was signing a petition against the trial of Alexander Ginzburg.

He has not been able to find another job, and now faces exile from the city as a 'parasite'. In any case, the K.G.B. officer had threatened him blandly, 'One more false move and you'll never see Leningrad again.' And although he is more bitter than ever, he is trying hard not to make that false move—to keep out of trouble in the hope that the K.G.B. will allow him to work again and remain in Leningrad.

'There's no alternative. If you want to be true to your conscience, you have to be willing to serve five years in a camp. I'm no Litvinov, I'm not ready to be a martyr. So I humble myself before my masters. I accept my impotence.'

*   *   *

Volodya is in the same circumstances as many Leningraders I know who have been identified as members of the dissenting 'underground'. As a foreigner I have been intermittently followed in Russia ever since I arrived; now they, too—people who have signed petitions or protests, who are suspected of being ideological defectors, radicals or 'cosmopolitans'—are being watched. They are followed; their telephones are (crudely) tapped; microphones, or neighbours acting as informers, invade the privacy of their homes. The flats of many writers, critics and artists prominent in the liberal 'movement' are kept under almost constant watch; occasionally their visitors are photographed and then followed in their turn.

Because it is unwise for one suspected person to be seen with another, these intellectuals often take conspiratorial precautions before meeting among themselves, even when they are planning social gatherings or talks about art. And when 'the situation' is to be discussed, nothing is said except *sotto voce* on a quiet street or in a park. Not even the taxis are trusted: it is assumed that roughly a third of the city's drivers are on retainer to the secret police. And when foreigners are present, even East European students at the university, the precautions often become bizarre—hence

Volodya's seemingly paranoiac arrangements for meeting me.

Even many simple folk in Leningrad, clerks and pharmacists with no interest in politics, have again begun to shun all but the most casual contact with foreigners, returning to the unwritten laws of ten years ago, before the Khrushchev 'thaw'. A considerable percentage of them walk away in embarrassment when told who I am; others ask my friends not to take me along to their evening gatherings — above all, not to their flats. For this is not the time to be seen fraternizing with foreigners, or to take other foolish risks. 'It's a very bad year,' said a librarian in the Museum of Russian Literary History. 'The signal for *this*' (finger drawn across the throat) 'has been given. We have very real things to fear.'

* * *

Above all, it is the 'boss' of Leningrad its citizens fear: Vasily Sergeevich Tolstikov, First Secretary of the Communist Party of Leningrad region. Many of Russia's highest Party leaders are called 'Stalinists' as a kind of shorthand, meaning hard-line bureaucrats who oppose all political, social and economic reforms that might weaken their stifling control over every word and breath. Judged by his public statements, Tolstikov is one of the most rigid of these supremely rigid men: an arch-conservative, opposed to any departure from orthodox Marxist–Leninist canons in politics, economics or the arts. But in Leningrad, Tolstikov is known as a Stalinist in a more literal sense. He is said to be made in the pattern of the megalomaniac Georgian himself: an ambitious, ruthless tyrant who revels in the accumulation and exercise of power, and will readily employ outright terror when the time is right.

D

Supported by four or five right-hand men in the regional Party secretariat, Tolstikov rules Leningrad as his personal fief—with an iron hand and a fierce determination to crush every trace of dissent. All regional First Secretaries have immense power and considerable autonomy, and the Leningrad Party, with its history of relative independence, is vitally important as a power base. But Tolstikov has extended these traditions: he is a law almost entirely to himself. No aspect of life in Leningrad, especially its cultural life, escapes his personal attention. He does not govern, but rules: *tsarstvovat*. Leningraders refer to him as a 'feudal despot', an 'eastern satrap' and 'Stalin's heir'. He even imitates some of Stalin's imperial habits, such as driving to work and official functions in a car for which traffic is stopped in both directions. This practice, common under Stalin, has been abandoned by the Politburo members in Moscow, who are usually driven unobtrusively through normal city traffic.

Russians themselves know painfully little about Politburo intrigues; and much of what they do know has been learned from Western short-wave broadcasts. But there are persistent rumours about Tolstikov and his ambitions—rumours repeated so often one supposes they have some basis in fact. He is said to be one of the most determined pretenders to Stalin's throne. Using the Leningrad party as his power base, he is jockeying ferociously for position (as these things are done in the Kremlin), building his personal following and preparing himself for the day when the collective leadership of Brezhnev, Kosygin, Podgorny and the rest dissolves or is overthrown. On the basis of his feudal rule in Leningrad, it is felt that Tolstikov is eager to do battle for supreme national power and, if he wins it, to drag Russia back to the rigid totalitarianism he likes.

His progress in this direction in Leningrad has been considerable. He has introduced a distinctly more rigid cultural atmosphere there, even compared to Moscow. Several plays and films approved by the censors for showing in the capital and elsewhere are banned in Leningrad. More significant, he has purged the Party and surrounded himself with a totally loyal, 'hard-line' apparat. He has extended and reinforced the network of *stukachi* (informers) that had been allowed to wane somewhat during the Khrushchev era. Stukachi are again everywhere—in all offices and factories, communal apartments, hotels, restaurants, even on the Nevsky Prospekt and principal squares—and are said to report directly to Tolstikov's office as well as to the K.G.B. Even in buses and the underground, Leningraders who are 'marked' talk in whispers and look over their shoulders.

The 'little people' of Leningrad, the vast majority of office and factory workers, are free of immediate surveillance of this kind, and of any direct pressure or threats; but they, too, are visibly more frightened than non-intellectuals and non-dissenters in most other parts of the country. On a trip back to Moscow last spring, I prepared to board the crack Red Arrow Express at about eleven o'clock in the evening. The conductress of my carriage, a slight young girl in the dark uniform of the railway worker, stood at the steps, white and trembling. 'It's Tolstikov,' she whispered. 'He's travelling in a carriage on this train!' Later she whispered that Tolstikov had indeed arrived shortly before departure (a stocky, vigorous, plain-looking man in his early fifties, accompanied by four pretty young girls who travelled in adjoining compartments), settled into his special carriage, and was not seen until morning. The trip was entirely uneventful, but the conductress was still uneasy when we said goodbye in Moscow. I had a glimpse—or was this only a faint shadow?—of the mass quivering of nerves under Stalin.

*   *   *

Tolstikov in Leningrad is a close match of man to job, for there is more dissent to repress there than elsewhere in Russia. A residue of St Petersburg's revolutionary tradition, always stronger than Moscow's, has survived the fearful pressures and punishments of fifty years of Soviet rule; and to be revolutionary now means, of course, to take a stand, if only a mental one, against the dictatorship. For the past decade at least, 'circles' of a few like-minded friends have been meeting underground in the city to discuss heretical political ideas, principally agrarian socialism and 'genuine' Marxism (as opposed to Marxism–Leninism). One such group was unearthed in 1965—it had circulated two issues of a slim, typewritten journal called *The Bell*, after Hertzen's celebrated emigré publication of the same name—and its nine members were sentenced to long terms in labour colonies. Reprisals were taken even against acquaintances of the accused who had no connection with the circle.

New trials were held this year, but information about them is scanty because they are held *in camera*, and the participants warned that 'spreading rumours'—in other words, talking about them—will be treated as subversive. Volodya himself, who is the best-informed man I know in Leningrad about all matters concerning the repression of dissenters, talks in terms of rumours and 'grape-vine' information. I have no way of checking this information, nor would I try if I had. For although, as I've said, my own freedom of movement is considerably greater than most foreigners in Russia, I know—I have been told—that 'they' (the K.G.B.) know roughly where I am and what I am doing at all times; and to investigate places I have no 'legitimate' reason for visiting would be foolhardy. More often than not, the best way of becoming informed in Russia is *not* to seek information. But this leaves many gaps, especially in a city one visits only briefly—and now, most of all, in Leningrad.

However, it is known with full certainty in the Leningrad 'underground' that dozens of people, principally students and young lecturers at the university, were convicted a few months ago of disseminating anti-Soviet propaganda, and exiled from the city. The most important trial took place in March and April 1968 in Leningrad City Court; the most prominent defendant was a man named Platonov, an orientalist at the university. No charges were announced; no news of the trial was published. Other defendants, apparently in other cases, were members of a 'Berdyaev Circle' that studied the ideas of Nikolai Berdyaev (an early twentieth-century Christian philosopher who wrote of the free human personality and of creativity as the central meaning of Christianity).

There is talk of more trials held since then, the harvest of a steadily intensifying round-up of dissenters. Leningrad intellectuals say these most recent proceedings—none of which have been reported in the West—are more 'rigged' and vicious than the *causes célèbres* involving Sinyavsky, Daniel, Galanskov, Ginzburg, Bukovsky, Litvinov and their co-defendants. Tolstikov is an active prosecutor; his policy is to 'search and destroy' dissent, rather than wait for it to surface.

The scope and thoroughness of persecution in Leningrad are beyond question, but it is often difficult to separate fact from fantasy in the stealthily told accounts of individual cases. Sometimes, however, a story circulating on Leningrad's complex network of rumour is partly corroborated by a verifiable fact. For example, Leningraders talk of a mass deportation of a hundred or more engineers and scientists who organized demonstrations in spring 1967 against the trials of Sinyavsky, Daniel and Ginzburg. One demonstration is said to have approached the proportions of a revolt, during which weapons were produced—souvenir rifles and pistols; it is not clear whether an attempt was made to use them—when the police arrived to disband the crowd. The revolt took place in a large housing development on the outskirts of the city. And, indeed, several blocks of flats were nearly empty for a week or so this spring; had they been occupied by the deported protesters?

* * *

Other stories circulating in the city are impossible to verify, and some seem plainly untrue. Russians are enthusiastic and sometimes imaginative rumour-spreaders, for in the absence of what is known elsewhere as news, rumour is an important source of information and entertainment. And even those Russians who are watched by the police, and whose fate one must lament and courage admire, are not above 'touching up' a good story to make it more dramatic and their own position more desperate. Nevertheless, even these tales have an ominous significance: a police state cannot operate without fear, and rumour is an important method of disseminating fear. Even exaggerated and fictitious tales serve as a powerful means of repression, since they frighten people back into the recently abandoned shells of he Stalin era.

The most remarkable story I myself heard in Leningrad

concerns Leonid Brezhnev, General Secretary of the Communist Party. Last winter, he arrived from Moscow for high-level consultations, and a ceremonial greeting was prepared on one of the city's larger squares. As often in these 'spontaneous' demonstrations, the 'public' consisted of K.G.B. officers and trusted Party and Komsomol members, admitted by special pass. At one of the entrances to the square, the guards detained two seventeen-year-old boys who had been trying to sneak through. One of the boys was carrying a tattered briefcase containing two amateurish, home-made bombs. The boys did not ask for mercy, but confessed their intention: 'Yes, we wanted to kill Brezhnev. We hate that ugly ape.'

Whether the bombs would have exploded is doubtful. In any case, the boys planned to toss them under the podium while Brezhnev was humbly thanking the crowd. The ceremony was not held, however; in its place, a kind of *ad hoc* tribunal met on the platform, with Brezhnev in the chair, and condemned the boys to death. Two hours later, they were publicly executed by a firing squad on a smaller adjoining square. Brezhnev left Leningrad almost immediately.

This story is often told in 'underground' Leningrad. It sounded unlikely to me, and still does: too fantastic, too much at odds with the Soviet passion for secrecy about dissent and its suppression. I first heard it from a well-informed journalist and he insists it was true: he had heard it from an intimate friend, a poet, who watched the executions incredulously from the window of his flat, and only later discovered their cause. I could not myself meet the poet; he left Leningrad, as intellectuals sometimes left major cities for the relative safety of the countryside during the worst Stalinist years. But the journalist is a thoroughly honest man, incapable of

lying—one of those Russians who care passionately about
personal truth because their professions require them to
lie. He himself questioned the poet remorselessly, then
confirmed the events from other witnesses. At first, he
was sceptical; now he is convinced. 'This is what we have
come to in this city. We are again on the border of
terror.'

If it is not true, it might have been. The mere existence
of this story says a good deal about Leningrad's political
state of mind.

*   *   *

Leningrad, thanks to its revolutionary traditions and to
Tolstikov, is particularly tense—but not uniquely so. Other
men known as uncompromising hard-liners have recently
risen to prominence in the highest Party and governmental
organs. The Department of Scholarship, Science and Education of the Party's Central Committee is now headed by one
Sergei Trapeznikov, a man best remembered as Stalin's
ruthless, ultra-loyal lieutenant in Moldavia. Trapeznikov
has immense powers in the whole field of research, scholarship and higher educational policy. General Sergei Shte-
menko, another of Stalin's favourites who was demoted and
banished to obscurity shortly after the dictator's death in
1953, was restored to high favour last summer. He was
appointed Chief of Staff of the Warsaw Pact forces shortly
before the invasion of Czechoslovakia.

Nikolai Mikhailov, the head of the Komsomol (Communist Youth League) when Stalin purged it ruthlessly,
then used it to help execute his policies in other spheres of
Soviet life, is now Chairman of the U.S.S.R. Committee for
Publishing. The man's biography and present post speak for
themselves. And General Alexei Yepishev, the current Chief

of the army's Political Administration – in other words, the supreme political commissar – was formerly the right-hand man of Lavrenty Beria, the person most directly responsible for administering Stalin's terror, and whose name is probably reviled more than any other in Soviet history. (Specifically, Yepishev was Beria's deputy director of the Ministry of Internal Affairs during the time when the secret police operated under the Ministry.) Yepishev has been one of the most hostile critics of liberal intellectuals, and in May 1968 was the first Soviet official to threaten Czechoslovakia publicly with invasion.

These men have immense influence on Soviet political life, and their reappearance, or resurgence, frighten those Russians who watch political manoeuvring in the Kremlin. But it is more than the shift in fortunes of individual Stalinists that worries them. Everywhere in Russia, in terms of policy as well as personnel, a full-scale retreat from Khrushchev's tentative (and, in the West, much misinterpreted) liberalism is under way.

The regression began around the middle of 1966, when the leadership made a discernible shift toward conservatism and orthodoxy in almost all internal affairs. At first, it was a change of mood more than anything. But the turn towards a 'hard' line developed rapidly into what is known as a campaign, and the campaign recently assumed the proportions of a massive movement. Its goal is to strengthen 'public order' – i.e. discipline – in all aspects of Soviet life.

The civic police, for example, have been reinforced in both numbers and powers, and newspapers are larded with lectures, sermons and thinly-veiled threats about the need for 'socialist civic consciousness' and order – again, discipline. The principle of 'democratic centralism' in decision-making – that is, dictatorial control from above – is again being praised as the cornerstone of all Leninist teachings. Appeals are made daily for the old qualities of vigilance, self-control and dedication, and against the old enemies of 'abstract' freedom and democracy and indifference to the demands of citizenship in a socialist state at war against rabid external and internal enemies.

But the principal attacks have been on the political and ideological fronts. They have resulted in the suppression of liberal intellectuals, scientists and students, the narrowing of personal freedoms for all members of the intelligentsia, and intensified censorship and demands for ideological purity in the arts. Russians themselves—those who are concerned about these things (the majority are not)—call the current phenomenon 'neo-Stalinism'. It is the most powerful of several such retrogressive movements since Stalin himself died in 1953.

In Moscow, there have been no mass repressions and no trials—no rumours of trials—unreported in the West. Mass terror and deportations, the infliction of direct physical pain and suffering, firing squads and torture techniques—in short, the horrifying aspects of Stalinism—play virtually no role in current measures of control; and in this sense, the comparison with genuine Stalinism is spurious. This distinction between neo-Stalinism and real Stalinism is by no means academic; it means that millions of people are spared shooting or slow death in labour camps. Nevertheless, in terms of personal freedom and security, the regression has been substantial. Neo-Stalinism achieves many of the social effects of its precursor, without the satanic measures.

The new repression is selective: directed, in the first instance, against people who know Solzhenitsyn or Sinyavsky who signed letters or petitions against the trials of Sinyavsky, Daniel, Ginzburg, Bukovsky, Litvinov and others, and the smaller number who protested against the invasion of Czechoslovakia (smaller because by August 1968 the repression had already done much of its work).

Punishment takes the form of personal and professional sanctions rather than imprisonment. The most common measures are dismissal from work, or demotion; expulsion from the party and Komsomol or severe censure, interference with academic and scientific careers; and retraction of privileges, including the privilege of living in Moscow.

Liberal scholars are ordered to abandon projects on which they have worked for years; appropriations for research are discontinued; scientists are demoted and transferred. I am told that several dozen young scientists of exceptional promise have been expelled from the Party and dismissed from their posts; heads of departments and their assistants in universities, institutes, editorial offices and laboratories have been demoted to the lowest rank and replaced by orthodox Stalinists; literally hundreds of liberals are summoned to K.G.B. offices and told outright that one false step will bring severe reprisals on them and, indirectly, their families.

Students have been expelled from Moscow University and other academic institutions—not all who protested, but enough to establish the principle that anyone who does risks permanent termination of his academic career. Several activists (those who drafted, rather than merely signed, protests) have been not only expelled, but exiled to distant provinces. A friend of mine is corresponding with one of the unfortunates, a former mathematics student who has been assigned to a construction site in the far north. Cautiously— because his letters are almost certainly censored—the exile describes his surroundings. 'It's not a labour camp,' my friend decodes, 'but that's the best you can say for it. He's at his wit's end already because his brain is atrophying. Life in the provinces is about two hundred years behind Moscow, and the stupid and brutalizing elements of the Russian village are still very strong. He may never be allowed to return to Moscow or finish his education. Mind you, his exile's not a criminal punishment, because he was never accused of a crime. It's simply the crushing of a good life by administrative measures.'

Very occasionally, these things come to the ears of incredulous foreigners. An elderly Belgian astronomer, Dr X, who came on a short professional visit, had long admired Soviet astronomy; now, seeing the institutes and their work at first hand, he was more impressed than ever. However, he was taken aback by Russia's grim living standards, the crude consumer services and public manners, and the maddening inefficiency (and mendacity) of the best of its bureaucracies, Intourist. 'Why do people put up with it? It's appalling.'

More appalling, however, was the revelation made just before his departure. Dr X had been looking forward to meeting Ж, a young Russian scientist whose papers he had been reading in Soviet journals. But Ж could not be found: he was no longer working at his old institute and none of his colleagues knew where he had gone. Intrigued, Dr X pressed his inquiries—but in vain; Ж it seemed, had simply disappeared. After a fortnight of persistent questions, an elderly Russian professor took him aside. Ж, the professor whispered, had been dispatched to a minor position in a provincial city, and it would be better not to mention him again. His career was gravely damaged—perhaps not permanently, but for the next five years at least and he might never go abroad again. He had signed a letter to the Politburo protesting against the Sinyavsky–Daniel trial.

Dr X was sceptical. Could this actually happen to a scientist of world reputation? He was convinced, in the end, by the demeanour of the elderly professor, who begged him never to disclose that he had talked about Ж, and never say a word about politics in his own office. 'Don't try to help, just believe me. This is what is happening now—again. I am an old man and it is shameful for me to talk to you like this.'

Dr X was puzzled by my composure on hearing his frightening story. But such tales are commonplace here.

Most of the victims remain in Moscow, however, physically unharmed but professionally paralysed. A graduate philologist at Moscow University, a Slavist of unusual promise, wrote a reportedly brilliant dissertation on the origins of the Polish language. His visa was postponed indefinitely when it was learned that he had signed a protest. It is doubtful now that he will ever gain his degree.

An elderly and highly popular writer of children's books and adventure stories, two years ago officially honoured with an elaborate testimonial dinner, signed one of the first letters of protest against the Sinyavsky–Daniel trial—and nothing of his has been published since. 'It's not so bad for me, I have enough royalties to live on for years. But some writers are without a kopeck, and blacklisted indefinitely. There's talk now that some people may be expelled from the union [of writers] which means it will be very difficult for them to publish, in addition to losing all the subsidiary privileges.' (There have also been expulsions from the Union of Artists, which makes it virtually impossible for the expelled artists to win commissions or have shows of their work.)

Novi Mir, the single 'liberal' literary monthly, champion of free literature and voice of virtually the entire intellectual community (it published Solzhenitsyn and Paustovsky) appears months late, emasculated by ever more stringent and blatant censorship. The journal is said to be succumbing to inexorable pressure from reactionary cultural officials who want it 'cleaned up'. The son of a prominent engineer lamented the position of Alexander Tvardovsky, the editor. 'He has received terrifying threats—they handled Dubcek with kid gloves by comparison.' To give a comparatively mild example, a recent target of the censorship was a long article on Fascist Germany which was withdrawn at the last moment because of its embarrassing, 'subversive', parallels to contemporary Russia. There are rumours that the editorial board is in great disarray, and the journal may be forced to cease publication entirely—a great tragedy for Russian letters.

A poet's room is searched by bullying K.G.B. officers. Several dozen books are confiscated, together with a trunkful of his own manuscripts. He is told he will never see them again.

The Chief Engineer of a huge machine-tool plant wrote a letter of protest to his local newspaper. He is expelled from the Party and reduced to foreman of one of the shops.

A dramatist who sent a personal letter to the Central Committee of the Party has two of his plays struck from the repertoire of almost one hundred theatres throughout the country.

An assistant professor of Russian literature is sacked without so much as rubber-stamp approval by the institute's Academic Council, and his contract for playing the principal role in a new film is torn up.

A former journalist who has worked in Moscow Radio for nearly twenty years went on holiday to find on his return that he no longer had a job. The Party Secretary of his department, a notorious Stalinist, smilingly told him the (unofficial) reason: ideological unreliability—meaning that he complained in public about Sinyavsky and Daniel. His fellow workers lower their eyes and say nothing as he clears out his desk.

A chemist in a research institute is dismissed from his job late one evening. He is not permitted to return to his laboratory to collect his notes and papers. Five years' work is lost.

One of my friends described to me his own summons to a K.G.B. office. His interlocutor was a well-groomed, fortyish man, apparently a K.G.B. major in civilian dress. 'Let me tell you,' the major said coolly, 'there's no mystery or doubt in this matter. I'm not going to argue about what *you* think about any trials conducted by a Soviet court or what *you* think the constitution says. Who do you think you are, challenging what has been decided by the responsible people in the Party? I'll tell you: a cheap little sensation-seeking subversive like the rest of them. And *our* decision is this: we are not going to put up with your dirty activities any longer. Traitors like you will never change. You just have to be dealt with so you can never be treacherous again. One more false move and I guarantee the only thing you'll teach your dirty politics to from then on is trees in a nice Siberian forest. We built up this country, made it strong and made it hard — and not for snivelling little intellectual woodworms like you to ruin from the inside. You've had your day; things are getting under control again; in another year or so, I guarantee, all you liberal wreckers with the smart-aleck ideas will be back where you belong. You're no better or safer than all your Sinyavskys and Litvinovs. We gave them what they deserve, and it will be a lot easier to deal with you.'

My friend was calm when he described his warning to me. 'There was no real argument,' he explained. 'The good major behaved with the full assurance he had total control over my fate. Which, of course, he had.'

Another friend, a young, emotional student, almost wept when he told me what had been happening in a prominent literary institute. His father and several of his father's friends—his own intellectual heroes—lost their jobs and are now beaten, frightened men. 'They were punished for their ideas. Purely and simply because they tried to follow their consciences and raise a tiny voice against the fraud of the trials. Many people are suffering. It's a terrible time.'

Russians estimate that between fifteen hundred and two thousand people signed petitions and protests against one of the trials or the invasion. Not all of them have been disciplined. Some are protected by international reputations: the Bolshoi prima ballerina Maya Plisetskaya for example. Others, like the Lenin Prize chemist and 'father' of the Soviet atomic bomb, Andrei Sakharov, are protected by the possession of vital skills—although even he has been dismissed from his post as chief consultant to the State Committee on Nuclear Energy. A few have been left alone for no discernible reason: they signed protests, even helped circulate them, but although summoned and warned—apparently no 'signer' escaped this—they have not otherwise been punished. However, the majority are now suffering the kind of retribution I've described. Literally hundreds of people have been expelled from the Party—which means, in addition to their personal hardship, that their influence on Soviet Policy has been reduced to virtually nothing, and the hope of reforming the Party from within has become that much more remote. And yet, ironically, the notion persists in much of the Western press that the protests are evidence of 'significant liberalization' in this country—'the first giant steps towards a new era of freedom'.

*   *   *

Several things stand out about the repression of liberals. First of all, the efficiency and thoroughness with which it is carried out. This efficiency is possible because a single organization has total control over where Russians work and live, as well as what they legally read and publicly say. Ordinarily, the inherent muddle of Soviet bureaucracy might give some measure of delay, if not protection, to potential victims: a decision to dismiss a man from his job, for example, might not be co-ordinated with revocation of his residence permit in a coveted major city. But Russia's most competent and prodigally financed central agency, the K.G.B., serves as co-ordinator in all matters of this importance. 'The K.G.B. is the real government of this country,' say my friends again and again. 'On the crucial decisions involving the fate of individual people, they always have the last word. It's easy enough to be fooled by all the government bureaux, committees, agencies and departments. They do all the running of the house. But behind them is always the K.G.B., the real power. When they want to ruin a man, all other governmental and economic organizations follow their instructions instantly. That's how a police state works.'

The repression is notable, secondly, for its secrecy; it is more 'underground' than the very dissent it seeks to eliminate. The K.G.B. dreads publicity. It wants to frighten and punish unofficially and anonymously, its role and power — usually supreme in any given situation, and understood by every Russian to be supreme — never mentioned.

It would be a hopeful sign, I suppose — one of the very few of this period — if this passion for secrecy derived from a sense of guilt. It may, indeed, somewhere in the political subconscious. But what the K.G.B. consciously fears is bad publicity in the West and among the uncommitted nations, which will smudge the image of the Soviet Union so painstakingly nurtured by the mammoth propaganda machine. An unfavourable report in an American or West German

B

weekly news magazine troubles the secret police far more than considerations of legality, justice, or democracy—or, it goes without saying, the fate of its victims. This, at any rate, is the assessment of Russian intellectuals: nothing, they say, makes K.G.B. officers more furious than leaks to the West of information about individual cases of repression. They have launched a determined campaign to stop these leaks (which accounts for the considerably stiffened customs search of anyone who is likely to have been friendly with a member of the underground). They are also determined to stop the—remarkably quick—flow of information about secret trials and similar events to Western radio stations, which, again quickly, beam this information back to Russia and Eastern Europe.

This assessment is confirmed by the victims of the K.G.B. I know. In many cases, they withheld details from me: they had been warned that 'squealing' would double their punishment. And instead of making public the injustices perpetrated against them, they concealed them. When, after long acquaintance, they finally approached this subject, it was in whispers, after imploring me never to mention their names. Several victims never talked about these things at all; I learnt their fate from friends. They are like the classic prey of the Mafia, whose terrorized victims never talk about their persecution.

Thirdly, the repression is notable in that the victims can get no redress at all. Lacking influence in high places, they have no means of protecting themselves, and their friends and colleagues fully understand that to protest against the injustice will only provoke reprisals against themselves, without in any way helping the victims. There is no public outcry against the repression not only because of the ignorance and indifference of the vast majority of Russians (workers and peasants who are not unhappy to see the intellectuals, whom they consider too clever by half, put in their place), but also because those who do know are impotent.

In spring 1968 it was Boris Zolotukhin's turn to experience this. Zolotukhin is the lawyer who defended Alexander Ginzburg at his notorious trial—a gentle middle-aged man who was Chairman of one of Moscow's collegia of lawyers. He was a Communist (whatever the endeavour or profession, Party members are likely to be selected for positions of authority, control and leadership), but a Communist of the humanist, rather than apparatchik, strain. In other words, he was a humane, honourable man, universally respected by his colleagues. He was known never to depart from principle in his defences, never to take under-the-counter payments from his clients, never to betray a subordinate in his collegium when police or prosecution applied pressure for conviction in a given case—a proud record under the conditions of the Soviet legal system. And in addition—although it seems almost fulsome to record it—he was called the *lyubimets* (the favourite, the darling) of the legal profession in Moscow.

His mistake was to conduct Ginzburg's defence with his usual skill, energy and high principles—protesting bitterly, among other things, against the intimidation of defence witnesses by the prosecutor and judge. His concluding speech, which exposed the political and moral evils, as well as the legal absurdity, of the writers' trials, was a courageous and, under the circumstances, brilliantly argued statement, equal to the highest standards of defence advocacy. After circulating underground for two months in Moscow, it was printed in *Le Nouvel Observateur*—and that, according to speculation in Moscow, was his undoing. He was expelled from the Party. (This, for reasons too lengthy to explain here, is tantamount to a criminal sentence: an expelled Communist is in many ways like an ex-convict.) This meant, of course, loss of his chairmanship of the collegium. Then, for good measure, Zolotukhin was expelled from the collegium entirely — which meant that he was deprived of his right to appear in court. He now works as a legal consultant to an enterprise in Moscow — earning enough to live on (perhaps a quarter of his former salary), but in other ways a ruined man.

Every lawyer in Moscow knows these facts. (And not only in Moscow. I first heard the story from a Leningrad lawyer while visiting there last spring.) The episode is referred to as a tragedy — not only because Zolotukhin was punished solely for honouring his professional obligations as counsel for the defence, but also because of his personal qualities. 'He was our *lyubimets*. It was a terrible thing, a tragedy for Soviet advocacy.'

Yet not a single lawyer protested, not a single letter or petition was signed. Why? '*Vse boyatsa za svoyu shkuru.* (Everyone is afraid for his own skin.) This was decided in the Central Committee. To protest against it would only ruin the protester. Believe me, it's hopeless.' But what if all the lawyers of Moscow signed a joint protest? 'You wouldn't get one hundred signatures before the K.G.B. found out — and even if secrecy were possible, half the lawyers would be too terrified to sign anything. And if five hundred lawyers signed, five hundred would suffer. They'd disband entire collegia if necessary.' Then isn't there anything at all that can be done? 'Yes: to try not to think about it. People cried when this happened to Zolotukhin. The kindest way, the only rational way, to comfort them was to tell them to forget.'

Fourthly, it is notable how much damage the repression has done to the concept of rule of law. In the fifteen years since

Stalin's death, slender support for this concept was painfully constructed in the quicksand of Russian authoritarianism and national attitudes. Now it has been washed away again, as has so often happened in Russian history. For most measures of repression have been either unconstitutional or illegal — performed, in the Stalinist tradition (if not with Stalinist brutality), outside the machinery of justice. Although there has been no mass terror against imaginary traitors, the K.G.B. has had a free hand to ruin almost anyone it wished. The trials themselves, as the transcripts circulating underground here demonstrate, were in many ways, both procedurally and substantively, cynical miscarriages of justice. To call them a 'wild mockery', as Litvinov did, is, if anything, an understatement. Several years ago, when public attention was focused on Stalin's crimes and the promise that the government neither would nor could ever again violate socialist legality, a few liberal jurists might have hinted publicly their disapproval of new violations of this kind. But jurists, like anyone else except a handful of young men and women willing to be martyrs, are now cowed; and, ominously, the Soviet press is now carefully rehabilitating Stalin's reputation.

As it happens, few Russians care about the rule of law itself — this academic abstraction has never appealed to the unlegal Russian mind. But they do know, all too well, about personal insecurity and lack of civil liberties, and all but a very few Russians are experiencing these now.

* * *

Other qualities of the current repression could be singled out: cynicism, ruthlessness, crudeness. Can it really be that the Soviet leadership operates so primitively, applying pressure so blatantly on obvious candidates like Zolotukhin, and violating so openly Soviet law and all civilized standards? Do they believe that the knowledge of what they are doing will not spread, that people will not see them for what they are?

But perhaps one should not be surprised after the conduct of the trials of Sinyavsky, Daniel, Galonskov, Ginzburg and the others, and the invasion of Czechoslovakia—nor, indeed, does it surprise people familiar with these qualities in Soviet propaganda and in so many aspects of daily life here. No one who has written half a dozen letters to a Soviet ministry and not received the common courtesy of even an acknowledgment, or who has been treated to outright lies by the Vice-Minister, will be bewildered by the loutishness of the K.G.B.'s tactics. The Polish, Czech, Hungarian and Yugoslav students I know are not at all surprised; it is only the Westerners, and occasionally the Asians, who are. The Russians themselves are accustomed to this kind of coarseness: the methods used in the repression are in full harmony with many other aspects of Soviet government. And whenever the dictatorship feels itself or its dogma threatened, it reacts in exactly this way.

How can they *do* things like that? I ask my friends after hearing the tales of repression. The question is rhetorical, but often answered in earnest. 'Because', as a graduate student in my hostel put it, 'they are crude bullies who quite naturally react to challenges in this way. Who do you think rises to power in the Party? Men who are hard enough, cynical enough and crude enough to best the competition. The apparat has its own requirements, and its own methods of selecting suitable people for running the Soviet dictatorship. It's the survival of the fittest.'

'Only narrow-minded, chauvinistic, anti-enlightenment

types — the worst of the Russian lower-middle class — can get to the top,' said a young abstract painter. 'Coarse and stupid men; third-rate minds of a degenerate ruling caste. And besides, they're afraid. They must bring the whole country down to their level in order to rule it. Even if some of the Party apparatchiks are a cut above that, remember, they've given control of law and order to the K.G.B. They're the people who actually run things in regional and district offices — who have operational control. And they are made in the classical gangster mould with the classical gangster mentality.'

*   *   *

In addition to the repression of the tiny minority who signed protests or otherwise stepped out of line, a massive programme of preventive measures has been started to dissuade others from committing similar transgressions. Surveillance and discipline have been tightened everywhere, and there are more stringent demands for Marxist–Leninist orthodoxy in all branches of scholarship and the arts. These measures have caused a distinct and calculated rise in the 'danger-quotient' of public life, and this directly affects every member of the intelligentsia. Honesty, creativity and quality are declining in proportion to the increase of pressure.

As usual, expression of opinion was the first victim. People with nonconformist ideas still talk freely to close friends; perhaps more freely than at any time since Stalin's consolidation of power. But it is again dangerous to say anything unorthodox at work. 'During Khrushchev's last year and the beginning of the Brezhnev–Kosygin reign, it had reached the point where you could talk and joke about these things on the job,' said an editor of a metallurgical journal. 'Now it is very bad again—worse than I've ever seen it. You simply don't talk about anything sensitive, certainly not about what's happening to the country at the moment. Even if you have a trusted friend at the office, you don't talk about real things there.'

This increased restriction is felt by everyone I know in Moscow: by teachers, actors, even research scientists, who usually enjoy greater immunity from control—or at least from fear—than non-scientists. The return of the old habits of self-censorship over a period of a few months early last year was a remarkable phenomenon to a foreigner. Even young professional men and women who had finished their education and begun working during the relatively freer Khrushchev years, and therefore had had no direct experience of repression, took up cautious habits quickly, if somewhat more reluctantly and with less alarm than older generations.

Moreover, the unwritten rule of silence on sensitive subjects was established well before this summer. 'On August 21st, the day after,' a chemical engineer told me, 'there wasn't a single word about Czechoslovakia by anyone in the lab. It was as if the invasion had never happened. And I, of course, played just as dumb. You must understand: no one knows what's coming next, we're all *frightened*.'

Most immediately, they are frightened by the renewed influence of stukachi. Informers had never disappeared from Moscow offices, but until recently, people felt their reports to the K.G.B. would not be acted on except in serious cases. Now, however, the stukachi have been told to intensify their work. It is taken for granted that one person in each office or department is passing observations and comments on to the K.G.B., and everyone, therefore, instinctively keeps his mouth shut. People are not afraid in the sense of physical trembling, but are constantly aware of the need for caution.

There are even more substantial reasons for the new caution. Everywhere in Soviet public and economic life, liberal or neutral chairmen, directors, managers, Party Secretaries, deans and heads of departments are being replaced by more conservative men. Not only in the Politburo, but in tens of thousands of factories, offices, bureaux, educational and research institutes, committees and commissions, the balance has swung sharply towards orthodoxy and the hard line.

Friends working in Moscow offices describe the change in a tone very characteristic of this period—more depressed than anxious:

'Outright Stalinists are very powerful again at the local level. A few years ago, they were holding their tongues and hiding themselves. Now they've crawled out of the woodwork and started taking over. They smell the old Fascist power again.'

'They are very bad people, real Stalinists, the worst. Anti-intellectual, anti-Semitic, totally uncivilized power-lovers. And they're just dying to lay hands on the liberals: to settle personal scores against them for their enforced retirement, as well as put things back in good Stalinist order.'

'I can name you ten offices in which the head men have been replaced because they were too liberal. The real reason is never given, of course, and if you ask, you get some lie about his new job, if any answer at all. Mind you, these replaced men were often not strong liberals, just middle-of-the-roaders. They presented a front of solid, reliable orthodoxy for public consumption. But with the door closed, they were willing to experiment—to meet foreigners for real discussions, say, and to let the real liberals speak their piece. The men who have replaced them are the drum-beating kind, to whom compromise and tolerance are dirty, "bourgeois-liberal" words.'

'They haven't taken over in every case—but they needn't in *every* case. It's the shift of direction and atmosphere that counts. Maybe that change seems subtle to you; to us its quite enough to make everyone shrink back into his shell. Everyone knows which way the wind is blowing. It's quite amazing—but logical—how slowly things go forward here, and how quickly backward.'

'The Khrushchev days are over—funny, they now seem rich in retrospect.'

Among the underground literature circulating in Moscow, the most talked-about new novel is Alexander Solzhenitsyn's *Cancer Ward*. (Russian intellectuals, unable to find out for themselves, frequently ask foreigners what has happened to Solzhenitsyn. They fear that a major show trial is being prepared against him, and that if he is not prosecuted, it will only be because he is well known enough in the West to generate an unacceptable amount of bad publicity.) One copy of *Cancer Ward* that was briefly in my hands—a type-script that had been passed from hand to hand among perhaps fifty readers, despite being an almost unreadable carbon—had '*Yes!*' pencilled in the margin next to this passage: 'The liars and slanderers, those who had criticized too boldly, the too-clever intellectuals—all of them disappeared, shut up or lay low while the men of principle, the loyal and stable men, Rusanov's friends and Rusanov himself, were able to walk with dignity, holding their heads high ... '

Solzhenitsyn is talking of 1937, the worst of the purge years: Rusanov, the novel's anti-hero, is a soulless official who came to power by denouncing others and who represents the middle level of the hideous Stalinist apparat. The

'*Yes!*' in the margin emphasized the relevance of this observation to the present political climate.

* * *

The repression did not come about spontaneously, of course. The campaign's rationale and general directives are proclaimed endlessly in all the media of mass communication. This is described as a time of 'intensified ideological struggle', when bourgeois propagandists are toiling harder than ever to erode the victories of socialism, and aggressive imperialism is on the march. Vigilance, political consciousness, and ideological purity must be increased; more intense efforts must be made against the cancer of bourgeois ideas and of indifference, especially among youth; more energy than ever must be devoted to rooting out the corrupting influence of 'liberalism' and 'the fraud of democratic socialism'. Greater discipline is demanded within the Party, and by Party members at their posts in all areas of public life.

Such 'lessons' and warnings as these are printed daily:

The April plenum of the Central Committee of the Communist Party declared that 'the present stage of historical development is characterized by a sharp intensification of the ideological war between capitalism and Communism.' Therefore, a merciless war with hostile ideology, in whatever form it might appear, assumes special significance in contemporary conditions. In the struggle between ideas, there is not and cannot be peaceful coexistence ... The clash of Communist and capitalist ideas has never before been so sharp and fierce. Today it is especially important that every Communist, every Soviet citizen, exercise ideological militancy, prepare himself to oppose the fictions of hostile propaganda with the truth of Marxist–Leninist teachings. Conditions demand an ever more active and uncompromising war against alien thoughts.

A huge variety of anti-Soviet organizations and services, founded by the imperialists, are searching out morally unsteady, weak, politically immature people. Sometimes people fall into their net who have sunk to indulging in egotism and self-advertisement — people eager to make themselves heard as loudly as possible, not through honest labour for the sake of the Motherland, but by any suspicious political means whatsoever, not even excluding praise of our ideological enemies. Renegades and turncoats cannot count on going unpunished.

Writers, in particular, are ceaselessly reminded of their duty in terms like these:

> Anyone who does not fully understand his responsibility to the people in a period of implacable conflict between the ideologies of socialism and capitalism cannot call himself a Soviet writer ...
>
> Writers, as well as all Soviet people, must be mobilized to strengthen their Communist consciousness and conviction, to fight indefatigably for the purity of Marxist–Leninist ideology and combat the attempts of hostile propaganda to exert its dangerous influence on people who are unstable and politically immature.

And on the hundredth anniversary of the birth of Maxim Gorky — who is called the 'forefather of Soviet writers':

> M. Gorky himself commented very tellingly on the wailing about art's 'freedom' from the needs of society,

and he did so not on the crest of the Revolution's victories, but in the most sombre reactionary period, in 1908: 'Literature, as expressed by the most talented writers, unanimously attests to the fact that when a petit-bourgeois, aspiring to complete freedom, bares his ego, a beast appears before contemporary society.' Much has changed since then in the wide world, and socialist literature, with its wealth of fresh ideas and talents, has appeared—together with the increasing victories of socialism, whose flags now fly over four continents. But M. Gorky's warning has lost none of its pertinence and urgency. For the petit-bourgeois writer, who is fighting for art's 'liberation' from the needs of society, from politics—from reality as a whole—and for his own ego as the final authority on everything—this petit-bourgeois is amazingly energetic in his role as a decoy, trying to entice drakes within range of a hunter whose name has long been well known ...

And, in a bitter and ominous denunciation of Solzhenitsyn in his role as a conscious tool of socialism's enemies:

History has charged Soviet writers with the great and noble responsibility of heralding the advanced ideas of of our age, the ideas of Communism, and of fighting for the social and spiritual values generated in the socialist system. This responsibility is to history, to society and the writers' own talents—which flourish only in the service of great goals, in the service of the people. This responsibility cannot be discharged by a detached observer of the contemporary world, or a grumbling nihilist, but only by a fighter for Communist ideals.

This language is unmistakable to every thinking Russian, and it is principally at the intelligentsia (a very small

minority) that it is directed. It is a mistake to assume all
Russia has been made tense by the campaign. On the contrary, the great majority of Russians are unaffected by it:
what happens in the war between intellectuals and bureaucrats hardly concerns them. In the course of their daily lives
in factories, on farms and in their cottages and flats, they
hardly even bother to read the outpouring of warnings. The
great majority of people are interested only in everyday life —
which here, even more than elsewhere, means the immediate
concerns of food and drink, good company and the football
matches on television. But everyone working in scholarship,
journalism, the arts — in any kind of intellectual endeavour
— is profoundly affected. Now more than ever (it is endlessly
preached), every poem, painting and narrative must be
mobilized in the offensive against dying capitalism, against
subversive bourgeois influences, attitudes and ideology.

There are times when the campaign goes so far as to
appear to be parodying itself. Its pronouncements and measures have a potentially comic quality; they are raw material
for the black humour that has become popular in the
vastly freer Eastern European countries. But they are serious,
and should be taken seriously, for they illustrate how different
Russian government is from what is considered normal
elsewhere in Europe.

At a recent conference of composers, for example (which
resolved that the principal immediate task of Soviet music
is to prepare for the hundredth anniversary of Lenin's birth),
musicians were directed to intensify their 'anti-bourgeois
vigilance' and the struggle against 'Western subversive and
decadent tendencies'. The Chairman of the Union of Composers announced the conference's full support of his
country's action in Czechoslovakia, and called for strict
observance of the principles of socialist realism in music as a

means of protection against Western attempts to discredit Marxism–Leninism. Western propagandists, stated the Chairman, have mobilized orchestral tours to the socialist countries as well as professional conferences and congresses (and of course, the press, radio, television and tourist visits) — all with the goal of preaching the 'de-ideologization' of art and its complete independence of politics. 'In reply ... we Soviet musicians announce to the world: No one can push us from the correct path. We are with the Party and people.'

The Chairman went on to warn about current dangers to Soviet music. Abstract (i.e. non-socialist-realist) ideas were too often allowed to penetrate the Soviet aesthetic. Propaganda for light music and jazz was uncontrolled. 'We must adhere to our own style in these genres, and not imitate foreigners. Already, we are producing too many frivolous and inept songs.' The greatest danger of all was the ideological one. 'We cannot remain indifferent when we see attempts to depart from aesthetic principles sacred to us,' (i.e. composers writing non-socialist-realist music) 'or when attempts are made to replace our Marxist–Leninist aesthetic by one of "pure art" ' (i.e. art divorced from politics).

This is what the public hear. What actually happens between the creative artist and the Party censor is even worse.

And if demands for orthodoxy in music appear somewhat obscure, perhaps ludicrous, the case with literature is more serious. Writers of both fiction and non-fiction are under very considerable pressure to comply in detail with the Party's requirements to increase 'Party-mindedness' and 'socialist idea-ness' in their work. More and more manuscripts are rejected because of ideological weakness, or returned to authors for 'improvement'. Even when no weaknesses are discerned in the manuscript, the stricter censorship takes considerably longer than before; anyone in a responsible position is cautious about approving a manuscript which may later be condemned. Why stick one's neck out, after all?

Many authors simply do not submit their best manuscripts. 'In times like these,' a young poet and critic told me, 'everything faintly unorthodox—meaning honest and interesting—is quickly abandoned. Anyone working on a meaningful idea knows it doesn't have a chance. The best he can do is put it away somewhere and save it. A thousand plans and projects have been aborted.'

Naturally, critics and scholars of contemporary Western culture suffer most. Their task is clearly stipulated: to expose the class basis of bourgeois culture and its role as imperialist propaganda. They find it virtually impossible to write even sections of their work honestly. 'Until recently,' said a critic of Scandanavian letters, 'I could at least reconcile my conscience by slipping in a few honest paragraphs. Now I have to completely prostitute myself, and denounce everything Western as rotten from start to finish.'

In at least one case, the cultural regression coincided directly with the propaganda requirements of the Czechoslovak affair. On August 17th, three days before the invasion, a young poet was summoned to the Union of Writers in Moscow. Two years before, he had submitted a collection of verses for publication. Roughly half the poems were rejected because of ideological weakness—a common occurrence—but a slim volume was published, including two poems in praise of Czechoslovakia, one set in Prague, the other in Bratislava. At the confrontation in the union, he was directed to write an article for a literary newspaper repudiating his Czech poems and his own political immaturity, and describing the social dangers of the country that he had wilfully concealed in his verse. Despite threats, the poet refused, and from that day his movements have been watched. He now expects to be presented with a trumped-up charge that will get him exiled from Moscow.

* * *

What caused neo-Stalinism is a matter for speculation. Freeze follows thaw in Soviet political life—hard freeze after short thaw, as in the Russian climate—almost as though following some natural cycle. Pehaps it could be, simply, that it's time for a freeze. On the other hand, Russian intellectuals cite several recent events that, in whatever combination, contributed to the current regression.

There is Czechoslovakia, of course. It could be taken for granted that the Soviet leadership would vigorously suppress potential internal opposition to the invasion; but the Czechoslovak phenomenon had a far broader effect in Russia. Since the Soviet dictatorship has always been justified by its stewards as socialism's indispensable defence against internal and external enemies, any attempt to democratize and humanize socialism is a potentially grave threat. For if it can be demonstrated, as the 'Czechoslovak spring' appeared to, that socialism can survive—indeed, can flourish and become popular—without repression, what of the traditional defence of the Soviet dictatorship? What, indeed, of the dictators themselves? Their very *raison d'être* would have disappeared. 'Our Politburo understood this, of course,' said a Leningrad historian, 'and reacted on one hand by invading Czechoslovakia, and on the other by clamping down in Russia. Both reactions were instinctive. The Czechoslovak virus had to be exterminated, and we here had to be immunized against it.'

'The Politburo's primary motive is always the simplest,'

F

said the historian's wife. 'Above all, stay in power. That's why our Communist Party fears Communism more than anything in the world. They can survive any other kind of attack or disaster. But Communism, in the sense of *democratic* socialism, would mean the end of their power. The idea terrifies them. A genuine Communist is persecuted here a hundred times more violently than in any capitalist country.'

Neo-Stalinism was born, however, well before the Czechoslovak spring. Russian intellectuals feel that the first signs appeared shortly after the powerful eruption of youthful challenge to authority almost everywhere in the West — and that the two phenomena were causally linked. The anger of Western youth, especially the young intelligentsia, disturbed the Soviet leadership. 'On the surface, for propaganda purposes, they appeared to be delighted,' explained a physics instructor. 'Students and intellectuals were revolting against everything bourgeois, demonstrating the wickedness of the Western world. But actually, they were frightened. Because challenge to authority and dogma is what worries them most. Everything Western students were saying about the stultifying role of the establishment and its slogans, the emptiness of contemporary goals and hypocrisy of the conventional patterns, the lack of freedom to develop — all that applies a thousand times more to this society than to any Western one. Here's where the real suffocation of human spirit is. But can you imagine a Berkeley free-speech movement or Sorbonne riot here? The Politburo shudders at the very notion.'

Far more serious, however, was the appearance of public dissent in the Soviet Union itself: the protests against the trial of Sinyavsky and Daniel. These two writers, especially Sinyavsky, are still the pre-eminent heroes and martyrs of liberal students and intellectuals. Their fate was more agonizing than that of subsequent convicted protesters (Ginzburg, Bukovsky, Litvinov) because the Russian intelligentsia is traditionally more moved and rallied by men of letters than by political activists or men of any other calling. That writers should suffer, and even worse, a writer of Sinyavsky's calibre and dazzling 'Russian' imagination, is the most hateful kind of injustice.

The number of protesters — 'signers' (*podpischiki*) as they are now called in Moscow — was in fact tiny. And 'protest' is a misleading term: the communications were in fact humble requests to reconsider the consequences of the trials. Nevertheless, there is evidence that the Soviet leadership was at first surprised, then infuriated, by the unprecedented challenge. (The story is told of Podgorny receiving a gift during one of his trips to a provincial city; on opening it and finding a petition, in place of the traditional honey-cake, he is said to have been seized by uncontrollable rage.) The Politburo decided to eliminate the dissent before it became a habit. 'Their reaction,' said my friend who had been called to the K.G.B. office, 'was the current squeeze. It was a classic case of over-kill.'

At the same time, international reverses were pushing the Soviet leadership towards one of their periodic bouts of internal repression — a well-established reaction among dictatorships. Recent events had indeed been sufficiently adverse to provoke sharp repercussions: China's hostility and the subsequent challenge to the Kremlin as the oracle of Marxism–Leninism; the humiliation of the Six Day War; the dissolution of the world Communist movement and the discrediting of Russia's image in non-aligned states; the immense loss of prestige, both within and without the socialist camp, after Czechoslovakia. In the classical pattern, the Politburo reacted to these reversals by shifting towards

conservatism and enlarging the K.G.B.'s power. The leadership seemed willing to sacrifice international goodwill — even
of Western Communist Parties — in order to strengthen its
control.

*   *   *

There is, of course, the argument that the current repression
is the beginning of the dictatorship's death throes: that the
old guard is losing its grip — as it must, in proportion to
Russia's material, scientific and cultural development. And
sensing the inevitability of liberalization and democratization,
it is fighting desperately and futilely to maintain control.

I have heard this hypothesis often enough in the West, but
never in Russia, neither from those who operate the dictatorship nor those who suffer under it. Whatever the dictatorship's prospects in the long run, there is little hope in Moscow
for its demise in the coming decades. Despite the alienation
of intellectuals and the almost total expiration of revolutionary and ideological fervour, the dictatorship is as powerful
as ever, and in many ways controls the country more completely than before.

'The only place I encounter strong optimism about
liberalization,' said a middle-aged teacher, 'is in the Western
press. The notion that protests against the writers' trials are
the forerunners of a great movement towards freedom is
wishful thinking. It's a Western analysis based on Western
conditions, and has little to do with Russian history and the
Russian environment. Genuine liberalization is impossible
under this dictatorship, and unless there is a war, or another
kind of cataclysm, there's no reason to hope the dictatorship will lose its hold.'

*   *   *

Probably the campaign's most oppressive aspect is not present hardship, but anxiety about the future. Among the liberals there is palpable fear that neo-Stalinism may slide into full Stalinism, with a deepening of Russian isolation and a return to some forms of mass terror. 'The campaign's gathering momentum all the time,' a university lecturer told me recently. 'No one knows where it will end. These things have a way of running away with themselves in Russia.'

And his friend: 'There are more and more blatant clues — the restoration of the M.V.D. for example — calculated to frighten the hell out of everybody. What frightens me in particular is that they've passed a certain line: they're not even trying any longer to reassure the liberals or pretend about the growth of democracy. They've decided to go on with the hard line and simply silence the people who disapprove.'

Of all these 'clues', perhaps Stalin's partial rehabilitation is the most frightening. 'The word's gone out to stop writing about Stalin's "mistakes",' a young editor told me. 'It's not a rumour, but an actual directive. People are not to be reminded about the cult of personality [i.e. the purges, terror and mass deaths before firing squads and in camps] any longer. And notice, it's barely mentioned in print now. The season for books exposing Stalin's crimes is over. Nothing will be published that suggests they were anything more than unfortunate "excesses". Stalin's our Father again, and we must be grateful to him for making the country strong against all enemies. It's a distinct change of tone. A dismal omen.'

Even to an outsider, untrained in the Aesopian and quasi-coded language in which changes in the Party line are made known, the shift in the official attitude towards Stalin is unmistakable. When I arrived, in early 1965, authors, editors and publishers were still going forward under the momentum of Khrushchev's de-Stalinization campaign, emphasizing the 'cult of personality' and 'violations of socialist legality' — although the horror of the purges, mass executions and arctic concentration camps to which these euphemisms refer was never fully described. After Brezhnev and Kosygin had consolidated their new collective leadership, however, mention of Stalin all but disappeared from print. This was not, according to most Russian intellectuals, to protect Stalin or restore his reputation, but simply to have done with this potentially explosive issue raised by the impulsive Khrushchev, to avoid embarrassing questions that could only serve to discredit the Party, upset the nation, and would do nothing for the building of Communism.

By mid-1968, however, Stalin had returned, and in a conspicuously new light. Books appeared praising his iron strength and dedication to the Motherland and socialist cause. Several were written by prominent marshals and generals, scientists, officials and members of the literary establishment, and serialized in leading newspapers, magazines and literary journals. Two aspects of his leadership are emphasized in the present reassessment: his role as commander-in-chief during the defeat of Nazi Germany, and the earlier role as commander-in-chief during the first five-year plans that transformed the country into a great industrial power. The essential point is that, despite his mistakes, Stalin was an immensely constructive Marxist–Leninist whose first concern was always the most important: to make the country strong. A decision like collectivization of agriculture, which is thought to have cost millions of lives, was nevertheless a giant step in the right direction, for a fully planned, mobilized economy would have been impossible without it. (And once again, the new line returned to sneering attack against Bukharin, Trotsky and other 'traitors' who suggested — or who were said by Stalin to have suggested — that collectivization and industrialization might be achieved in less brutal ways.) In short, Stalin was right on all the major decisions of his regime, and the twenty million or more people who lost their lives under it represented no more than a temporary 'distortion in the life of Soviet society'.

Nor is this reassessment of Stalin an accident; books on subjects as sensitive as Stalin and Stalinism are published only after authorization by high, and perhaps the highest, Party authority. In this country, history of all kinds, but particularly this kind, is a political issue of supreme importance.

Recently, a journalist friend of one of my close friends was commissioned to write a chronology of the year 1953 for a new year-by-year historical series by the publishers of a children's encyclopaedia. This was the year of Stalin's death, and in his account, the journalist mentioned the notorious funeral procession in Moscow. On March 6th, hundreds of thousands of people pushed their way into the centre of the city in hopes of catching a glimpse of Stalin's coffin, which was lying in state in the famous House of Columns. The pressure became so intense that people were literally crushed to death against trees, walls of buildings and signposts. There was only one way to avoid mass panic and substantial loss of life: the Army trucks lining the streets and squares had to be moved to allow the pressure to dissipate. But although people pleaded with officers to move their equipment and help control the human tidal wave — pleaded even as they were crushed and trampled in agony against the trucks — the officers did nothing: they had had no orders to move. Many of the officers themselves were hurt, and others wept as they watched the terrible suffering and heard the cries. But they were powerless to help; they had had no orders. It was a particularly shocking day; perhaps because the deaths could have been avoided; perhaps because the dictator seemed to be taking sacrificial victims with him, like an Egyptian pharaoh; perhaps (as Yevtushenko describes in his autobiography) because the soldiers and policemen, in refusing, against their own will and common sense, to help their own people, seemed to symbolize everything abhorrent in Stalinism: senseless, inhuman orders executed to the letter because reason, compassion and good sense had been extinguished by tyranny and bureaucratism.

This was the point the journalist most wanted to make about the funeral. But he was instructed by his editor to delete all mention of the deaths of that day. It was necessary, he was told, to stress the deep sense of loss felt by the Soviet people and to record the display of mourning; but not necessary to include details that might cast aspersions on Stalin for no sound reason. The writer protested — a rare action — and, when this produced no results, he raised the matter to the encyclopaedia's editorial board. A heated and prolonged dispute ensued, ending in the writer being sacked and the project being assigned to someone else.

When I met this man several weeks after his dismissal, he was still bitter and depressed by the affair. 'The attitude towards Stalin,' he said, 'is absolutely crucial. It's a reflection of the whole problem of authority and the individual, of the difference between what Bolshevism was supposed to be and what it turned out to be — of a hundred things only Russians can fully understand. The main point is, Stalinism wasn't an accident and wasn't temporary; much of it — the theoretical and intellectual aspects, the *tone* — still weighs us down. And we're not going to break free unless we act, which is just what the Party has decided it cannot or will not do.

'I myself remember the day Stalin died very clearly. I was

eleven years old. During the war we'd been evacuated from Moscow to a little village where my grandmother lived, and I went back to live there in 1953. When the announcement came through, everybody was absolutely devastated: we all thought it was the end of the world. Life without Stalin was simply unthinkable—unbearable. Schoolchildren wept, even our teachers. We organized a guard of honour round his bust. We all thought of him as a kind of personal god: our great leader, our *rodnoi* (our own dear) Father. Ever since we'd been able to talk and read, we'd talked and read about him. We never had enough to eat, and I remember the wind ripping through my rags; and yet we all chanted, "Thank you, dear Comrade Stalin, for our happy childhood!" as we were taught. And we meant it. They might have taught us to say, "Thank you, Comrade Stalin, for the trees, for our rain, for Tchaikovsky and Turgenev;" we'd have believed that too. We're a fantastic people—we bless our gods and leaders for our rags. That's what I was trying to undermine, in a small way, in the account of Stalin's funeral. That's the crippling heritage of Stalinism in the long run. As for the short run—the polishing up of his image by the Politburo—the danger of that is obvious enough. It means a tightening-up of authority.'

When the neo-Stalinist movement began in earnest last winter, there was a surge of fear it would develop into full terror. Then, after a month or so, it became clear that it was going to stop well short of authentic Stalinism and the fear subsided somewhat. Now, however, the tension is steadily mounting again, keeping pace with the growth of the movement itself. 'Stalinism could return tomorrow,' said the stepfather of one of my closest friends recently. 'Do you know why some people have stopped seeing you? Because they're afraid a new Stalin is in the wings, and when he takes the stage, friendship with a foreigner—even someone like you, who's been invited here—will be enough to send them to a labour camp. I myself don't think it will came to that, obviously, and you're welcome to continue visiting us. But who can be sure? People say it can never happen again because we're a different society at a higher level of development. That's wishful thinking. In this country, there are no guarantees.'

As I write this, however, many liberals are less pessimistic about the immediate future. Most people feel there will be no mass terror so long as Russia's international position does not suffer drastic reversals and collective leadership is maintained in the Politburo. 'But if a single man gets control again,' said a young instructor at my institute, 'nothing will stop him. In fact, he'll be forced to eliminate his beaten competitors and discredit everyone around them. This could easily lead on further to another period of madness like the 1930s.'

'But what if the single man who takes power is a liberal?' I asked.

'There are no liberals at the top. Not in the Politburo. No Soviet Dubceks in sight, and no viable faction within the Party that would support one. That's the worst of it. Czechoslovakia will bounce back one day, no matter what we do to them. Russia will stay true to her character. Which means keeping a tyranny roughly like this, with periodic witch hunts more or less like this one.'

4 NOTES ON A WINTER IN RUSSIA

LIVING here year after year, trying to observe and understand, searching for explanations, one slowly refines and reduces one's theories and hypotheses to a simple statement: Russian life is a reflection of Russian winter. Nothing I had read or heard prepared me for it. In Leningrad, frozen fog hangs in layers round the old tsarist palaces and ministerial headquarters; the Neva is a metre of ice. Moscow is drier but much colder—so searingly cold that Muscovites themselves are startled and embittered by it. It is a romantic mistake to assume that Russians have become somehow immune to the cold. Not long ago, a pretty young chemist with a fondness for Shakespeare shattered this illusion once and for all. 'No, we do not get used to it just because we're Russian. For are we not human? If you freeze us, do we not shiver?' She longs for what any girl of any nationality would long for in the circumstances—warm boots and a fur coat.

In 1968, the cold was crueller than at any time since the famous winter of 1941–2, which helped stop the Wehrmacht at the gates of Moscow, laying waste its men, materiel and morale. The first heavy snow fell in early October; by December, one's shoulders ache from the weight of one's overcoat; skin flakes and cracks, and a muted, universal depression hangs over the city: the hardest period has only just begun. The radio blandly announces temperatures of minus thirty to minus thirty-five degrees centigrade (minus twenty to minus thirty degrees Fahrenheit) in the Moscow region, and minus fifty degrees centigrade (minus fifty-eight degrees Fahrenheit) in the Urals.

Russian winter is not simply colder than winter elsewhere in Europe; it is so much, and so immutably, colder that the difference becomes one not merely of degree but of kind. Long grey months of iron cold that heavily tax energy and nerves: it is unfair; man cannot win.

A sense of being under siege and of fighting overwhelming adversity creeps into your consciousness: something is *wrong* with this land: higher forces want to punish you. When a trip out of doors is unavoidable, you bundle yourself in a mountain of clothes, hunch into your collar and trudge resentfully through the beleaguered city, conscious at every slippery step and burning breath that this is a land where hardship is a way of life.

Yet somehow, things work. Miraculously, the rattling old buses keep moving in thirty-five and forty degrees of frost. Armies of workers, deploying immense modern machines and the muscle power of peasant women, clear the streets of heavy, daily snowfalls—the most impressive display of efficiency and organization in civilian life. The city's movements are slowed down by the great cold, and enormous reserves of strength are consumed simply protecting oneself against it; but Russians have become expert in keeping their houses warm and operating machinery under conditions that would make other nations despair. Often I marvel not at how little is accomplished here but—considering the hostile environment—how much; and I feel a warm pride, as if I myself were part of it, when I see construction cranes moving and bricks being laid on a viciously cold morning. There is something uplifting simply in staying alive and in motion in defiance of this weather.

And there are compensations. The rare sunny days can be

exhilarating, and on Sundays I take the metro with my friends to the outskirts of Moscow and spend the day cross-country ski-ing. The city stops suddenly where the last raw housing development cuts into the woods, and we are in the Russian countryside, in touch with the ageless Russian spirit. The landscape makes us think of Berdyaev: 'There is that in the Russian soul which corresponds to the immensity, the vagueness, the infinitude of the Russian land; spiritual geography corresponds with the physical.' The little ramshackle villages with their disintegrating churches exude an extraordinary, almost mystical aura. I have felt it once before, but can't remember when ... at last I remember: at my first sight of early Chagall. The villages, like those in his paintings, are decrepit, eroded, sunk in snow, mud and holy fatalism; yet fantasy and a free human spirit soar and dance in them somewhere, like Chagall's figures floating between the thatched rooftops and the moon. I cannot explain the effect of this combination of backward wretchedness and profound peace, of hopeless disorder and limitless hope. But it is there, as it has always been — at least since Russian writers began describing it.

At first the Russian countryside meant nothing to me, and I could not understand the fuss Russians made about it. Every writer and poet (almost every member of the Russian intelligentsia is a — possibly unpublished — poet) sings its praises with lyrical emotion. Unlettered people, too, as I quickly discovered, have a deep, half-mystical attachment to the Russian earth and air. A day in the countryside, they say, is a supreme kind of joy. It refreshes the spirit and cleanses the soul: it is communion with the world and oneself.

These writers and waiters with their urge for a day in the country are obviously not propagandists; and yet the Russian countryside appeared to me ordinary to the point of dullness, and something rang falsely sentimental in their praises. No rugged mountains or virgin forests, no breathtaking views; nothing spectacular, or even exciting. Just tired old woods and slopes, eroded river banks, and meandering paths made by five centuries of tired feet, leading to an abandoned shack or two, to complete the air of utter neglect.

At last I understood. It is precisely for this ordinariness that the Russian countryside is so loved. Nature here is not for show, but for *use*. It is like a large, old, uncared-for country house, totally unpretentious and welcoming. Disorder, lack of splendour, utter naturalness—this is what makes one at home in a way one can never be in the far more dazzling Alps or Black Forest. Erosion, untidiness, sadness, a motley juxtaposition of trees, cart tracks and a decaying fence ... It is old Russia again: artless, wholly itself, demanding nothing at all from you, but putting you at peace.

Even in winter, when much of the countryside is concealed by a heavy white blanket, this feeling persists. We ski along the paths over fresh snow, panting because there are few hills, and all the motive power is our own. It is not ski-ing as I have previously known it, but a kind of messing about and playing in the snow. There is no competitiveness, and not a single item of special ski-ing clothes—and the skis themselves are as worn-looking as the countryside. Large numbers of Moscow couples, groups of friends and entire families, are spending their Sunday in the same way. When the sun shines—a brilliant ball that gives light but no heat; at its zenith it is perhaps ten degrees above the horizon—we occasionally see a young man stripped to the waist, in spite of the thirty degrees of frost. On the way home, we stop at a large food shop, each of us standing in a separate queue to help amass the provisions quickly. Arms full, we return to someone's flat to thaw out; and in the evening, we stuff ourselves with hors d'œuvres, home-made borscht and shashlik, and drink Moskovskaya vodka and Georgian wine in quantities to match the food and cold. It has been a splendid day, without a care in the world, without a thought about the world's future or anything else unconnected with ourselves and our feelings.

My friends have never travelled in the West and probably never will, but their comparisons are accurate, nevertheless. 'Our life is simpler. Harder, yes—very much harder. But simpler. We don't have the Martinis and sophistication—but we don't have to smile when we don't want to. You're never far from the elements here, and from a certain understanding of the human condition. And the human condition is sad, after all. Seven months of winter.'

*   *   *

One of the most unexpected things about Russian life is its enervating mixture of foreboding and serenity Nothing can be done about the weather. Or the government; or Czechoslovakia; or the poverty. The likes of us are powerless against the huge, predominantly hostile 'outside' forces that shape our destiny—and so my Russian friends and I remain on the 'inside' as much as we can, busying ourselves with the struggles and pleasures of our daily lives. The passiveness of centuries is in the air and bred into our bones; we eat, drink, do as little work as possible, and try to wangle passes for the closed showing of *Cassanova 70* for Party officials and the cinema elite. A bottle of French cognac or a kilo of oranges, magically procured, is cause for a celebration. Or an anniversary, a pay-day or birthday—even Lenin's birthday—serves as a reason for yet another party. Even the liberal intellectuals who are in danger spend dreamy, self-absorbed days in the Russian manner. No single quality of existence here is as important as the underlying spirit: the inevitability of things, the heaviness and closeness of fate. If you want to know the feeling of modern Soviet life, read not journalists' reports, but the nineteenth-century Russian novelists.

*   *   *

The persistence of immemorial Russian attitudes into Soviet society is what most surprised me my first winter here. One of the most curious and fundamental qualities of life is that the dictatorship's control and repression, vicious though they often are, have not enforced personal or social regimentation except in distinctly political areas of activity. (This is easier to appreciate when one abandons the naive notion that another country's politics are its life.) There is a long tradition of political apathy in Russia that makes the Praesidium's mastery of political life a natural, or at least understandable, phenomenon. But there is an equally long tradition of personal and social self-confidence that gives Russians a natural immunity to many of the de-humanizing pressures of twentieth-century life. In many ways, Russia is the least conformist society of the seven or eight countries of Eastern and Western Europe in which I've lived—not to mention America, the land of the free, where the pressures to be successful and all-American make it painfully hard for anyone to be simply himself.

Take, for example, the minor matter of uniforms for schoolchildren. They are obligatory and identical throughout the Soviet educational system—not so noticeable in winter, because then they are covered by non-uniform overcoats; but every schoolchild wears his uniform every day.

For girls it consists of a black pinafore over a dark, preferably brown, dress, white cuffs and collar, and a red neckerchief— the emblem of the Pioneers, to which every schoolchild belongs almost without exception. The boys fare much better in a simple grey suit with a mandarin collar and brass buttons—rather like a Mao Tse-Tung or Nehru suit—and a furazhka, the traditional military-style cap with the stiff peak, which in Russia has always suggested something much more imposing than a postman or a bus driver. (The uniforms, in fact, are almost exact copies of the gymnasia uniforms of tsarist Russia, just as Soviet military uniforms, legal codes and many social customs and conventions, are almost precise replicas of their tsarist precursors.)

But what strikes me about all this is the rarity of a child in full uniform. A pair of trousers has rubbed through in the seat and Mother hasn't had time or money to buy a replacement; a brown dress is kept three weeks at the dry cleaner's instead of the five days promised ... one or another part of the uniform is always missing, and the substituted articles are varicoloured enough to ensure that a group of schoolchildren never looks in the slightest way military.

I once asked a teenage girl what happens when pupils come to school out of uniform.

'Nothing happens. Why should it?'

'Doesn't the teacher complain?'

'Sometimes she says something if you're not in the full uniform for a few days running. But you just tell her your dress had to be washed or you need a new one, or something. It isn't the army, after all.'

Even her final point didn't carry much weight: to a foreigner, the Russian Army seems in many ways distinctly unregimented. A column of Russian soldiers marching (excluding the painstakingly rehearsed demonstrations in Red

Square) is a curious sight indeed: it has a lackadaisical, almost lazy air that would not be tolerated in any other army I've seen, except perhaps the Israeli. There is a certain amount of order and regularity, of course, but it is kept to a minimum. The soldiers do not march in step, nor do they all appear to be in full uniform. They chatter or daydream, hold their bodies and rifles at various angles, each man seems to maintain his own expression, pace and attitude towards life. One almost expects to see wives, sweethearts and mothers walking alongside the columns, bringing comfort and carrying bundles—as they did until not very many years ago. (True, the army, more than most Soviet institutions, is saturated by political propaganda, and each company is infiltrated with political-section stukachi to report on 'anti-Soviet' attitudes and behaviour. But this does not seem to affect personal relationships or behaviour.)

In all aspects of 'private' life, there is a remarkable absence of conventional standards and pressure to conform. One is not looked down upon if one is ugly, smells strongly, looks or behaves oddly; nor if one argues with a bus conductor, slurps one's soup, or otherwise departs from the standards of the glossy magazines. And this—despite the tyrannical government—gives an extraordinary sense of freedom to ordinary, non-political Russian life. Freedom from tension and pressure; freedom from the thousand signals that direct the lives of 'outer-directed' Western man. It is well known that personal behaviour is determined more by a country's conventions than its laws or police. In Russia, the conventions permit far greater individual freedom than what the state can grant or take away.

And this is why a walk in central Moscow, after reading a particularly belligerent and ominous call to discipline in *Pravda*, restores one's sense of balance. Moscow traffic is a better guide to the Russian character than the Soviet press; and nothing is more anarchic than the traffic here. Drivers must be careful, for the penalties for infractions are extremely severe. But pedestrians walk about as if in the countryside or a market village. No one pays any attention at all to the 'Stop' and 'Walk' signs placed at great expense on all major intersections. The great masses simply surge forward at will. That is their way: they do not lend themselves to regimentation of this sort. For this is Russia—not Germany or China.

* * *

Another aspect of Russian life that surprised me as a newcomer was the attitude to work. I had expected discipline and regimentation: a dedicated—or frightened—people who report to work on time and are pushed hard at the job. I expected this because I had been reading the Russian press before I came—and should have known better. Why would *Pravda* publish all those dreary, didactic articles, exhorting everybody to be more disciplined at work, cajoling them to fulfil their norm, pleading for greater concentration and productivity, preaching the five-year plan—why all this if Russians were already punctual, regular, disciplined workers?

In fact, of course, the opposite is true. I've never seen such a negative attitude towards work, or such lackadaisical performance. No one I know is driven by conscience to get the job done, or feels compelled to go to work when not in the mood. (And, if one must report, there is always a good chance of persuading, bribing or otherwise convincing the supervisor that this day must be skipped.) The pace is far slower than any I've seen before, and to mention enthusiasm at all, except in connection with creative people, would be misleading. The objective is to do the minimum, and the rules—the unwritten ones—are bent to match the goal.

Again, the ninetenth-century novelists give us the important clues to the Russian character: the traditional torpor and procrastination—on the part of managers as well as workers —easily predominate over twentieth-century propaganda and the efforts of the Communists to instil Western habits of industry, production and the need to keep busy.

One morning I telephoned an official at his office. After the usual fifteen minutes mechanical trouble, I got through to the number and a sour woman answered my ring. Comrade Я, she informed me testily, was on holiday on the Black Sea; call back in a fortnight. I called back in an hour because I knew Я was in Moscow. This time I got through in ten minutes, and another woman, younger but equally sour, said that my man was not at his desk but somewhere in the building—ring again in an hour. Subsequent calls produced the information that: Я was abroad on business in a socialist country; and at a conference in another ministry in the city. The fifth attempt produced the only honest answer of the day: a man admitted he did not know where Я was or when he would return—nor did anyone in the office.

This incident is extraordinary only in degree. Я is the head of a department of a U.S.S.R. ministry, at least the equivalent of a vice-president of a huge corporation. He was not trying to avoid me (in such cases the lies are impossible to penetrate and may continue for weeks) but simply did not bother to tell his colleagues where he was. They themselves could not reach him. He had no personal secretary. This kind of thing is the rule, not the exception, in Moscow offices: chaos rather than regimentation, *je m'en fiche* rather than even an appearance of concern.

'On any given day, in any given office,' says a friend of mine, 'eighty per cent of the staff are in the corridors, gossiping, going out to pee or comb their hair, or making a glass of tea. Before lunch, all effort goes into the battle with hunger; after lunch into the battle with sleep. No one *works*. No one has to. It's almost impossible to be sacked—so hardly anyone can be promoted. You just sit there and put in your time.'

My friend feels all this is caused by the sluggish Russian consumer economy and the near impossibility of getting ahead, either on the job or outside it. 'No matter how well or rottenly you work, you have your one hundred roubles a month, maybe a hundred and ten. That's enough to live on, but barely. If you work a lot harder you can get a bit more —but what for? It's never enough to make any difference. If you scrimp and save, you can put together a tiny bit of money—but again, what for? You can't invest, can't really get anywhere. So everybody works as little as possible and spends every kopeck. All this would change overnight if there were some incentive.'

But most of his friends and mine disagree on his last point. Most Russians have worked, or not worked, in this way throughout Russian history, and the general opinion is that the attitudes are so ingrained that generations will pass before they change. Even if radical reforms were introduced tomorrow in the organization of work and the opportunities for rewards and scales of incentives, Russians would long retain their traditional nonchalance. For in these matters—the development of the inner discipline so devoutly desired by the Communists and their predecessors—national character resists change with the inertia of centuries.

*   *   *

Some day I am going to write a treatise on why Russians work so badly. Why are they so undisciplined, uninterested, unwilling to take on responsibility? It is an immense subject with many interwoven, and sometimes contradictory themes, and if explored at the length it deserves, it would explain a great deal about the conditions of Soviet life and the traditions of Russia; about the inter-relationship of religion, wages and the price of bread. Here I can only mention one or two of the factors.

One of the reasons Russians work badly is that they are surprisingly content with their lot—content, at least, compared with what Westerners would be living at such a meagre level. It is true there is very little of real value to buy, and the prices are outrageous; but it is also true that most Russians do not want much in the way of material goods. (But they want little because they cannot imagine themselves having more—and so the circle goes round.) 'Are you satisfied with your standard of living?' I used to ask Russian workers whenever I could. The average answer ran something like this:

'Satisfied? Why not? I've got my wife, got my own room. A television set, table and chairs and a bed. How many tables do you need, after all? My son's in school, the daughter's got a good job, better than me. What more can I really use besides an extra half-litre [of vodka] now and then? Too many things just get in the way.'

And what does an Intourist chauffeur buy in a hard-currency shop if he's given a dollar by a Western tourist? He rarely saves towards a radio or a nylon shirt, but almost always blues it on a litre of his favourite brand of vodka.

Russian workers have this remarkably low level of expectation and ambition partly, at least, because they do not live in a competitive society where advertised riches are constantly dangled before their eyes. They have never felt a strong pressure to be successful and keep up with the Joneses.

Their frame of mind is still that of the *Russian* peasant, to whom the notion of worldly success and riches is as far-fetched as a holiday in Nassau.

Oddly, there is much in the popular Russian attitude towards work—and acquisition, and certain other aspects of social relations—that reminds one of the southern Catholic countries, whose people are more preoccupied with sin and redemption than commerce, thrift and progress. It is the Protestant, especially the Calvinist, countries of the north that have given the world the concept of work as a means to salvation. But the so-called Protestant Ethic never came to the Russian masses. (Nor, incidentally, did the north's deep-rooted sense of guilt about the pleasures of the flesh.) Salvation in Russia has nothing at all to do with discipline and industry, but with an intangible, mystical goodness—something that concerns infinity and the soul, and is almost the opposite of proving oneself by worldly success and hard work. So the pace is leisurely and the delays taken for granted, and *mañana* is nearly as fundamental an attitude here as in the Latin world.

The contrast between Russian insouciance and the ambition of the rest of northern Europe cannot be over-emphasized. Russian writers have described it again and again. 'It's a curious thing. The Russian peasant is intelligent, quick and full of understanding ... But it's no use at all ... He's never developed that—how to put it?—love of work.' (One of Turgenev's characters in *A Month in the Country*, 1855.) 'Did you ever notice what makes Russian literary heroes different from the heroes of Western novels? The heroes of Western literature are always striving for careers, money and fame. The Russians can get by without food and drink—it's justice and right they're after.' (One of Solzhenitsyn's characters in *The First Circle*, 1967.)

Years ago, I had dinner in the restaurant Moskva in Prague, a well-run establishment where the service was equal to the highest international standards. (The Russian cuisine, too, was on a higher plane altogether than I've encountered in any restaurant in Russia itself.) After the meal, my waiter and I fell into conversation. It turned out he had spent two years working in the restaurant Praha in Moscow—one of the city's best. The waiter told me he could not quite believe, at first, the size of the Praha's staff. I have forgotten the figures, but the Praha had some five times the personnel of the Moskva in Prague. 'On each shift,' said the waiter, 'there were administrators and assistant administrators, several categories of cooks and assistant cooks, apprentices, salad-preparers, washers-up, supervisors of washing-up and, of course, twice the necessary number of waiters.' Still, the Praha's service was the usual maddening farce—a forty-minute wait for the menu alone—and the Moskva's, with one-fifth of the staff, was excellent. 'Because Russians hate work,' said the waiter, 'even when they could double their tips. They don't *care*. Otherwise they're splendid.'

This is not to say that Russians cannot or will not work when they are moved. They can work harder, longer and on less food and rest than anyone I've seen. Millions did it during the first five-year plans, and millions more during the Second World War. And I have seen several workers do it on an individual scale, when they were moved by a friend's need or the challenge of an interesting project. But the point is, they *must* be moved, whether by some special cause or person or idea. Their imaginations must be touched; they must be made to feel a sense of personal involvement. The daily routine, doing the work well for its own sake, is alien to the Russian spirit. This, more than anything, is what makes Russia a pleasant place to live in—and a frustrating, maddening place to work. The slightest task—repairing a pair of shoes, buying a pad of paper, applying for a library card—takes two or three times more time and effort to accomplish here than anywhere else. One becomes exhausted and infuriated. And learns to put off these tasks until tomorrow, like everyone else.

*   *   *

Three 'case histories'—people I met while I ate my lunch one day—say more about the unwritten economic rules and popular economic attitudes than all the scholarly articles I've read.

I am in a small cafeteria near my hostel—the standard kind, with the standard menu of thick soup with black bread, greasy macaroni or fried potatoes with a hunk of unidentifiable meat, and dried fruit compôte served in a thick, chipped glass. The man sharing my table is wearing an ancient flapping suit and a striped shirt with a frayed collar and no tie: the uniform of the 'haute proletariat'. He is, he tells me, a former factory machinist who, for reasons of health, has recently qualified as a chauffeur. Soon he will look for his first job, in a taxi park or government pool or the personnel office of some enterprise, he's not sure which. Isn't he afraid, I ask him, he might not find a job?

'Of course not. It's their job to take me. After all, I'm a qualified driver, aren't I?'

At this point he left, and I did not have time to discuss the details of job-hunting with him. But his point was clear enough. It is the state's *obligation* to find him a proper job. He will not earn much at it—he has no ambition to earn much—but he will be assured of a steady income. It is unthinkable that the state or its agents will not provide a place for him. And this is deeply comforting. Most Russian workers fear unemployment more than they desire to get ahead. And while the propagandists' brag that Russia has no unemployment is not true, it is in fact very low: because millions of people are employed at make-work jobs, and it is virtually impossible to be made redundant. This makes the economy very sluggish—and very safe. This too is how the Russians want it; in these things 'rugged individualism' is hardly their style.

Then, at the table next to me, I overhear the case of an old man who is slurping a big bowl of kasha and milk. He is a thin, stooped cutter in a shoe factory, and quite ill with high blood-pressure and a weak heart. He has worked for nineteen years in this factory; only one more is needed for a pension. He has trouble now making his way to the job, and once there, can hardly pretend to work. But the factory keeps him on so that he will get his pension—and this is done without question, as a matter of course. Who cares what the rules say? This is our old friend Arkady, and he has a family to maintain.

Then there is the mousey girl who serves behind the counter, ladling out soup, cabbage, meat and potatoes—a sweaty, dreary job that earns her sixty roubles a month, hardly enough to live on. But she smuggles out food to take home, and feeds her husband and daughter *gratis* at the cafeteria. The supervisors close their eyes to this: of course she must take care of her family—it would be inhuman to interfere. What's wrong with a bit of harmless stealing when life is hard and people have to be fed?

These three cases are typical; paternalism, protectionism and a blind eye to the bending of the rules are entrenched in the economy, as they always have been. To the vast majority of Russians, economic security is more important than economic opportunity, and the reasons are historical and geographical. For lurking in the Russian consciousness is the threat of failure, and until recently failure here has meant not simply not 'making it'; it meant famine, starvation and trying to survive a winter without fuel or stores. To be protected against this, to have a guarantee of the essentials of life — the minimum requirements of food and warmth — is still a great comfort and a great achievement. If economic opportunity — initiative, independence and competition — carries with it the threat of failure, most Russians would rather not take the risk. Above all, one must be secure in the knowledge that one will have one's daily bread.

*　　*　　*

What is to be done? This is Russia's question of questions. It is the title of Chernishevsky's famous political novel which startled the Russian intelligentsia in the 1860s. It was borrowed by Lenin for his equally famous treatise on the nature and needs of the revolutionary party which startled the intelligentsia again in the early years of this century. The question implies, What is to be done about her age-old misery? About delivering her from her backwardness, enlightening her peasant masses, curing her ills? In one way or another it is asked by everyone, Russian and foreigner alike, who cares about her. But perhaps the only answer — or the wisest — is to do nothing.

' *"What is to be done?" asked an impatient Petersburg youth. What a silly question: what is to be done? If it's summer, there are berries to pick and jam to make. And if it's winter, there's tea to be drunk with this lovely jam."* ' (Vasily Rosanov, 1899. Rosanov, of course, is one of the Russian authors not published in the Soviet Union.)

*　　*　　*

If socialism has changed little in the Russian approach to work, it has probably changed even less in the traditional attitude towards class. This too is a puzzling aspect of Soviet society. In some ways, Russians are the most egalitarian, least class-conscious people in the world. One sees this in the way they approach strangers: anyone in any station of life can talk to anyone in any other, and the exchange is carried out with remarkable ease and candour, and a total lack of concern over accent, dress or rank. And in the way Russians share public facilities like restaurants and buffets. An unshaven peasant who has sold some of his private produce advantageously, and drunk enough of the profits to transport him into a damn-tomorrow spree, will plant himself in his shirt-sleeves at a table in Moscow's best establishment and order herring or champagne, without the slightest self-consciousness about his own appearance amidst the columns, vaulted ceilings and high society in its finery.

This is an inborn sense of equality—deriving probably from the feeling that they are all children of the Russian earth, and brothers in the Russian family—which the Communist ethic has surely reinforced. No people can have heard the continuous sermons about proletarian solidarity, the brotherhood of man, the elimination of exploitation and the classnessness of Soviet society without being affected by them. This has clearly given them a dignity and sense of individual worth.

Other aspects of the Soviet system, however, have reinforced a caste consciousness so archaic and rigid that it makes a foreigner blush. I do not only mean the vastly unequal salaries, prerogatives and privileges attached to different kinds of jobs; many economists have described this. But although scientists earn twenty times as much as unskilled workers—and for peasants the difference is still greater — probably overall the gap is smaller than that between the rich and poor of Western Europe.

However, many of the privileges Russia's upper crust arrogate to themselves would not be tolerated for a moment under the most unrestrained capitalist economy. Theatre and airline tickets, hotel rooms and places in resorts not sold to the pleading crowds *in case* an official or foreigner appears at the last minute to claim, by right, the best of everything. Drivers waiting all day in the cold outside Party and government buildings while officials, their masters, are at work — or enjoying themselves at the specially stocked buffets — inside. Entire stretches of the Black and Baltic Sea coasts and large tracts of the most picturesque countryside reserved for official villas, and not even visible because they are protected by high fences. Caviare, foreign travel, imported furniture, private railway carriages, private hotels ... a hundred luxuries and privileges are reserved exclusively for men of rank. And the Russian masses, struggling in shops, shivering in queues, do not protest or even question this anomaly. No Rockefeller, and not even a Rothschild, could get away with the kind of disdainful high-handedness taken for granted here. But the 'classless' Soviet system is in some ways as class-conscious as the tsarist one, and both surely were derived partially from the Oriental obsession with rank.

The most blatant of the new forms of privilege is the network of hard-currency shops and counters in the major cities. Here, domestic and foreign goods ranging from Scandinavian vegetables, ermine coats and Italian shoes, to Volga motor cars, are in full supply and offered for anything from a third to a fifth of the rouble price, even assuming any of these items can be found in ordinary shops. (This, incidentally, is one reason why there is such enormous demand for hard currency on the black market.)

These hard-currency shops make a cruel mockery not only of socialism and equality, but of any notion of justice and democracy. Yet there they are, dangling unobtainable goods in front of every Russian, and ninety-nine per cent have become inured to the temptation.

One day, however, I witnessed an unpleasant scene at the hard-currency counter in the foyer of a well-known hotel. A burly Russian worker tried to buy a Japanese transistor radio there, but was brushed away haughtily by the saleswoman because he had 'only' roubles. He began to walk away, then stopped suddenly, scarlet with rage. 'What country is this?' he shouted, '*Whose* country?' He held up a ten-rouble note with its engraving of Lenin. 'Whose portrait is this? Is this our Soviet money or not? You tell me: why did I fight five years at the front? You think my mates died for this? *I'm going to buy that radio.*'

But he did not of course; he was led away by a policeman.

I myself am often embarrassed by the special treatment, even obsequiousness, shown me simply because I am a foreigner with a bit of hard currency. It is paradoxical that in no capitalist country does the colour of my money open so many doors and 'earn' me so many of the good things. Some of this may pass when the shortage of goods is alleviated; but I think the curious juxtaposition of egalitarianism in some things and a caste mentality in others will persist.

*   *   *

'There is only one area of production in which we're ahead of the West,' a friend of mine likes to brag, 'not counting propaganda, of course: political jokes.'

This is certainly true in terms of numbers. *Anekdots* abound about the follies of Communism and the Politburo leaders.

Some of the funniest stories—judging by my friends' laughter
—escape me because they allude to events and slogans I don't
know about. I understand best the slight stories that bring
slight smiles.

Communism is at long last achieved in the year 2000,
and little Sasha wonders about the mysteries of the harsh
past.

'Daddy, what was socialism?'

'That was when you had to pay for things with money,
instead of getting everything distributed free, according to
your needs. If you wanted some butter, for example, you'd
stand in a queue at the cash desk, give the cashier some money
for the proper chit, then stand in the queue at the counter
to exchange the chit for butter, if the salesgirl was in a good
mood.'

'Daddy, what's butter?'

A threadbare but distinguished-looking man is making
his way slowly up Gorky Street. Tall, gaunt and slightly
stooped, wearing steel-rimmed glasses he is the picture of
an established academic. After a time, he notices a man
walking at his side and studying him furtively—a swarthy
peasant in a quilted jacket and boots caked with mud and
manure.

'Excuse me,' says the peasant in a hoarse whisper. 'Are
you a member of the Party?'

The professor is surprised, but the question cannot be
dangerous and he answers matter-of-factly, 'Yes, I am a
Party member.'

'Oh wonderful,' says the peasant, rubbing his hands in
anticipation. 'Tell me then, what year did you join the
Party?'

'Well, 1925.'

'*Very* good. Excellent!' The peasant's eyes become greedy-crafty again, and he draws closer and softens his whisper.

'Well then, sir, did you ever take part in the left deviation?'

Now the professor is more than curious, he is beginning to feel apprehensive. He peers down at his muddy interlocutor.

'No, I did *not* take part in the left deviation.'

'Splendid! Simply splendid! Then tell me this: did you ever take part in the right deviation?'

'My good man, I never took part in *any* deviation,' says the professor with more confidence than he feels. 'My record happens to be unblemished.'

'Oh very good indeed, perfect.' Now the peasant is literally breathing down the professor's ear. 'Then tell me, please, where's the lavatory around here?'

The scene is the auditorium of the club attached to a large Moscow factory, during the regular Wednesday political lecture. Machinist Second Class Vanka Ivanov, the salt of the Russian proletariat, is sitting at the back, slipping a bottle of vodka from under his overalls from time to time and gulping cautiously as the professional agitator, reading from a standard propaganda text, drones on. The workmen around Vanka are dozing or arguing about last night's soccer game, and he too settles back in the hard chair, for this is his favourite hour of rest.

Then something in the lecture captures his attention. He perceives the agitator is not talking about Lenin's childhood, dialectical materialism, or the Communist future of mankind; but Chinese insolence and insults to Mother Russia.

'That's what those traitorous Chinamen are doing to us. After we gave them everything they have, thousands of millions of roubles and our best technicians — after we gave them our sweat and comradely love — they spit in our faces. Accusing *us* of distorting our own dear Lenin. And treacherous ingratitude isn't enough: now they're shooting into our borders on the Amur. They openly claim parts of our own dear native Siberia. Comrades! The Party calls upon each and every one of us to recognize China as a great danger to the Motherland and Marxism–Leninism!'

Vanka Ivanov is moved. 'Those dirty Chinese!' he fumes. 'Attacking Russia like that after all we sacrificed for them!' By the end of the meeting, Vanka's bottle is empty and he tight — and very angry. He decides he's going to *do* something for once, to strike a blow for Russia. He is going to find himself a Chink and show him what for.

But it is no longer easy to find a Chinaman in Moscow: since the Sino–Soviet split, almost all have departed. Vanka searches for an hour before finding an Oriental face.

'Hey, you. You're a Chink, aren't you?'

'Oh no, I'm a Tadjik — one of our own Soviet nationalities.'

Vanka moves off, disappointed. During the next few hours, he stops half a dozen men with suspicious Asian faces — but with no luck. A student from Outer Mongolia, a visiting Japanese businessman, a doctor from one of the minor nationalities in Soviet central Asia.

Finally, in a queue for bread in the new south-west district, near the heavily guarded Chinese Embassy, he spies a small man with distinctly oriental features.

'Hey you, yellow-face — are you Chinese?'

'I am indeed.'

'*At last.*' Vanka jumps on the alien, pummels him and pushes him into the snow. Then he rubs his hands and, for good measure, plants a kick in the fallen man's ribs.

H

'That'll teach you, you dirty Jew.'

There is also a new vogue for black humour and Staliniana.

Stalin summons Molotov to his office. Molotov is nervous —the call was urgent. Seated at his desk, Stalin plays with his pipe and stares in his own inimitable way at his sweating underling.

'Listen, Vyacheslav Mikhailovich, something very disturbing has come up. I've been hearing rumours you're a Jew.'

'But ... but ... Comrade Stalin, dear Joseph Vissarionovich. You know that's not true. It *can't* be true. You've known me all these years.'

'Yes ... perhaps.' (Draws on his pipe and pauses ominously.) 'But all the same, you'd better think it over.'

An interval of silence precedes the laughter whenever this joke is told.

*   *   *

My friend exaggerated, of course. Russia is conspicuously ahead of the West in many categories. In the reading of serious literature (the unendurable quality of television helps). In serious drinking. (The ingestion is staggering. I have been told that the annual *per capita* consumption of vodka in the Russian Republic is 10·5 litres—roughly two and a third gallons. Compare this with the *per capita* consumption of spirits in the United Kingdom—roughly half a gallon. And since a Russian can drink nothing for weeks, and puts down his yearly total in a series of monumental binges, the figure is still more extraordinary.) In walking and participation in outdoor sports. And in the enjoyment of pre- and extra-marital sex.

The conventional image of Soviet prudery is nonsense—of all Western misconceptions about Russian life, this is probably the most far-fetched. Behind the appearance of severe modesty and decorum (and this is an old Russian tradition, not a Soviet invention) Russia is considerably more permissive than any Western society I know. Almost all hostels of institutes of higher education are co-educational—boys and girls in adjoining rooms—and it is taken for granted they do not remain in their own rooms at night. Lovemaking is extraordinarily casual, in the emotional as well as physical sense. There is almost total freedom, with very little talk about it, and less guilt. A locked door is rare (supposing one is lucky enough to find an unoccupied room), and so is embarrassment if a friend walks in without knocking.

'We call it socialist realism,' says a university student. 'A certain number of girls don't sleep with men the first night as a matter of principle—about fifteen per cent.'

There is no Pill; only one girl in a hundred has so much as heard of it. ('They'll never introduce it here,' said the prettiest girl in my hostel. 'The birthrate's too low, and this worries them. In the cities, one child is the maximum now. No room or money for more—people want to *live* at last.') No diaphragms either, although a few university girls do know about them. And although condoms are available, they are ludicrously coarse, as their slang name, 'galoshes', implies. No man I know has ever used them. 'We just get on and ride,' says a Leningrad engineer, summing up the evening activity of his circle of friends—fresh girls having been corralled on the streets half an hour before the riding.

Yet both statistics and one's own observation indicate that there are extremely few births. In 1960–5 the world average birthrate was thirty-four per thousand, and in Western countries, twenty-one per thousand. Compared with this, the birthrate in Russia as a whole fell from twenty-five per thousand in 1960, to eighteen per thousand in 1965, and in Moscow itself the birthrate in 1965 was only eleven per thousand. These figures profoundly alarm the authorities.

And in spite of the free and easy attitude towards sex, there seem to be extremely few unmarried mothers. What's the secret? An old antidote: the girls jump up and douche after intercourse. And a modern remedy: legal abortion on demand, which is usually free; the average city girl has had several before marriage. A few go, illegally, to private doctors to avoid the registration, red tape and possible embarrassment of a health-service operation. Private fees range from five to thirty roubles—nothing to worry about. Some girls slip their health-service doctors ten roubles for an anaesthetic injection. Whatever option is selected, the easy availability of abortion encourages an easy-going attitude towards sex.

But I think the attitude would be easy-going in any case, and probably always has been, even under Stalin's much less liberal laws. 'Russian girls are wonderfully submissive,' says the son of a diplomat who has lived in Paris and London. 'If you appeal to them in the right way, they just can't say no. Otherwise, you just *tell* them you won't take no for an answer.'

Yet officially, in public, and especially in the press, the appearance of utter decorum—even prudery—is maintained. I remember a recent *Izvestiya* article by the chief customs officer at Brest. It described the customs service's high moral purpose, and their eternal vigilance against poisons that imperialist agents and decadent bourgeois tourists tried to sneak into the Motherland. Among the literature recently confiscated from foreigners at the Brest 'front'—most of it 'anti-Soviet political propaganda' (books about Russia disapproved of by Soviet authorities) — were several issues of *Playboy* and its competitors. The customs officer professed to be outraged at this attempt to corrupt Soviet morals; yet sexual life in the major Russian cities is free and exciting beyond the imagination of any *Playboy* writer or editor.

*   *   *

Here and there in the self-righteous, prudish press, snippets of light humour and even frivolity appear. (Occasionally, too, there is a first-rate film that manages to avoid sentimentality and sermonizing — even politics altogether. No one seems able to explain how or why these manifestations of 'pure' art, some of them very good indeed, manage to pass through the bureaucratic cultural machine.) Here is a squib from the magazine *Youth*, whose political bias is progressive in the Soviet context. It appeared in the miscellaneous section (called *pilesos*, vacuum cleaner), and is one of the cleverest little comments on this aspect of Russian life I've seen. It is also instructive for those who read between the lines. Any Russian reader understands, for example, that 'necking on the first night' is a euphemism.

ASK A SILLY QUESTION — GET A SILLY
ANSWER
(*From the Correspondence of Galka Galkina*)
Dear Editor,

I'd be very interested to know what kind of opinion chicks have of themselves. People are always writing things like, 'She refused to dance with a man who was drunk,' or, 'She slapped his face for using bad language.' Huh! That kind of thing never happens. I've tried it for myself more than once. Came to dances not exactly sober, and used plenty of bad language about all sorts of things — anything and everything, no holds barred! Started necking on the first night, and not one girl has ever tried any slapping. What's the matter, are they afraid or something? And what's more, I never pick out my chicks, but simply walk up to anyone who interests me the slightest bit.

There's not a grain of strictness in any of them. That's how it goes: an evening with one girl, the next with another.

There you are, they like fellows who know how to *act*.

Two years ago I wasn't like this at all, and they didn't pay me any real attention. Now I'm 'celebrated' in the town as a lady-killer — although, as far as I can see, there's nothing special about me at all. The chicks themselves ask me for dates, and I've had too much of it all, I'm sick of the whole business.

I'd like to get rid of them all, but no matter how you push them away, they keep coming back for more.

Please advise them in your magazine to have a little more pride, then men will have more respect for them.

YURI E——OV
City of Troitsk
Chelyabinsky region

Dear Yura,

I must confess your letter agitated and disturbed my maidenly soul. My heart actually skipped a beat, as they say.

I immediately dashed to the editor-in-chief and began pleading to be sent to Troitsk city. I dreamed about seeing you, Yura! But my request for the assignment was turned down.

'No, Galka,' they told me, 'you're a young girl, a weak creature. Sending you would simply be too dangerous. Just suppose you meet this Yura when he's tight — how would you be able to resist his embraces? Or he'll say something vulgar to you, and you'll melt in his arms. And he'll start necking on the first night! Nothing doing, lovey — you'd better play safe at home.'

In short, they wouldn't let me go.

And how I was longing to try out your fascination on me! How I wanted to see you: so super, so well-built, so marvellously boorish. I can just picture how you'd come up to me with your charming, swaggering strut and intriguingly announce, 'Hey, stupid, let's dance ... '

Good heavens, my heart would simply burst with joy!

But at the same time, I'm worried about your fate, Yura.

Don't you see you're going to ruin yourself this way? Do you think your kind of irresistibility is a joke!?

Perhaps you could try plastic surgery? ... But no, I'm afraid that wouldn't work! You'd still have your boorishness and presumptuousness ...

No, Yura, we'll have to think of something more clever ... Try becoming polite, considerate and occasionally sober. That frightens away the girls like nothing else!

And most important, don't write any more letters like that to the magazine. There was so much conceit, cheap moralizing and cynicism in your first one that after its publication, you'll be absolutely overwhelmed by the female sex.

But it's not worth ruining your nerves for our sake.

If we like you, Yura, then as, they say, we deserve you!

> Regards — from someone who's
> lost her mind over you,
>
> GALKA GALKINA

P.S. I haven't written out your name in full because, judging by your letter, everybody knows you in Troitsk.

And this item from the writers' newspaper, *Literary Gazette*, dated August 21st, the day of the invasion. It is obviously satirical, and 'wine' here surely stands for something stronger. But the point it makes about contemporary attitudes of Russian girls (at least those who live in the major cities) is fairly obvious. The action takes place in Leningrad.

IT HAPPENED ONE EVENING

The volunteer-communal sociological committee of our district has questioned several bachelor-fathers, and as a result has discovered the process by which a young man becomes a bachelor-father. As an example, we shall cite the history of twenty-year-old Anatoly Shumaev.

This is what Slava S. (as A. Shumaev asked us to call him) told us:

'I made the acquaintance of Lusya K. (this is her real name) accidentally on the street. She approached me and suggested we get to know each other. I, of course, immediately refused, because one does not make acquaintances on the street. But at this point, it turned out I had nothing to do that evening and she had two tickets for the cinema. To cut a long story short, I was persuaded.

'When I accompanied Lusya home from the cinema, she tried to kiss me in her doorway. I, of course, wanted to end our acquaintance immediately, but at this point, it turned out that Lusya plays jazz on the electric guitar and has a motor scooter. To cut a long story short, I realized that she was an interesting person, unlike the other girls who try to pick men up on the streets.

'I saw Lusya again once or twice—I don't remember exactly how often—and on Saturday, she invited me back to her place. I, of course, immediately refused, but at this point, it turned out that she had some new records and her parents were in the country for the week-end. To cut a long story short, I went along. At first everything was fine: we listened to the records and then Lusya opened a bottle of wine ... I, of course, immediately refused, but at this point, it turned out the wine was mild and Lusya suggested we drink to love. To cut a long story short, I drank two or three glasses—I don't remember exactly how many.

'We began to dance, and Lusya put out almost all the lights. I, of course, immediately decided to go home, but at this point, it turned out my head began to spin a bit from the effects of the wine. To cut a long story short, I stayed with her. Alas, that was my mistake.

'After a while, Lusya informed me that I was going to be a father. I, of course, immediately burst into tears and said that if she's an honest person she must marry me. But at this point, it turned out she didn't want to burden herself [this is a play on words: 'to be pregnant' is literally 'to burden oneself' in Russian] with a family and *I* myself should have thought of the consequences. To cut a long story short, I became a bachelor-father, and I'm ashamed now even to appear at dances.

It turns out that my father's right: you can't trust a girl until she marries you.

'Everything that happened to me could have been prevented if the schools had instilled in us, from child-hood on, a sense of manly honour and pride ...'

The histories of the other bachelor-fathers questioned by our volunteer-communal sociological committee are all more or less the same, and differ one from the other mainly in the names involved and the amount of wine consumed.

The mini-skirt can serve as an example of Russia's social attitudes and environmental pressures. In the major cities, skirts two or three inches above the knee are now tolerated, along with imitations of the shake, cool jazz, imported juke boxes in three or four cafés in the centre of town, and several other novelties that had been denounced as dangerous bourgeois decadence until a year or two ago. If these few items of swinging life seem feeble and sometimes pathetic to a foreigner, they are events to young Russians, and are greeted happily, both for themselves and as symbols of the kind of new man and new society they want. Designers even publish sketches of skirts four or more inches above the knee. (But what is published in magazines and what is worn on the street seem to have even less relation to each other here than elsewhere in the world: I have not yet seen a single Russian woman who is well-groomed and smartly dressed from head to toe in all of Leningrad, Moscow or Kiev.) But genuine mini-skirts are not manufactured, and no girl would risk wearing one in public.

'Why not?' I asked a bleached-blonde shop girl who had seized my copy of *Paris-Match* and was transfixed by photo-graphs of her Western counterparts exposing nine inches of thigh on the streets of Paris and London.

'You just wouldn't. It isn't done.' (Incidentally, in the privacy of a friend's well-heated flat, this girl has less modesty about nudity — even in the presence of strangers — than a thousand ultra-mini-skirted English girls.)

'But what would happen if you *did* do it?'

'You'd get arrested. Or sacked. No policeman would let you past on the street; maybe even the crowd would stop you. And if you got to your office, you'd be called in and told that's not the way Soviet women dress, and don't come back until you've learnt how they do. Believe me, the idea is just ridiculous. No girl would try it.'

'But how can you be sure? Maybe nobody tries it simply because no one else has.'

'Well, it happens that a few really cheeky girls *did* try it last summer. They planned it for weeks. Then walked out from their flat into the street in their home-made minis, about six inches above the knee. They were so self-conscious they wanted to die. The first policeman who saw them took them to the station, and they were almost relieved. The whole experiment lasted two minutes. It was a farce, and they knew it all the time.'

She paused for a moment, looked at the photographs of the swinging London birds again, and sighed. 'Besides,' she added, 'what's the good of a mini-skirt in *this* weather? You could wear it for maybe three weeks a year. The rest of the time, you'd just *freeze.*'

The point applies to a hundred aspects of Russian life: the 'system' or 'regime' is only partly and secondarily responsible for the restrictions, prohibitions and severity. It is the geography, history and above all the climate that sets the tone and lays down the fundamental rules. A coat that does not come below the knees is really worth very little here.

*   *   *

The attitude towards marriage and divorce, as towards sex, is remarkably easy-going—and, once again, this is encouraged by surprisingly liberal laws. Divorce is granted virtually on demand: last year (according to a Russian newspaper article) almost ninety per cent of the couples requesting it in the courts of the land had agreed beforehand to the step— and over ninety-six per cent of the requests were granted. Granted, moreover, in a matter of minutes when the case was actually heard before the court; except in unusual circumstances, the court's decision—based on a simple statement that 'I do not love him/her any longer' or 'I just don't want to live with him/her any longer'—is virtually automatic.

Marriage—that is to say, its formal registration—seems to be a correspondingly insignificant step in many people's lives. Great numbers of couples—those lucky enough to find a suitable room—live together without bothering with the formalities of registration. The young do it for the reasons young people everywhere in the world do. (Except perhaps more of them do it for less reason; less importance, fuss and coyness is attached to it, and fewer explanations to oneself and others are needed.) Older people do it because of the dislocations of the war: women in their forties and fifties heavily outnumber the men, and this was recognized by many of the sociologists, psychologists and jurists who debated the new Code of Marriage and the Family, recently enacted. Men are so scarce that many Russian women of that age can have no permanent relationship with one, and many feel an illegitimate baby is better than none. (The new code, which removed all legal disadvantages from illegitimate children, was another piece of admirably liberal, adult social legislation.) But the special pressures of Soviet life give rise to curious 'arranged' marriages. A number of marriages are entered into because the man has an opportunity to go abroad in the diplomatic service or on one of the many economic and technical missions. The authorities are extremely reluctant to send bachelors to any post abroad — Soviet honour might weaken under temptation — and some young men marry the first available girl when they hear of an opportunity for foreign assignment. (I'm told particularly attractive girls are never chosen as Aeroflot stewardesses on international routes, for similar reasons.)

A greater number of marriages are contracted because one of the partners is a legal resident of a city where the other wants to live. Moscow, Leningrad and several of the republic capitals and Black Sea resorts, are 'closed' cities. That is to say that one can move there only by securing a job that carries with it a residence permit or — considerably easier — by marrying a man or woman who has one. This is why a large number of undergraduates whose homes are in the provinces seek marriages of convenience during their final year of study. 'I'll marry any old hag,' said a student at my institute. 'It doesn't matter, as long as she has a Moscow permit. I'll do anything to stay in the big city.' This attitude is widespread, and the 'permit-marriage' is so widely accepted that money is often paid to the partner with a coveted police registration. It is not unlike the political marriages by which people contrive to leave unpleasant 'closed' countries.

A well-known Moscow story illustrates this point nicely. Two men, old acquaintances, meet on a street. One has heard the other was recently married. '*Nu*,' he asks, 'how's married life?' 'Not bad,' replies the newly-wed. 'But the window faces the courtyard.'

Not long ago, the results of a questionnaire sent to five hundred recently divorced couples in Leningrad were published in *Izvestiya*. Sociological research of this kind is a great novelty, and the article attracted considerable attention. The questionnaire revealed that 'living space' was the major cause of marital disharmony: forty-one per cent of the couples said arguments with in-laws played a role in the divorce. (Most young couples live with parents-in-law for at least the first few years, and although Russians seem to tolerate cramped quarters and lack of privacy better than most people, it can get on their nerves too.) One in five said continuation of the marriage was impossible because of the other partner's constant drinking. Thirteen per cent had married for economic, 'residence-permit' or 'living-space' reasons, and thirteen and a half because they had been expecting a baby.

Only sixty per cent said they had definitely loved each other before marriage. Twenty-four people said they didn't love the partner at all, and seventeen that they just didn't care. Over a third of the couples had known each other for less than six months, and ten couples had been acquainted only a few days. The most telling evidence of the easy-going attitude towards marriage was the fact—reported in the same article—that ten per cent of the people who had booked the solemn ceremony at the Palace of Marriage did not appear.

Statistics like these are quoted by doctors, psychologists, jurists and the handful of new sociologists who write in the popular press, urging careful thought about ways to elim-inate the 'frivolous' attitude to marriage of a certain segment of the population. In general, these articles are by liberal-minded authors, who call for sex education and courses on marriage and the family (which are unknown). But there are also suggestions that the waiting period between the appli-cation for marriage and the ceremony itself be extended from one month, the present statutory minimum, to three.

These suggestions, however, are dismissed by people whose opinion I respect. 'The government just wouldn't risk it,' observed one of my friends. 'Why? Public opinion — there'd be too much indignation. On things like these, they really do take people's feelings into consideration. Just like vodka: they could raise the price to whatever level they want to reduce consumption, or simply cut down supplies to the shops. But do you notice that in spite of all the furious campaigns against drunkenness, every food shop, no matter how bare its other departments are, is always stocked to the ceiling with vodka? Because for one thing, cutting down on supplies would immediately lead to a huge increase in the production of moonshine. One way or another, the vodka is going to be drunk. The government knows this, and would rather make the money on legal sales. But they know they have to keep the shops fully stocked for another reason: a deficit in vodka would produce a lot more tension in our life, and that would lead to mass discontent, maybe even riots. Easy vodka, easy marriage and employment, an easy-going life — that's what the people really care about.'

*   *   *

The issue of whether to tighten marriage requirements is an open one, with frank and intelligent debate in the press. But Russians — their instincts sharpened over decades — are often more interested in what is *not* publicly reported and discussed. Clues, rumours and deductions from between-the-lines reading are the major sources of information and often the major topics of discussion.

'I always fly Il-18s,' says a friend of mine who makes

frequent trips to construction sites. 'Why? Because the Politburo boys always do. If *they* pick that plane above all others,
that means it's safe.'

It is a minor example of the Soviet sixth sense in inter-
preting news and recognizing clues. Soviet plane crashes are
never mentioned in the Soviet press. (Western crashes are
fully reported.) Which planes, then, are safe? Sharp observations are made, the necessary deductions arrived at, and the
good word travels fast.

*   *   *

A thin African boy, obviously a student, boards a crowded
Moscow bus, looking morose in the bitter cold, and sadly
incongruous in his collective-farm hat with the flapping ear-
covers. The woman sitting next to me, a spreading, middle-
aged matron with a beautiful plump child on her lap,
shudders demonstratively. 'Those dirty blacks. Disgusting.
I can't stand them.'

More and more frequently and openly one hears gratuitous
comments like this. Russians used to whisper their revulsion
for black Africans, conscious that they were guilty of something faintly anti-Soviet and, perhaps, anti-humanist. But
casual acquaintances now broach the subject openly, as if
proud to share an accepted local prejudice. Many Russian
girls announce that they are upset by the sight of black skin —
and would be sickened by the touch of it.

To some extent, this disgust has been caused by the behaviour of the Africans themselves — who, although not
usually as bad as the stories about them make out, often are
insulting to their hosts. Russians say the African students
are selfish, uncivilized boors who do not know how to behave
(especially with Russian girls, whose favours they openly

buy with Western clothes and trinkets) and who are blatantly ungrateful for Russia's bountiful hospitality. One day a chauffeur lectured me on the Africans' faults. 'The savages. We sacrifice a lot for them, keep out much better qualified Russian boys and girls to give them places in our universities, give them twice our grants, all sorts of allowances and privileges—and they insist on wailing to the world about how awful Russia is. Why don't they leave, then? Who wants them?'

But there is also enough pure racial comment about skin, smell, inherent inferiority and abnormal sexual appetite to satisfy any small-town sheriff in the American South. 'Blacks are simply disgusting to look at,' said a young secretary. 'I wouldn't want them here even if they didn't behave like animals.'

The disgust extends, in a milder form, to other coloured students, journalists and diplomats in Moscow. 'The Arabs and Indians aren't as repulsive as black Africans,' said a university student, 'but they give me the creeps all the same.' Here too, the reaction combines deep racial prejudice with resentment over Russian generosity to 'inferiors'. The most disliked of all Russian foreign policies are those that seem to threaten war with the West. Second on the list is aid to under-developed countries. Since Arabs seem to get the most aid, Arabs are most disliked. Propaganda photographs of Russian trucks and machinery being unloaded in Arab ports do not provoke pride in comradely aid to less fortunate brothers. On the contrary, Russians become bitter when they see their own goods being 'wasted on' coloured—and un-grateful—peoples. 'It isn't as if we're a rich country, you know,' said the university student. 'Here we are, struggling with our own damned shortages, and we send a boatload a day of our best stuff to countries that'll stab us in the back as soon as they have the chance. Every Russian knows that every item sent to Africa and Asia comes right out of our own mouths and off our own backs.'

The resentment against the Arabs led to a surprising reaction here during the Six Day War. Despite deafening, and often vicious, anti-Israeli propaganda, the Israeli victory provoked interest and admiration out of all proportion to the Russians' sense of involvement or the importance of the event. I was not in Moscow when the war took place, but my friends told me about it with some amusement on my return.

'It was amazing,' exclaimed a young sub-editor. 'The radio and newspapers were screaming about the capitalist-imperialist-Nazi aggression of the blood-sucking Israelis — and everyone in the entire city, even the muzhiks who are ordinarily wildly anti-Semitic, was on the side of the Jews. For the first time, it was fashionable to be Jewish in this country.'

A dentist told me this story: 'I got into a taxi one day near the end of the war with a girl who was Jewish, and looked it. The driver, a real peasant, the kind who's usually always cursing the "dirty Yids", beamed at the girl and shook her hand. "Your people are really giving those Arabs hell, aren't they dear? It's about time." '

It was not so much love of the Israelis that provoked this reaction as a greater resentment and dislike of the Arabs. Nevertheless, the Six Day War did much to stop the talk of the stereotyped, cowardly Jew who is terrified of battle and gets a soft (and profitable) job behind the lines. Since then, I am told, anti-Semitism among the peasants and workers, where it has flourished for centuries, has subsided slightly but noticeably. Among the intelligentsia, it has never been a problem: in the artistic and intellectual circles of Moscow and Leningrad, Jew and Gentile mix more easily and thoroughly than almost anywhere in the West. But in the government, anti-Semitism has again gained momentum. 'More Jews than before are arranging to have "Russian" instead of "Jewish" entered on their children's passports,' Edik (whose own friends are largely Jewish) explained. 'It's really just an added burden to be officially identified as a Jew. On the other hand, more Jews than before have become proud of being Jewish.'

Proud, but not happy. The conditions for pogroms still flourish in Russian life.

*   *   *

For the moment, however, the hostility of most Russians is directed squarely against another national enemy: the Chinese. Hatred for China and the Chinese unites all sections of the Russian people as few other issues do, and perhaps no other international issue.

To explain why the Russians dislike the Chinese so cordially, one would have to review three hundred years or so of Russian history. The propagandists say it is because the 'Mao clique' is distorting Marxism–Leninism, and inflicting grave damage upon the causes of socialism and international proletarianism. These reasons, of course, are almost entirely spurious. The intelligentsia distrust the Chinese because the Great Cultural Revolution is a frightening reminder of Soviet cultural life under Stalin. Maoism is too ominously close to Stalinism. The working class dislikes them because they are foreign, yellow and a threat to Mother Russia — reasons one would expect from a nationalistic, only partly developed people. The government dislikes them for obvious reasons: they are a danger to the nation, poised to swarm into Siberia in suicidal waves. Everyone is angry because, having accepted thousands of millions of roubles from Russia, they are now arrogantly and openly contemptuous of her.

Russians have never liked the idea of alliance with China against the West. It reversed the natural order of things. Russia is — or must become — a Western, European nation, not an Eastern, Asian one. Ever since the reign of Peter the Great, Russia has looked Westward. And, paradoxically, the fact that Russia was partly Oriental provided an even greater stimulus to become Westernized: it was never something to be taken for granted. Russia had to push hard and consciously in the direction she wanted — towards European culture, manners and wealth.

During the time of the alliance with Peking, there was a deep, underlying fear that Russia would be dragged in the wrong direction — Eastward and backwards, instead of Westward and forwards. The break with China five years ago came as a great relief. Even the increasing threat of war with China is a relief: although it represents a real danger, it means that Russia will avoid a much greater danger — war with the West. Inevitably, the threat of war with China will push Russia Westward.

'If war were declared tomorrow,' said a student friend, 'there'd be a roar and a charge to the army recruitment offices. It would be the most popular thing the government could do, except, maybe, lower the price of vodka. People would actually cheer the Politburo. Everybody's longing to get at those spiteful yellow runts.'

None of this is particularly surprising. What *is* curious is that I should ever have entertained the notion, as I did for years, that simply because they were temporary ideological allies Russia and China were great friends. What was printed in *Pravda* and *Kommunist* between 1949 and 1960 about the eternal Sino–Soviet proletarian–internationalist friendship had virtually nothing to do with people's true feelings. Russian attitudes to the Chinese, as to everything else, spring from personal feelings developed over centuries of conditioning.

There are hundreds of jokes about the Chinese, all mocking the despised elements of their national character: rigidity, asceticism, fanaticism, hero-worship of the Leader and devotion to sterile ideological Marxism and state power, rather than the pleasures of warm-blooded life—mocking, in other words, most of the qualities Westerners attribute to Russians themselves. There is a certain amount of irony in this, and a certain amount of truth, which makes Russians dislike their Chinese comrades all the more. Chinamen work on empty stomachs, building dams with hand-shovels, rather than taking it easy and sitting down to a good meal. They chant Mao's sayings rather than sing gipsy songs and play Beatle records. They study all night rather than drink vodka and make love. They are less like Russians—like *real* people —than anyone in the world. In fact they are not human beings at all, but worker ants—or indoctrinated robots. And what is more, they are *poor*.

As emphasized in some typical Moscow *anekdots*:

In Peking, a very rich man dies, and since he has no heirs his property is sold to a second-hand dealer on a central street. The dealer proudly puts an announcement of his new goods in the window: SIX-PIECE BEDROOM SUITE FOR IMMEDIATE SALE! The suite consists of one straw sleeping mat and five portraits of Mao.

In Peking, Chairman Mao summons his Minister of Defence to discuss the overall strategic plan for invading Russia in 1970. Chairman Mao outlines his intentions: 'On the right flank, we'll hit them with six hundred divisions. On the left flank, we'll attack with nine hundred divisions. And in the centre, we'll break through with the tanks.' Minister of Defence: 'Both tanks, Esteemed Chairman Mao, or just one?'

Question: 'What's the only animal that hasn't been exterminated in China during the clean-up campaign of the Great Proletarian Cultural Revolution?' Answer: 'Cats.' 'Why Cats?' 'Because they're the only animals that say Maooo.'

*   *   *

The *dramatis personae* of Russia: so much less regimented than I had pictured; so much more fallible and intriguing, even when they perform ugly jobs. Each character with a story of a partially 'underground' private life that is not only fascinating in itself, but illustration of the essential anarchy and simplicity of Russian society behind the grey and uniform public image.

The K.G.B. officer based in Tula who is in love with a local actress and sells his influence to buy her chocolates because his wife appropriates his monthly pay.

The notorious Stalinist publicist who, after an ominous tirade against liberal students, waited until we left the meeting, took my arm, and asked for a packet of Gillettes.

Now an army major, a jolly, balding man with a Ukrainian accent, Mexican moustache and winter coat that falls to the top of his boots. He has come to the Moscow city Soviet for some vital information. In June, a new Code of

Marriage and the Family was enacted that provided, principally, for full legal equality for illegitimate children. But the Ukrainian major is worried. He has not read the new law (he explains to the elderly, shuffling official into whose office he is admitted after a two-hour wait in the corridor) but has heard disturbing rumours about it. Is it true there's a return to the 'bad times' [the Stalin era]? 'I heard that if a girl gives birth and just two witnesses say you're the father, you have to support the kid until he's grown up. Two witnesses—that's a laugh. Two half-litres [of vodka] and any girl can get two witnesses to swear to anything. This means a man can't have any fun with girls any more. It's going to be awful. Well, you understand, don't you.'

The old official calms the major, searches for a copy of the new code, and together they read the relevant paragraphs aloud. Fatherhood, it states, can be proved only in court, on the basis of a shared household or other positive evidence ... Profoundly relieved, the major grins broadly and pumps the old official's hand. 'This means I'm safe, then. I'm being posted to the Urals, away from the wife. What a time I'm going to have!'

Leningrad City Court. A tiny room for criminal appeals. The convicted man is a thirty-three-year-old machinist's helper, slightly retarded, who lives (as a number of Leningraders still do) in a workers' hostel. Early one Sunday morning, he pulled on his trousers, staggered from his bed to the lavatory—staggered because he had had his vodka binge (as a great number of Russian workers still do) on Saturday night—and then made his way to the communal kitchen for a long drink of water (Russian vodka is particularly dehydrating). Perhaps because he only meant to stay in the kitchen a minute, perhaps (as the prosecutor argued) because he was anti-social, perhaps (as his counsel pleaded) because his right arm had recently been partially paralysed and he had not mastered the art of buttoning up (Soviet trousers are never made with zips) with his left hand—for whatever reason or combination of them, the man was 'hanging out', as the judge put it, when he stumbled over for his drink.

The kitchen was of course empty at that early hour. But as luck would have it, the hostel director, a self-righteous, zealously patriotic type, was passing on an inspection of the grounds and, glancing through the window, the first thing he saw was the exposed member. Enraged at this flagrant disrespect for hostel rules and Soviet society, he summoned a passing policeman and together they dragged the feebly protesting offender to the police station. They covered him with a raincoat, but prevented him from buttoning up until the police sergeant had taken notes: material evidence. After investigation of the case and trial, the defendant was sentenced to eighteen months in a labour colony for 'malicious hooliganism'.

The appeal is heard by a youngish woman judge; a younger and strikingly pretty girl in a tight pink sweater is the defending counsel, and an older, uniformed woman the prosecuting counsel. Together they analyse the case in the fullness of detail it deserves: Was he drunk or sober? Criminally motivated or simply negligent? Could he have buttoned himself, given the hour, the arm, the measurements of the member? They manage to preserve straight faces for most of the discussion, but succumb, finally, to giggles, and then to roars of laughter. The appellant himself has not been delivered from jail for the appeal, but his mother is there, an ancient, wrinkled babushka in the traditional threadbare

black shawl, and she is not laughing, but moaning and be-
wailing the fate of her only surviving son.

In time, the court announces its decision: a full acquittal
(the only one, says the young lawyer, she's ever won in two
years at the bar). The old woman weeps all the louder now,
struggles to the dais, crosses herself in the Russian Orthodox
manner, and, bowing almost to the ground, blesses comrades
judge, lawyer and prosecutor in turn.

However, these things are rarely so amusing, or end so
happily.

*   *   *

The excitement of Russian life, almost all its interest, colour
and warmth, consists in what might be called do-it-yourself
entertainment. It is people and people's life stories that make
this country fascinating. By contrast, public or commercial
entertainment—fashion, publicity, personalities, swinging
places and things; the whole world of *bon ton* and the *dernier
cri*—is quite remarkably subdued. The whole sprawling city
of Moscow has fewer restaurants—and these are of far
poorer quality—than, say, two hundred metres of Zurich's
Niederdorff. There are no genuine film personalities, no pop
groups, no new dances, no crazes of any sort, no far out
trends or glittering people—and only three cool jazz records
have been pressed *ever*: one a year since the first disc in 1966.
In this respect, it is unquestionably the dullest major city
in the world.

The most talked-about popular singer at the moment is the
baritone ballad-singer Muslim Magomaev, a tall, dark,
self-consciously handsome Azerbaidzhan, who affects exaggerated gestures, and has a voice that seems to contain
built-in echo chambers. Magomaev appears frequently on
television in the new, amateurish entertainment revues, and

sings each song with the same deafening melodrama, like a young Mario Lanza. Like Lanza, too, he has difficulty keeping down his weight. It is said that he studied in Milan under eminent opera teachers; that he is a homosexual (something relatively rare here, and hardly ever discussed); and that he is a big bore, despite his booming voice, 'but the best we have'.

For people who care about these things—which is almost everyone under thirty—the trend-setters in songs, dances and every sort of popular fashion are almost all Western. Russia simply has no one in the league of the Rolling Stones, Bob Dylan or Aretha Franklin. And since all the means of public communication are operated by the state in the interests of building Communism, a star cannot be 'made' even if he is 'born'. There can never be the necessary publicity to generate excitement over someone new and transmit it to the public. The very notion of a genuine pop star is implicitly anti-Soviet: it distracts from the job of increasing productivity and building Communism, competes with the leaders of Party and government, and is a manifestation of decadent and dangerous bourgeois 'individualism' and 'hero-worship'. So young Russians who want to be with it follow the fortunes and sing the tunes of the popular Western groups, whom they hear on short-wave radio; their records (bought from the occasional Western tourist) change hands for fantastic prices on the black market, and their songs proliferate at an astonishing rate on tape-recorders in people's homes.

The fact that there is something slightly anti-social and risky, if not quite illegal, about listening to these Western stars hardly harms their popularity. A young man who can boast the latest tapes of the Beatles is a man-about-town indeed; an evening spent listening to them is exciting in a way it could never be where the records are sold in every other shop and broadcast on every other radio station. 'Forbidden fruit is sweet,' goes the old Russian saying.

And this popularity, in turn, makes the Soviet leaders yet more wary of the potentially subversive pop world. A number of Western singers are invited to tour Russia, but they are always second- or third-rate entertainers, almost unknown in their own countries, and very tame—and very dull. The real stars are never invited.

'They can't be,' say my friends. 'Because if they were, there'd be an absolute riot here, the like of which no one's ever seen in the West. Can you imagine the Beatles here? Every kid under twenty would go absolutely mad.'

Western readers must understand that Russian propaganda often means the opposite of what it says. Thus: it is precisely because of the Beatles' popularity and their potential effect on impressionable Russian youngsters that they cannot be invited—not, as the newspapers make out, that the high moral tone of Soviet youth places them above that kind of thing.

*　　*　　*

But it is not only the pop, mod and hippie worlds that are sacrificed; it is also people. Earlier, I've described several of the casualties of the recent political dissent; these have grown more numerous and serious since the appearance of neo-Stalinism. There are, however, other kinds of casualties: those inflicted by the broader interests and policies of Soviet rule, which have been suffered for decades. The cases are many and varied; but they are all of the same basic pattern.

A young assistant in a geology laboratory is corresponding desultorily with a Dutchman she met at an international conference in Moscow. She is summoned to the office of the

partorg (Party Secretary) of her laboratory and told to dis-
continue the correspondence immediately. 'But I was *asked*
to make friends with people at the conference. I was *assigned*
to this work.' 'Well, you are now assigned to stop this friendship. Or aren't you interested in keeping your job?'

A thirty-five-year-old mechanic is excluded from a trade
delegation to an under-developed country. He is incredulous
when he discovers the reason: a brief affair, two years ago,
with a Polish girl on an official visit, whom he'd picked up
on a Moscow street. 'But she's *Polish*,' says the mechanic,
'from our ally, our brother socialist republic.' Nevertheless,
this blot on his record will be erased (according to the universal understanding of the unwritten rule) only after a
minimum of three full years of exemplary conduct. Shortly
thereafter, the mechanic learned he had been turned down
for a small promotion, as well as rejected for foreign travel.
'It could be worse,' he says ruefully. 'She could have been
Czech.'

A Moscow painter is invited by a Zurich gallery to stay
there for a month and exhibit his new work. The invitation
is addressed through the Union of Artists, and opened and
answered by the Party Secretary. The young man in question, the official writes, must regretfully decline for reasons
of health and pressure of work. The painter himself craves
a trip to the West because, in addition to all the usual
reasons, he is a surrealist and therefore will probably never
exhibit in Russia. ('No painter I know of any interest has
any hope at all of showing during his lifetime,' says the best
Russian critic I know.) But he never so much as sees the
invitation, and learns of it by sheer accident. When he does
hear about it, he merely shrugs his shoulders and smiles.
'We are conditioned to these things. We've long passed the
point of frustration.'

A radio operator on a cargo ship is allowed ashore in capitalist countries for no more than four hours at a time, and always supervised by one of the K.G.B. agents in the ship's crew. 'Every step is watched. Every ship has special men responsible for surveillance, and there are men watching *them* in all ports. If you even ask to go ashore alone, you only create suspicion.' Still, she is one of the fortunate ones: roughly fifty per cent of the crew has a so-called 'second visa' which prevents them so much as stepping ashore in capitalist ports. But catastrophe overtakes her: her best friend marries a Frenchman in Moscow, and, after the usual difficulties, joins him in Paris. A month later, the radio operator is reassigned to ships serving Soviet ports only—in a less responsible position earning one-third less pay. Then she is summoned by the K.G.B. and told she will never again have the privilege of sailing on an international route. She is also warned never to correspond with her girl friend, 'the traitor'. She now hopes the girl friend has the good sense not to attempt a correspondence. 'Things are bad enough. That's all I need now—letters from Paris.'

In Leningrad, a thirty-year-old physician calls on И, an art historian, in his flat, and after some hesitation (caused by my presence) says that he has heard from a close mutual friend that И has obtained a copy of Freud's *Sexuality and the Psychology of Love*. The doctor very much wants to read it because he is working in the psychiatric wing of a large hospital and considering specializing in sexology. But he is not yet a specialist, and therefore not 'cleared' to read Freud. И produces the book, published in 1922 in St Petersburg, powdery and yellow far beyond what is usually meant by these tired adjectives, and the young doctor immediately leafs through its crumbling pages. He is, he says, certain there will come a time when scientific pressure will force the

Soviet regime to permit the study of Freud again, just as it has recognized cybernetics and genetics (both banned until recently). 'When might that be?' I ask. 'I'm an optimist. Certainly within the next hundred years.'

A Moscow journalist describes how foreign news is written for Soviet newspapers. Every day, all newspapers are supplied with the Tass bulletin of world events. (Tass, the official Soviet news agency, is administratively subordinate to the Department of Propaganda of the Party's Central Committee.) Except for the handful of newspapers that have their own foreign correspondents, this is the single source of foreign news—and editors may not alter a single word of the copy. This bulletin is printed in purple ink.

But there is also something called 'White Tass'. It, too, is circulated daily—but only to a select circle of top editors and commentators. White Tass is a comprehensive summary of world news: 'Just the facts, the kind of reporting done in the West—and much of it's actually taken from Western news agencies.' Then directives are given to sub-editors on how to present and interpret the material. 'A demonstration in, say, Greece, is either "progressive" or "reactionary", depending upon the latest line. The writer then fits the story to this slant. He knows the necessary formulas, phrases and slogans by heart, of course; he can write the story in ten minutes with the required outrage about the Fascists, or elation over the vanguard of the working class—either way. But nobody dreams of using White Tass straight. This is prohibited. You can only quote from it where necessary to support *our* arguments and "demolish" the bourgeois position.'

But beyond this, there is yet another level of truth, reserved for a yet more select circle of editors-in-chief of the four or five most important newspapers and members of the Central

Committee who need to know the facts. This is called 'Red Tass', and all its sheets are marked secret. 'It contains the truth about things like commentary on the Soviet Union and Soviet policies by foreign governments, and, of course, only the top people are trusted to see it. Thus socialist "democratic" truth is fed to the people. Oh my God.'

(A parallel system operates for books. A friend who works in both a research institute and a government office says that every Western book of any political or cultural importance is translated and published in a limited edition of about four hundred copies, and distributed as secret material to top government and Party leaders. A recent example of this kind of book is Robert Kennedy's account of the Cuban missile crisis. 'In the old days they lied in ignorance; now they know a great deal more — and lie more effectively.')

A former Moscow University student lived in the same hostel as a visiting American, who subsequently wrote a book about Moscow student life — not unflattering, but far enough from the official image to provoke the usual enraged reaction. The Russian student is required to sign a three-page typed statement refuting the 'lies' in the book and recounting the American's (imaginary) connections with the C.I.A. and (imaginary) dissolute life. 'But I never even saw that boy take a drink,' the student protests, 'and as for the book, this is the first I've heard of it. Let me read a bit before I attack it.' His interlocutor departs, enraged at this 'insolent' anti-social behaviour. Later, the student is told by a K.G.B. officer that he will not be accepted for post-graduate study unless he signs. After a week of reflection, he does.

A young athlete (who cannot be identified more precisely) is struck from the list of a team preparing for an international meeting to be held in the West. On his last trip abroad — to a socialist country — he had remained friendly with two West

German competitors, in spite of being warned to drop them by the team's political overseer. His behaviour was reported as being 'unreliable—not reflecting credit on the Soviet Union'. (The athlete, incidentally, plays for a major sporting club in Moscow which 'bought' him from a smaller club by means of a higher salary. He is of course officially an amateur and has a nominal teaching job, but in fact he is paid over twice the salary of a skilled factory worker. 'Big sport here is professional through and through,' he says. 'Amateur status is one of the biggest fairy-tales around.')

A young architecture student while on holiday met and briefly courted a girl from a neutral European country. The boy is caught in the girl's hotel room (against hotel rules) and made to sign a confession and humiliating recantation. The romance had been carefully watched from the first by K.G.B. agents, and the violation of hotel rules eagerly seized upon, in an attempt to incriminate the girl's journalist father. Despite his admission, the boy is debarred from his institute, refused permission to continue higher education and ordered to remain permanently in his native town beyond the Volga; here he has found work as a fork-lift truck driver. A year later, the local K.G.B. officers inform him that the girl has been expelled from the country and her father sentenced to eight years in a labour colony for espionage; he is ordered to supply more information about the family's 'subversive' activities. The boy has no way of knowing this is a total fabrication— both father and daughter are still living in their Moscow flat —but refuses nevertheless to sign anything. Whereupon the K.G.B. officers inform him he will spend his life as a semi-skilled worker, and never be allowed to live in Leningrad or Moscow.

A twenty-seven-year-old unmarried woman wishes to join her father; her mother died of starvation during the siege of

Leningrad in 1943, and her father, taken prisoner by the Germans near Kiev in 1942, has remained in the West. (Many Russian prisoners of war refused repatriation for fear of vicious reprisals—which were in fact carried out—against soldiers 'traitorous' enough to surrender, and he is still afraid to return to Russia because he is a Soviet citizen, and, according to Soviet law, subject to punishment for desertion.) The woman has applied seven times for permission to join her father in Holland, and was refused without explanation each time. He is her only known living relative. He is chronically ill, and getting worse; she fears she will not see him before he dies.

A middle-aged cinema enthusiast has seen only one of the recent prize-winning Czech films, *The Shop on the High Street*, and has no hope of seeing the others, not to speak of the best-known films of Fellini, Antonioni and Bergman. Even before the events of 1968, the most important Czechoslovak films were not shown in Russia because they were not 'Soviet' enough—that is, they were ideologically weak or dangerous. 'You can read blistering attacks on these films in our literary newspapers and magazines, but you can't see the films themselves, of course.'

A librarian who married a West German exchange student last year against her widowed mother's wishes, was, as expected, immediately dismissed from her job. She is now undergoing threats, humiliations and psychological examinations prior to being granted, or refused, an exit visa to join her husband in Munich. The mother, too, was sacked from her administrative position in the office of a large factory. 'I worked there for sixteen years without a moment's trouble. But it didn't depend on the factory—word came from the K.G.B.' She will never have an administrative job again.

A Leningrad nurse as beautiful as the young Deborah

K

Kerr is engaged to a Belgian journalist. They fell in love, both for the first time, during the White Nights of Leningrad's summer. The journalist's reports about Russia were less than flattering, however, and he was indiscreet enough not to disguise comments made by her. Five weeks after the publication of a particularly frank report, the girl is summoned to a K.G.B. office, cursed, slapped, humiliated, threatened. 'You whore, you'll never see that Belgian scum again. You're a filthy whore who sells her Motherland for a few rags of clothing.' During the subsequent sessions with the K.G.B., intense efforts are made to force the nurse to give damning evidence about the journalist's activities in Leningrad — and if no damning evidence can be remembered or invented, to sign a statement (already typed in several copies) describing him as sexually depraved, hysterically anti-socialist, and in league with West German editors close to military and industrial circles. The girl holds out for weeks, teeters, tells her best friend (and begs her to tell no one else), then slashes her wrists. Five months later she remains in a mental hospital because, although physically recovered, she is still suicidal.

*   *   *

No more mass terror, no midnight knocking on the door, no tens of millions of near-corpses in labour camps. But careers ruined, families broken, lives mangled — not with sorrow, but a kind of glee — by the K.G.B.

Of course, these are exceptions — the stories one remembers. The great majority of Russians never experience a traumatic confrontation with police or Party; life goes on calmly, if humbly, without the pain of injustice or loss. But this is because the great majority live the intellectually stunted lives of which the dictatorship approves. The entire country is cut off from the best (as well as the worst) of contemporary world culture, ideas and information — reduced to the level at which the Politburo feels safe. It is only when one tries to step out of line, to spend time with foreigners, or travel abroad, read serious political literature, or ask serious questions about Russian literature and history, that one is slapped back into place. Or when one happens to have friends who have 'betrayed' Soviet ideals in these ways.

And the victims of the K.G.B. are not surprised or indignant; these episodes are commonplace, the normal sanctions of Soviet life. ('Normalization', the Soviet euphemism for reimposing tyranny in Czechoslovakia, has become a fashionable ironic expression among the Russian intelligentsia. 'The situation is normalized,' means that another senseless restriction has been imposed or another person hurt.)

But what does this brutality accomplish? If it helped secure material, cultural or spiritual advantages for society as a whole, the argument that the end justifies the means *might* be used in support of it. But, naturally enough, the government that inflicts these humiliations and injuries on its people makes a mess of almost everything else — everything, that is, that doesn't contribute directly to its military and dictatorial power. The bungling is endemic in every department and section of the bureaucracy, but most glaring in the management of the economy.

A babushka in the inevitable black overcoat and woollen shawl is fighting the daily battle for the family's groceries on a central Moscow shopping street. Food shops in the city are closed from 1 to 2 p.m., but the old woman takes her place in the crowd at the locked doors of a fish shop at 1.40. At two o'clock, some sixty people are there, chiefly pensioners like herself, clutching tattered shopping bags filled with purchases wrapped in old *Pravda*s. Finally the door is opened (one side only of the double doors; no one ever bothers to open both sides, no matter how large the crowd), and there is a bellicose murmur as the crowd surges forward, elbowing and shoving viciously, crushing people painfully against the narrow opening as they are propelled through. The old woman is brutally tossed about, but fights back, not giving an inch. In three minutes she is in one of the long queues that have formed at each of the counters, the leading person in each exchanging snarls with the shop assistant behind it. She herself snaps at the shop assistant, cashier and other customers. Ordinarily, she is a gentle soul, but in shops, the law of the jungle obtains. It is every man for himself—everyone fighting with the bitter determination bred by perpetual shortage.

This is the scene in almost every Moscow shop. As it happens there is no shortage of fish at the moment. (In frozen, salted and tinned form, that is. Fresh fish is difficult to find, as always, and the waitress in a sea-food restaurant in Leningrad—almost within view of the Baltic Sea—snapped at me to 'stop clowning' when I asked if anything on the menu was fresh.) But the mentality of scarcity persists; shoppers never approach their task calmly, even where supplies are adequate.

But if there is plenty of fish, other staple items are in short supply. One week there is a shortage of soap powder, the next of kettles, then of razor blades. No one knows why these 'deficits', as they are called, occur. One day, the shelves and counters all over the town are empty of a given item, the assistants haven't the slightest idea when new shipments are expected, and will turn their backs or hiss an insult if you ask a second time.

Yet the situation in Moscow is incomparably better than

anywhere else in Russia. The capital is known here as 'the shop window' of the Soviet Union, and is untypically and deceptively well-stocked and rich. It is at the apex of the zoning system, according to which cities and regions are assigned their supplies of goods and services. Moscow receives the choicest supply of everything, and people come sometimes hundreds of miles to do their household shopping here, often returning home by train the same evening.

A plump, jolly woman is at the head of a queue in a grocer's shop that looks as attractive as a railway station canteen. The queue is for processed meat, and is of average size for this time in the afternoon: eighteen people are ahead of me, and it takes nineteen minutes to be served. The woman asks for four kilograms of a cheap grade of sausage. 'Why so much?' asks the impatient young man behind her. 'Stocking up for the next war?' The irony escapes the woman, and she explains soberly that sausage is never supplied to her town. She lives some fifty miles north of Moscow, and comes to the city once a week for all the family's meat.

The shortages and shoddiness of even the most everyday goods makes shopping a frantic task. (The verb 'to buy' has virtually disappeared from conversational Russian, replaced by other words—'to get', 'to obtain', 'to find'—more descriptive of the whole difficult process of acquisition.) On Moscow's Petrovka Street, a three-hour queue stretches out raggedly in the cold at the doors of a shop selling English nylon stockings for five roubles a pair—two days' wages for a factory worker. Across the street, the corridors of T.S.U.M., a less elaborate cousin of G.U.M., are like stadium runways after a football match: the crowds are pushing, shoving, fighting towards the counters to buy pencils, pants, pickles, *anything*, before supplies are exhausted. The queue for a shipment of Czechoslovakian boots will last an entire day, and women who actually achieve a purchase will be delighted with their victory.

It is as if the Second World War ended only a year or so ago. I once asked a secretary in an office I was visiting for a paper clip. She produced one—but reluctantly. 'They're as rare as gold-dust,' she sighed. And paper is still rationed to publishers in this land of unimaginable timber resources.

*   *   *

But Russia's consumer economy is not entirely stagnant. On the contrary, the quality and variety of goods in the shops, and of the clothes on the shoppers, doggedly improves. Anti-wrinkle creams and rinses for greasy hair have appeared on shabby cosmetic counters—primitively made and packaged, but giving the surging crowds who fight for them a taste of luxury and feminine adventure. The windows of G.U.M. and three or four lesser stores are brightly and in some cases even thoughtfully arranged (even if the clothing is often only for display, and not intended for sale), providing a hint of high-street atmosphere in the otherwise sombre streets. Fabrics can often be bought without having to queue (although the services of a tolerable tailor, like any other craftsman, are appallingly expensive).

And the progress in housing has been even more substantial. The immense housing developments on the city boundaries are squat and dreary, but provide hundreds of families with long-awaited self-contained flats. Although extremely cramped and already crumbling, they are a vast improvement on the stifling, nerve-fraying rooms in communal apartments where these families have bickered with their neighbours for decades. In short, Russians have never 'had it so good'. By their own standards, they are doing fine.

But much as it has improved, this second richest country in the world is still hopelessly, bafflingly poor. Every structure and article of manufacture is crude and cheap; buildings everywhere—even the new, showpiece airports—are peeling, flaking, cracking. The only high quality I have seen for a year was in the tanks, armoured cars and missile-carriers that rolled along Moscow's dark central streets night after night, rehearsing for the November 7th parade in Red square. This equipment looked sinister, but superb.

*   *   *

Then there is the cheating. The staggering corruption, embezzlement, swindling and outright theft practised at every level, ranging from counter girls who give short weight, to robber barons who have organized factories, wholesale outlets and sales forces involving hundreds of employees in illegal private enterprises. Construction bosses steal and sell lorry-loads of timber on the black market, while workers are filching tools and nails. Restaurant cooks put less meat than they should in the borscht and sell the surplus on the side, while managers are taking bribes for tables. Directors of taxi depots sell used windscreen-wipers for private profit, and turn a blind eye to the drivers' manipulation of their meters.

It is a rare enterprise that does not contain an inner, moonlighting operation of some kind that is busy siphoning off the profits from the state system and bribing the army of inspectors, controllers, auditors, watchmen and criminal investigators appointed to stop the leaks. The workers in these enterprises usually know of the existence of the *sub rosa* operation, if not all its details. But they rarely protest. It is expected that those who are in a position to cheat will do so. The indifference is as massive as the cheating itself.

For example, a young lorry driver who works at one of the giant Moscow depots tells me that he and his fellow drivers steal as a matter of course whenever documents can be doctored or mislaid. (Transport is one of the best fields for cheating, covered as it is by a mass of conflicting documents. It is said that ten per cent of the goods simply disappear — and about that much of the petrol, which drivers siphon from their tanks and sell to car owners.) 'The stuff's not mine, it's not yours — it's nobody's, and nobody cares unless he has to answer for it. That's why the shops are so bloody empty all the time.'

I have saved the *Izvestiya* of August 21st, 1968, the day of the invasion, and I now notice by chance an article — one of thousands of such feature stories and feuilletons every year — that illustrates the petty-cheating problem better than anything I could write. It was this article, entitled 'Their Souls Are in Their Purses', that attracted the knot of readers round the wall-frame I passed in the early evening of the 21st. This is the kind of reporting that captures the Russians' attention, not because it tells them something new, but, on the contrary, because people enjoy reading about themselves and familiar situations. It was a look at the Russian *byt* (the reality of daily life) and the part played in it by petty cheating.

The article was an attack on the city bazaars which so often are the *locus criminus* for speculating and profiteering on 'deficit' goods that are smuggled out of factories and warehouses and sold privately on the black market. The author's points were made largely by means of quotations from letters by people who had been victimized by or profited from the cheating. The typical cycle of shortages/black market/theft from state enterprises/selling stolen items at bazaars was repeatedly described. For example, a Muscovite complained about a shortage:

It's a cheap item—a base for a Volga jack. But try and buy one! They make you take the whole jack, even though it's always the base that breaks. If there are any car owners among you *Izvestiya* people, you can continue the list of this kind of item yourselves ...

A schoolteacher from Kaluzhskaya region, just south of Moscow, pointed out the connection between shortages and profiteering:

Recently I was in one of the largest cities in the country (it's embarrassing even to mention it by name) to do some shopping. My husband had asked me to buy him one of those ties with the shiny threads in it. But there were none in the shops. The black markets in this city had also been closed down by the authorities long before. And then (excuse me for mentioning it) in a public convenience, I suddenly saw a real-life black market. There they were, whole bunches of these ties in bags, like so many dried perch. I'd been prepared to queue for hours in the shops, I was ready to pay a bit more for something fashionable. But why under the counter? Isn't it obvious we're supporting not only all sorts of illegal traders, speculators and pilferers—we're helping *professional* parasites to make a living? Is that clear? And by the way, I'm behind the times. When I said how disgusted I was, people looked at me as though I was something out of the ark ... And so I came home very depressed, and thought to myself, Who's really the fool? After all, I hadn't managed to do my own good husband the favour he had asked me ...

A woman from Odessa had much the same problem, but felt less anguish in dealing with it:

It's the season for bottling vegetables and fruit again.

And there are no lids for the bottles! Do you think everybody in Odessa is sitting on their empty bottles and tearing out their hair in despair? Oh no—we make it our business to get our hands on lids somewhere. Chaps turn up who sneak them out of the bottling factories. And just think, everybody has just what he needs. Only the lids cost us not two, but ten kopecks apiece ...

What exasperated the author of the article was that pilferers add nothing to the economy, but merely play havoc with the distribution of goods through the regular channels, and multiply the cost of each item. 'If you can't find something in the shops, it doesn't mean the item doesn't actually exist somewhere in the economy.' The goods are often there; the profiteers have merely transferred them from over the counter to under it.

I can recall [the author went on] a casual conversation some time ago in the factory committee of the Perovsk locomotive repair plant. ('Of course we have pilferers. What factory doesn't?') Once it was all the rage to dismantle shelving made of the finest beech, sneak the wood out of the shop plank by plank, then glue them together again and sell the 'product' on the black-market. Then the fashion changed, standard lamps became the latest thing, and everybody was furiously making them in the same way. And, of course, sneaking out a light bulb in your pocket is the most natural thing in the world. Once a search party found a whole barnful of them at the factory switchboard operator's place. ('Well, yes, we did prosecute him—but you can't go to all that bother over every little trifle!')

The author was more distressed by the general public

attitude towards pilfering than the abuse itself. The feeling that everyone does it, and that it's not really a crime, swelled his journalistic indignation.

The pilferer is not really a thief, we assure ourselves. If he'd taken money — of course! But as it is, just a piece of metal, fabric, or wood, we're embarrassed to make a fuss about it. We call the culprit a 'pilferer' rather than a crook. And if we do say 'crook' it's always with the reservation 'petty'. And in so doing, we also make petty our responsibility for these things — your responsibility and mine ...

The last letter quoted was full of contrition. It was from a pilferer named Nikolai P., a thirty-eight-year-old father of three children from Gorky:

I never speculated at the market with the stuff I sneaked out. I sold everything for less than I could get — just to finish the transaction as quickly as possible. And the wife only yelled at me when I came home [drunk] on all fours. Please take my word for it: everything that's smuggled out of the factories, all the 'under the counter' stuff, is converted into vodka and *drunk up* right on the spot. And that seeps right into the blood — you get to work in the morning and start thinking not about how to do your job better, but how to 'cook something up' ... They arrested me when I was transporting some smuggled-out piping on a truck.

Then, to conclude, the customary sermon by the author of the article:

Did he deserve his arrest? But just understand that every arrest is a reproach to you and me as well — a reproach for our endless, loquacious condescension to this urgent drama we so often witness; a reproach to our indifference and lack of concern. Somehow, we don't consider our attitude towards a drinking driver or a man who smokes near petrol tanks excessively strict. In cases like these, we don't go in for sermons. These people are dangerous! They jeopardize many lives! But take some kind of swindler, someone who entices people with the lure of an unearned rouble, someone who spreads the poison of acquisitive selfishness everywhere around him. Doesn't he cripple many people spiritually—the lives of adolescents, of your children and mine? ...

This long-winded discourse on petty cheating on the day of the invasion is itself an example of the constancy of the 'inner qualities' of Russian life. The author complained indignantly that, although a storm of indignation is whipped up almost daily about pilfering, nothing is done about it. His own article, however, was a classic example of the very thing he decried—and he surely knew it. Exposés of black-market operations in the Soviet press are rather like complaints about the weather. Nothing is done about the situation, and the revelations, carping and lecturing acquire an almost soothing, small-talk effect.

Take, for example, those hermetically sealed lids for bottling about which the housewife from Odessa complained. Five or six years ago, a campaign was launched to encourage families to preserve their own fruit and vegetables: it was intended to help ease the shortages of commercially produced tinned foods. Understandably, there was a shortage of lids the first autumn. And since then, the same shortage suddenly becomes acute in the autumn—*every* autumn. It is as predictable as the flurry of indignant articles investigating the shortage. Every year, dozens of these articles appear, posing the traditional question: What went wrong? Who's to blame? Why this again? A friend of mine thinks that a factory for manufacturing these lids could have been built on the fees paid to journalists for these exposés alone. Yet nothing changes: everyone knows there will be a shortage again next year, and some housewives begin hoarding lids in the spring. So, too, with fuel for heating houses and apartments: every autumn, the spate of indignant articles appears about the failure to lay in enough for the winter. What went wrong? Who's to blame? Why this situation again? The whole thing has its comic as well as its exasperating aspects. For the massive petty cheating on all levels of the manufacturing and distribution system is as integral to Russian life as cabbage and kasha.

*   *   *

Besides this petty cheating, there is the deeply entrenched, flourishing corruption in the sprawling bureaucracies. One hears only second-hand stories and rumours about the cheating and nepotism (people in high places are well protected from press and publicity), but everyone is certain it exists on a massive scale. And this is only natural, for corruption of this kind almost always flourishes in a dictatorship once ideological fervour has been exhausted, as it has been in Russia. The absolute power of the bureaucracy, the secrecy and the protection against disclosure by mere citizens or journalists provide the perfect conditions for cheating within ministries and industrial and distribution enterprises and trusts. The Soviet system is in fact a hothouse of corruption—of many of the vices associated with South American dictatorships—and this is both made possible by and prolongs the shortages of consumer goods.

This massive cheating in high places does much to keep Moscow shopping streets on their jungle level.

*   *   *

A pretty young secretary is shopping for a pair of party shoes. Pushing through the crowd in a second-hand shop, she finds a pair that pleases her among the rows of worn and pungent clodhoppers one would be ashamed to give to a rag-and-bone man. They are black English Clarke's, almost new, but inexpensively made and in the old-fashioned stiletto-heel style. In England they would have sold, new, for about five pounds. The price is fifty roubles; the secretary pays it happily. Her salary is seventy-five roubles a month.

It is traditional for Western reporters to quote prices in Russian store windows — an exercise of marginal value because supplies of attractive items are instantly exhausted, and others are so ungainly and ill-made they remain unsold at any price. A more accurate guide to real value (the meeting of the supply and demand curves) is the prices in the municipal second-hand shops. It is here, rather than in the department stores, that Moscow's *beau monde* shops for high fashion, for the unusual — that is, Western — item.

A thick Italian mohair sweater in good condition: seventy roubles. A lambswool sweater, with a Marks and Spencer label, which has had a year's hard wear: thirty-six roubles. (It probably sold new in England for forty-five shillings — four hours' work; here, barely wearable, it costs two weeks' wages.) A knitted dress in a synthetic fibre, probably East European: ninety roubles. A mohair scarf in excellent condition: forty-five roubles (value: fifty shillings; cost: almost three weeks' wages). A pair of English tights: fifteen roubles (a week's wages). A pair of French boots, worn two winters: thirty roubles ... And the demand for these fashionable items is so great that the assistants in second-hand shops earn extra money by informing regular customers when a pretty article is put on sale, or arranging with members of their family to buy it for private resale later at a profit.

The prices of articles bought and sold privately roughly match those in second-hand shops. A huge trade in used clothing is carried on in this hand-to-hand fashion, citizen Б selling or buying a sweater or pair of shoes from citizen Г. Everything, no matter how old, has its value, and every girl is a part-time businesswoman who knows within five roubles the value of any item, depending on style, age and quality. Thus Communism has produced the strongest private-enterprise consciousness in the world.

Boots, incidentally, provide a useful guide to the progress of the Soviet consumer economy. I am told that after three years of intense effort, domestic production has at last somewhat relieved the desperate shortage, but that Soviet-made boots are so cheap, crude and dowdy that anyone with the opportunity and money will gladly pay six weeks' wages or more for a good imported pair. The price of these privately sold boots, as of most other Western items, has actually *increased* during the past three years, because the demand for pretty (that is, Western) things is growing faster than the supply. In the course of 1968, private savings in Soviet savings banks grew from twenty-seven million roubles to over thirty-two million. This dramatic increase (which was recorded by the Central Statistical Bureau) testifies officially to something everyone here knows instinctively: savings are available and people want to spend them, but the quality of goods is so poor that they cannot entice customers, even in this protected market.

The inflation is also reflected in the heavy demand for

hard currencies, especially dollars, on the black market. A few years ago, there was an intensive campaign against economic criminals, including currency speculators, and a fair number were shot. But recently the campaign has abated (although the death penalty is still applicable to large-scale economic crimes). And with the easing of the campaign, a thriving black-market trade in hard currency has resumed, in which the dollar is gaining steadily against the rouble. It now fetches five to six times the official exchange rate, and, interestingly, has reached virtually the same prices offered in financial centres like Geneva and Vienna. Thus, while the Soviet press gleefully describes the weakness of the franc, dollar and pound sterling, the rouble, on the free market, is under greater pressure than any of them.

The inflation in black-market — that is to say, real — prices is most dramatic in the case of motor cars. The official price of a new Volga is roughly six thousand roubles, but an almost-new one fetches twelve to fifteen thousand on Moscow's black market, and as much as eighteen thousand (or fifteen years' wages for a factory worker) in provincial cities. Incidentally, the waiting list for Volgas — the new model that will soon appear, almost two years late — has already been closed; but according to rumour, it is now ten years long.

However, it is only the very rich who have use of cars, the very rich being principally high Party apparatchiks. Having surrounded themselves with luxuries as unobtainable for average Russians as those of Texan millionaires for residents of Negro ghettoes, they spout slogans about the morality of Communism and the interests of the working class. The members of the working class I know think not about cars, but real things: Lemons, for example: a good one costs a factory worker about forty-five minutes' wages. It is a reckless extravagance, but occasionally indulged in because a slice is so good in a glass of tea. Besides, lemons are often the only fresh fruit available in winter. Fresh vegetables are roughly as scarce and expensive, but tomatoes can occasionally be spotted in the peasant markets—a pound costing about two hours' work. These are wild luxuries, obviously, but the prices of staples like potatoes, cabbage, onions, kasha, unidentifiable cuts of meat, not to speak of butter, eggs and cheese, are so high that the average family spends approximately half its income on food for a diet that it is generous to describe as grim.

A middle-aged couple working together in the same factory, she as a lathe operator, he as a repair mechanic, earn together two hundred roubles a month—well above the national average—of which about one hundred goes on food for themselves and their daughter. Rent, lighting, heating, taxes and transport, hair-cuts, cinema tickets and other incidentals are very inexpensive, and the husband rarely splurges on vodka (unusual for a Russian). In a good month, watching their budget carefully (again, unusual), they have almost fifty roubles over for purchases.

But a tolerable pair of women's shoes, even domestic-made, costs forty roubles. A shoddy suit costs a hundred and twenty-five, an overcoat, two hundred and fifty. Three purchases like these virtually exhaust the family's yearly income—but it is in fact expended principally on dressing and prinking the child. Mother's and Father's overcoats are at least ten years old. A white shirt or nylon stockings are important purchases.

How is it, then, that a secretary will spend a week's salary on a French brassière? A novelist friend of mine who has vast experience with secretaries has long pondered this question. 'Because', he says, 'they're so desperate for something that

L

will make them stand out of the crowd, they'll literally go hungry to buy it. You must understand their psychology. All their lives, they're surrounded by drabness. What does it matter if life's one degree harder for a few months? It's their one chance to have something *pretty*!'

*　　*　　*

But why all this concern with the standard of living? A poor country is not necessarily unhappy, after all. (The converse, at least, is certainly true: a rich country is not necessarily happy.) Russia preserves much of the simplicity, warmth and unspoiled virtues of a pre-industrialized, pre-'Americanized' society, and if this were another country, one would be extolling its charms, not harping on its shortcomings. Besides, the causes of its consumer poverty lie far deeper than the bungling of the present system and leadership. Feudalism never worked properly in this country; nor did capitalism. The inherent anarchy in the Russian character and disorder in Russian life — the 'backwardness' of social relationships and civilization — severely retarded the development of both these systems. There was no reason, then, to expect socialism to succeed. On the contrary, what progress there has been must be applauded, for every civilizing movement, every centimetre forward, requires many times the sweat, sacrifice and pain expended in the West. That is the burden of Russian history.

It is not Russia's poverty that irritates one, but the denial of it. Every day, hundreds of times a day, we are told that the Soviet system is brilliantly successful, and that life in the West is one of misery for the common man. The Communist Party constantly proclaims itself a glorious success, an inspiration and example — the cynosure of the entire world.

The signs and slogans written by the Party are every-where: in neon lights, on red cotton, hand-painted and mass-produced, in new mosaics and flaking paint:

'WE HAVE OPENED A NEW ERA FOR ALL MANKIND!' 'THE GREAT OCTOBER SOCIALIST REVOLUTION IS THE GREATEST PRIDE AND HOPE OF ALL MANKIND!' 'GLORY TO THE SOVIET GOVERNMENT!' 'GLORY TO THE SOVIET PEOPLE, BUILDERS OF COMMUNISM!' 'GLORY TO MARXISM–LENINISM, WHICH SHOWS US THE TRUE PATH!'

Glory to the Communist Party—proclaimed by the Communist Party! The simple-minded religiosity and crudeness of it all is exasperating.

*   *   *

But the laborious efforts to conceal incompetence in a garb of holy infallibility is worse. These efforts are centred round the name of Lenin. Since the moment of his death, Lenin has been treated not as a man, but an object of worship. But now, with the start of the campaign to celebrate the hundredth anniversary of his birth, the propaganda is over-whelming. (For a fuller treatment of the preparations for the centennial of Lenin's birth, see Appendix 2.) His name is invoked, his memory hallowed, his deeds immortalized, his words quoted and his political message (or whichever of his messages is most appropriate at the moment) is repeated literally a thousand times every day. New books, museums, films, plays, stamps, memorials are planned. His portrait hangs in every office, and mass-produced statues and busts of him are everywhere.

Perhaps this can be explained in terms of necessity. Most of the other principal Old Bolsheviks—with the exception of relatively second-rank officials like Sverdlov, Dzerzhinsky and Kalinin—were executed as traitors, enemies of the people and the cause of socialism. Obviously, heroes cannot be made of Trotsky, Kamenev, Zinoviev, Bukharin or Radek (a few of Lenin's closest collaborators), all of whom are still in posthumous disgrace. Nor can Khrushchev, Molotov, Malenkov, Bulganin, even Stalin, be properly honoured since all of them, according to the normal pattern of dictatorships, have been denounced at some time by their successors. And since every state needs the trappings of mystical legitimacy—particularly this state, which has demanded so much sacrifice from its people—Soviet propagandists are left with Lenin.

Whatever the reason, the campaign to sanctify his name is extraordinary. Its intensity, fervour and piety beggar description. Lenin's every gesture, every article of clothing, every word and thought (except those that might embarrass the current Politburo) are the holiest of holy treasures in the Party sanctum.

Here is a summary of *one day's* 'news' stories in the press:

'The Search Continues: Eternal Echoes' (concerning yet more research into Lenin's writings). 'Fidelity to Traditions —Rural District Prepares for Lenin Anniversary'. 'Cherished Image' (about publication of another book of photographs of Lenin). 'A Chronicle of Glorious Achievements' (a Ukrainian newspaper announces publication of a new daily section on Lenin, in addition to its daily column of readers' letters about him). 'Ilyich in Smolney'. 'Lenin and Youth' (Lenin's writings systematized for Armenian teachers). 'More pages of Leniniana: Our Subject is Limitless' (about new films in production for the Leninist anniversary). 'Greeting the Lenin Anniversary' (Party organizations in the Ukraine meet to discuss propaganda preparations for the anniversary). 'In Honour of the Glorious Date'. 'Eternally

Living and Creative Teachings'. 'Millions on a Leninist Vigil: The Workers of Moscow Prepare' (a section of Moscow's clothing industry resolves to fulfil the five-year plan in time to honour the anniversary of Lenin's birth—i.e. two months early). 'Our Ilyich—an Inexhaustible Source of Knowledge and Guidance'. 'In Ilyich's Native Land' (on the preparations of Ulyanovsk province for the hundredth anniversary of Lenin's birth). 'Lines of Love and Hope' (description of the circumstances surrounding two letters by Lenin). 'The Ulyanovs Lived Here' (story of the school where Lenin's father taught). 'Together with Us' (four poems about Lenin's life and legacy). 'Artists Discuss Lenin's Anniversary' (preparations of the Artists' Union for celebrating and propagandizing the event). 'Made Brilliant by a Great Life: Land of His Youth' (description of Ulyanovsk, city of Lenin's birth). 'No Subject is More Important'. 'Towards the Hundredth Anniversary of V. I. Lenin's Birth—Twelve Million Books'. 'A State Farm Prepares for the Glorious Date'.

Every newspaper and every magazine carries two or three articles about the anniversary, and every day's broadcasting more than matches this outpouring. The stories smack of an almost nauseating idolatry: women in clothing factories sew their garments as if for dear Vladimir Ilyich himself; captains of fishing vessels find bigger catches than ever in honour of the coming event; steel workers volunteer for extra shifts because they want the Leader to be proud of them. Every moment in the country's life is linked to the sacred date; every movement in Lenin's life (except any unsuitable one) is told and retold, in tones and terms of the most fervent idol worship. 'Lenin is with us!' 'Lenin is more alive than the living!'

To someone outside the Marxist–Leninist faith, this

whipped-up adoration for a mortal—and highly contro-
versial—political leader is pathetic or abhorrent (as indeed,
it would have been to Lenin himself). But it is curiously in
harmony with many other aspects of the Russian national
character and Russian society. Lenin is the Saviour who
explains, justifies and promises sympathy and heavenly
rewards for all the hardships of life. And although most
Russians are, in one sense, fed up with the incessant agitprop,
they are also comforted by it; life without the hum of the
hive would be too bare, perplexing and frightening.

To change the metaphor, Lenin is an icon, borne aloft
by the officials who organize mass propaganda, almost
precisely as saints are borne aloft in the feast-day processions
of the Orthodox Church while the Russian peasants
genuflect, and the old, spent women touch their foreheads
to the ground. And although admiration and affection for
Lenin is genuine and virtually universal in Russia, none of
the preparations for his worship are accidental, as Marxists
like to say. They are all planned and executed by the in-
credibly huge (if clumsy) empire of Party political instruction. No aspect of Soviet rule is more revealing than this
secular canonization of Lenin. And none more clearly illustrates the continuity—even the reinforcement—of the backward as well as the progressive elements in Russian life.

But even the agitprop and Lenin-worship are tolerable;
one develops reflexes which enable one to shut them out. It
is the outright lies that one cannot avoid. Not the lies about
the West or internal Russian developments; one simply
learns to ignore the distortions and inventions of the press.
But when one's own companions are involved, one begins
to understand the viciousness of this system.

A close friend of mine was denied permission to attend
an important international conference in Brussels to which

he'd been invited. He is an honourable, apolitical man, and his application was rejected simply because he is not among the one in a hundred 'Soviet' enough to be trusted with a passport. And then there is the girl who has been waiting three years for an exit visa to join her husband in a Western country. She may never be allowed out. She is given no reason.

The very afternoon I last saw this girl I was talking to an official of the Ministry of Culture, who assured me soothingly that all Soviet citizens are entirely free to travel whenever and wherever they want; the only restriction is the availability of hard currency. After all, he boasted, this is not America, where restrictions on travel to Cuba, Albania and China are stamped on the passport itself; this is the Soviet Union where democratic freedoms — genuine freedoms — are guaranteed by the constitution.

I said nothing; I've lived here long enough to learn when I must keep my mouth shut. It is liars like this who rule Russia. The lie is an essential part of the Soviet system of government, and to challenge it for no good reason is senseless.

*   *   *

And yet this is one-sided. To be fair, one must record also the supremely tender, sensitive and sensual elements of Russian life. And one must do justice to the Communist rulers too — even to the hyper-chauvinistic, brutal and ignorant apparatchiks. It is often said by foreign students of the Soviet Union that its admirable 'human' qualities are a legacy of the old Russian life, the traditional customs and modes of behaviour, for which the Soviet system and leaders can take no credit. And that the ugly elements, the lying, the preaching of a political line and the silencing of anyone who departs from it, are characteristic of the Soviet system and leaders. But surely this is too simple. Surely the Communist Party and all it stands for has done immense good as well as immense harm.

Often, on freezing winter evenings, I think of what life was like in old Moscow: the working people in rags in their huts and basement doss-houses; the ignorance, brutishness and despair. And I realize how far Russia has come in fifty years. The Communists have killed many people, crushed many good ideas, destroyed many good schemes, but they have vastly improved the general standard. There is not the slightest doubt about that. However poor Russia is, it is incomparably richer than it was. Above all, the general level of education is immeasurably higher.

And the people who have supervised these changes and who rule this country deserve the praise they so desperately thirst for. There is not the slightest doubt that they sincerely want good things for their country, and a better life for their people: more parks, more theatres, more schools, even more cafés. They are proud of what they have done, and plan to do much more.

The trouble is, they are impatient, intellectually and culturally limited, and intolerant. They are also in absolute control of all punishments as well as rewards. So that when other men, like Boris Zolotukhin, speak out, also wanting good things for their country, but disagreeing about what they are and how they should be achieved, they are whipped back into line, or entirely destroyed. The leaders cannot understand why this provokes dismay and anger: after all, anyone who (in their eyes) impedes the building of the Communist society deserves his punishment.

*   *   *

I confess that I can no longer strike a proper balance between what is good and what bad in the Communist Party and Soviet system; between the great progress and the terrible cost. It seems that the Communists have delivered Russia from one kind of backwardness only to plunge her into another. And I no longer care. I will never be able to answer the big questions about the good and evil of Communist rule in Russia; and anyway, they now seem irrelevant.

But I have leaned this: that after hearing the tale of a mangled life from a friend, or a cynical lie from a Communist official, I can forget my anger ski-ing with my friends in the ageless, melancholy woods outside Moscow. We go almost every Sunday, with the minimum of paraphernalia—just warm clothes, an old pair of skis, good company, and food and drink. We are very happy together. The sun rarely breaks through the dark, low layer of cloud, but I am relaxed in a way I have never been elsewhere. It is always a perfect day.

5 NADEZHDA NIKOLAEVNA

I STOOD there in the burning cold for almost an hour, moving back from the main road to the minimal but welcome protection of the nearest doorway when no headlights were in sight. It was an arctic night, the elements demonstrating the frailty of the human body. When the wind drops, the Moscow cold is usually bearable, but a snow-storm had been raging since early evening, blowing stinging pellets into my face and down my neck through the mesh of the scarf. I'd missed the last bus to my friend's flat, and was trying to hail a taxi, the only remaining means of transport. Five of them had passed, three empty, the other two with plenty of room for another passenger—but none did me the honour of slowing down. Then a sixth approached; the driver switched on his main headlamps when he caught sight of me running into the road—and swished past me almost silently in the snow. It too was empty.

I can't explain the deep-rooted reluctance of taxi-drivers to pick up passengers; their fondness for demonstrating not simply disinterest in, but deliberate rudeness to the public they are supposed to serve. But it is one of the conditions of Moscow life, and always worse—or at least more noticeable —after dark. Unoccupied taxis speed by, their little green 'For Hire' lights shining brightly, their unshaven drivers clenching *papirosi* between their teeth, sometimes utterly oblivious, sometimes aware enough of their surroundings to direct a look of profound contempt at anyone who attempts to hail them. They seem thoroughly pleased with themselves and their cars, as if they were masters rather than servants — which is, in fact, the case.

If you stand directly in front the driver may slow down enough to shout, 'To the garage,' through his closed window. This can mean that his shift is over and he's going in to hand over the car to the next driver, or that he simply can't be bothered with you. Perhaps he's already fulfilled his daily plan. Perhaps he doesn't like your looks. In any case, he needn't stop; however poorly educated he may be, he instinctively recognizes the situation: a seller's market in which shortage is always the principal determinant, and anyone who offers anything or any service for sale is in full command. He can take his pick of whom he wants to drive — or go for a spin alone if he's in the mood. The taxi in Moscow is a neat microcosm of the country's economic system.

But once he lets you into his car, once human contact has been established and you are no longer a customer but simply a person, the driver may speak to you with a familiarity, intimacy and frankness unknown in the cities of the world where taxi manners are more formal. You sit beside him in the front seat, and you are not driver and passenger, but two comrades, linked by the common struggle against hardship, common desires and shortcomings and by open *sympathie* unimaginable outside Russia. Once again, you realize that discipline, job etiquette and all normal forms of politeness and good order count for nothing in this country, while making personal contact and talking *po dusham* (from the soul) is everything.

*　　*　　*

I stood near the top of Kutuzovsky Prospekt, shivering in the burning cold … At last a taxi pulled smartly over to the kerb.

It was an old green Volga with a motor that coughed as it ticked over.

'Where to, *synok* [little son]?'

'Electrolitny Prospekt, please.'

'On the far side of the university?'

'That's the one.'

We picked up speed, passed the Hotel Ukraine, turned right under the Novoarbatsk Bridge, then cruised along the broad Milovskaya Quai towards the new south-west district. On our right, squat office buildings were shut tight against the cold and hung with icicles. On the left, the river was almost completely frozen over. The university loomed like a giant stalagmite, its red warning lights for aircraft barely visible through the swirl of snow. It was well after midnight; except for a few construction lorries, the road was empty. The taxi felt dizzyingly warm after the sharp cold outside, and reeked of grease from the driver's quilted cotton jacket. She was a thick, kerchiefed peasant, strong in face and body, massive and solid, an unmistakable product of the Russian earth.

'Not used to the Russian winter, eh my lad? I'll turn up the heater. What do you think of Moscow?'

'Please don't start on that. I'll go mad if I hear that question once more. I've been here three years. Ten people ask it every day.'

'Fair enough then. Three years—I expect you've become one of us. What's young life like these days? You look like a healthy type. Have you been to the countryside? Do you go to the theatre? Do you mix with our girls?'

'The girls are wonderful.'

'Yes?' She grinned with pride. 'In what way? You find them pretty?'

'Not so much pretty as womanly. I don't know exactly—

they're unspoiled. They have a way of making things very relaxed.'

'Because they're natural. That's the main thing. A Russian girl doesn't like to fake.'

'They're uncomplicated and friendly. Good-looking too — I think they're very attractive.'

'Yes, our *girls* are fine. But only the young ones. Oh, you don't have to tell me: Russian women *my* age are a sight. We don't take care of ourselves. We don't know how to dress. But you see, we wouldn't have time to dress even if we knew what to put where. We *work*, you know — work pretty hard. Then we run a home. Shop. Stand in queues. Do the washing. Mind the children or grandchildren. Then back to work. We hardly have time to look in the mirror after we're married and girlhood is over. And we're all fat from years of bad food. Ech, we just let ourselves go, become like me, heavy like horses ... But our young girls are the best in the world, yes? You should marry a Russian girl. They make the best wives.'

She drove deliberately, conscious of each movement of gear lever, accelerator and wheel as if remembering the sequences from training manuals. She was one of that breed of Russian for whom machines are a new kind of wonder, deserving solemn respect. (Nevertheless, she rode the clutch incessantly with a heavy boot, a weakness of three-quarters of Russian drivers.) Her big black eyes never left the road and her big round hands — gloveless — gripped the steering wheel as if it were slippery. Like most of her kind, there was something faintly Neanderthal about her big protruding mouth.

'And how do *you* like Moscow?' I asked her.

'Moscow? It's my own city — I love it, I adore it. Not only all our new construction and fancy modern places. I love the old parts too, the crooked market streets, even the rotten old log cabins they're busy pulling down. Look at that church over there! It's an old one, built before Napoleon. And I dare say you've seen our new Kalinin Prospekt—not a finer street anywhere in the world, I'll bet you anything. This is *my* city, my Moskva; of course I love it ... Not that I know any other city well, really; I've never even been to Leningrad, to my shame. But I *know* nothing could replace Moscow. You can keep all your Parises and Warsaws and Berlins. Moscow has a soul ... '

Suddenly she interrupted herself and looked at me sheepishly. 'But I haven't insulted you, have I? Where is your homeland?'

'You're sure I'm not Russian?'

'Sure as I'm not Chinese, thank God. No one will ever speak without an accent unless he's born here. You're Czech, I suppose. Or Polish. From one of the democratic countries. Came here to study in one of our institutes.'

In contemporary Russian usage, the 'democratic countries' are the six Warsaw Pact nations of Eastern Europe that elsewhere used to be known as satellites. I said I was from none of these, and expected to continue playing the guessing game that is a daily part of my life here whenever I meet strangers. A West European is still rare enough to provoke curiosity and excitement, even among taxi-drivers, the city's working-class cosmopolitans. But the woman seemed uninterested in pinpointing my nationality. She glanced at my shoes to confirm that I was a Westerner, and nodded her head.

'It's all the same to me where you're from. I say let you young people from everywhere in the world come to us to study and learn. You'll get your knowledge here, and if you're honest and decent, you'll go back with it and help your own people ... Not long ago, you know, it was very different. Not long ago, poor Russia had to send its lads to the West for a real education. Now you are coming to us to get the best. Well, it's wonderful, I think it's wonderful. Some people resent the expense, especially for all those black students we have now. But I say, let any young person of the world who needs a real education and seeks the real truth come to us, and welcome to all of you.'

She accepted a cigarette from my packet, rolled an end between her fingers in the Russian manner before putting it in her mouth, and bent forward towards the match. 'What's your name, then?' she asked. I supplied the Russian version, which was the christian name of several Romanov tsars. 'I'm Nadya,' she announced in return, and for a time we talked about her full name and patronymic: Nadezhda Nikolaevna.

'It's all the same to me, where you come from,' she repeated as we drove towards the university (Nadya referred to it as 'our university' as we approached, in the same way she would speak of 'our' Lenin, 'our' new Il–62 jet and 'our' new television tower). 'People are the same everywhere, aren't they? Basically the same. They all want the same things, after all. You and me, for example—we understand each other. All ordinary people everywhere want good things for themselves and their children, and to keep away the bad. It's as simple as that.'

She was silent for a moment, and in the sleeping grey-and-white city, the only sounds were the motor, running smoothly now, and the muffled whirr of the worn tyres on the packed snow.

'You know, I can't understand it—all this hostility between us and you people in the West. We want to live in peace—you know that, if you've been living here. We want peace more than anything in the world. And you want it too,

I'm sure of that. The ordinary people everywhere want peace, because they suffer terribly in war. We have nothing against you, you can see that. I think it's better to take off your hat and bow low three times than to start a fight that kills people. The Cold War is terrible. Who benefits by it, after all, except for a few capitalists? It's only a wicked waste and a shame. A stupid, idiotically expensive shame.

'And we're not so badly off here, are we? Is life so terrible behind the "Iron Curtain"? Do you see anybody hungry here? Suffering? Unhappy? Can anyone really think over there in the West that we want something from them besides being left alone to build our own lives?'

Of all the questions Russians ask foreigners, none is more embarrassing or difficult to answer than the request to confirm that their own life is not unusually poor. One does not want to lie, yet to tell the truth—that life here is indeed vastly poorer by material standards than in any major country of East or Western Europe—would be a painful insult when the question is asked this way. To change the subject, I asked Nadya where she was born.

'Born and bred in Moscow, and, God willing, here's where I'll live out my life. I've watched this city suffer, seen her grow. Felt her picking herself up by the scruff of her own neck when she was down. And she was down plenty of times, maybe that's why I love her so. There's something special about her—have you been able to feel it?'

She looked down at my proffered packet of cigarettes and shook her head. Just at that moment, the rear of a motor-cycle and side-car carrying three policemen in huge sheep-skin coats appeared out of the snowy greyness of the road immediately ahead. It was travelling very slowly, no more than twenty metres in front of us, and we were bearing down on it quickly.

'Careful Nadya! I don't suppose you want to crash into the police, of all people.'

She applied the brakes heavily and chuckled. 'Why not? If you have to run into someone, they're the best people. Nobody likes those layabouts. We call them *musor* [garbage] ... And what about over there, in the West? Does everybody love the police like they're supposed to?'

'Hardly.'

'Of course not, I just asked. People are the same everywhere, after all; nobody likes to be pushed around and lectured to by a puffed up turkey-cock in a blue uniform.' She brushed a few wisps of greying hair back under her kerchief and frowned for some minutes, either in thought or in an attempt to shape what she was thinking. 'What baffles me,' she continued, 'is how you people over there put up with capitalism. You're so progressive in other ways. You could overthrow it if you really tried. You just have to follow our example—no! you can do it a lot *better* than our example. And we'd help you too, of course. If you just got started on it, you'd have every Russian worker fighting alongside you for the sake of the world revolution. And with all your wealth and learning—just think what a magnificent life you'll have when you overthrow capitalism and toss out the capitalists.'

'A lot of people over there wouldn't understand you. They're not doing so badly, either. What's so wrong with capitalism?'

'What's wrong with capitalism? It's contrary to human nature, that's what's wrong with it. It's backward and vicious. I'll tell you something: we know the West is rich, really rich. That you live far better than we do, that everyone has a car. But I wouldn't swop for anything. I'd hate to live under capitalism. Not so much because of the exploitation and lack of freedom and all that, but the *feeling* it gives you: the awful

M

knowledge you're a kind of second-rate person. You know the country doesn't belong to you, you only exist to do the work of the capitalists and follow their bidding. You sit in a park somewhere or walk along a street, you look around you and realize it all belongs to someone else—even you yourself belong to someone else. I couldn't stand the idea of working in a capitalist factory. Think of it: I'd actually be giving my labour, my own body, to somebody else ... And besides, capitalism eats a person and cripples him psychologically. It's an evil thing.'

'What is it exactly that cripples people?'

'Private property. You know what private property means. It means jealousy and greed and hate, and it's *got* to mean that. Your neighbour gets rich for no reason on dividends; you feel insulted and bitter. Is he better than you? Not a bit! Then why should he have more? Because he's crafty or cruel, or dishonest or lucky. You might work twice as hard and give society twice as much—and get a tenth in reward. *Why?* Because he or his father owns shares, something like that. You want an explanation, then you want revenge. It eats at your mind and makes you an animal. It's not decent or fair— not *human*. Not even efficient. No thank you, that's not for me. When the principle is evil, the whole system and society are wrong, no matter how rich it makes you. That's the trouble with capitalism. That's why I want to help build Communism. Communism is a fair society, the hope of the future.'

'Are you a Communist, then?'

'Me a Communist? That's a laugh. I'm a worker—simple working class.'

'How do you know what private property means if you've never left Moscow?'

'I see it here. It's ugly. Some people in this city have cars and seven-room dachas, eat caviare and live off the fat of the land. And others—well, you've been to the villages, you've seen how our peasants live. The difference ought to be obvious enough.'

'But whose fault is all that? You've eliminated capitalism. If you hate inequality so much, why not just give everyone an equal share? Then everyone will be happy and there'll be no evil.'

'It's nobody's fault. I don't know. It's the fault of history. We can't have equality yet, not even under socialism—it just wouldn't work. For one thing, there's still too little of everything: if you gave everyone an equal share, no one would have much of anything. There'd be nothing big or beautiful at all, no cars, no nice houses. Besides we've still got to *stimulate* people to work by offering unequal rewards— precisely to make enough of everything. Kosygin is right, you know, in stressing personal rewards. All the present propaganda about individual material incentives is just what we need. Years ago, they'd shoot you for saying that the way to get a man to work is to tempt him with more money. Kosygin has an understanding of human nature. That's the way people are, especially on our collective farms. Nobody does anything for nothing.

'Anyway, private property infects us too, I can tell you. Take a typical flat—you know, two or three families in adjoining rooms. One man earns his bread honestly in a factory, and hasn't got a kopeck to spare. His neighbour supposedly works too, but suddenly buys a car. Where did he get the money? He cheated or stole from the state—that is, from the people. He embezzled funds from his office, ran an illegal scheme, speculated on the black market or had his hands in some other dirty business. And how does the honest fellow feel? Soon he hates the cheater, then they hate each other. I see it all the time.

'That's private property, and that's what will be eliminated under Communism. People will get what they need, and they will be *honest*. Completely, absolutely honest—in thought as well as deed.'

'You mean you have to cheat to buy a car?'

'Not always. Some people get paid enough without cheating.'

'Who, for example?'

'Well, military officers. The Air Force colonel I drove this afternoon. He's fifty, and *retired* on two hundred and fifty roubles a month—twice my man's pay. And he's got another job besides. And his wife works. *He* might be able to save for a car without cheating. The military brass always get on all right ...

'But I'll tell you something: the ones who live well aren't the real Communists. They're interested in themselves; so long as they're all right, to hell with everyone else. They might as well be capitalists. The real Communist is the ordinary worker, who has nothing but his bottle of vodka on Saturday night—which he shares, because his mate's hard up. We want Communism and we're willing to sacrifice for it because we live it and we *believe* in it. We believe in equality and brotherhood; that's natural to Russian workers. We don't want to live better than the next person, or live off someone else's sweat. Give a worker the choice between a wad of money and Communism, and he'll take Communism every time, even when it means less to eat.

'But you can't say that about the high-ups—they'll choose the fancy life over Communism. Take Stalin's daughter, for example—that Svetlana woman. Did she have to go without anything here? Didn't she have more than enough to make any normal woman happy? But no, she had to have that million dollars offered by sensation-mongers in New York.

She had to travel around and make a big name for herself in the West. A woman in her position, doing something like that! It's a disgrace. A terrible slur on her father's name and the working class.

'Or take that writer from Siberia, that what's-his-name who decided the other month he liked life in Paris. Did you hear about that? It was the same story: a man who has everything, who's been given everything on a silver plate, turns his back on his Motherland when he sees the chance to grab something bigger.'

'Do you mean Dyomin? How did you hear about that?' (Mikhail Dyomin, a well-known Russian writer, defected during a visit to Paris in July 1968. Like most such cases, it was wholly ignored by the popular Soviet press; and very few Russians read about it.)

'Don't worry—word gets round. I drive all kinds of people all day—there's always some interesting talk. We're not *quite* as ignorant as you might think.'

This time she took a cigarette without even noticing. It was snowing more thickly now, and we were the only car in sight. We had slowed to a near-crawl.

'It's always the same kind of people who turn their backs on Russia, and always for the same reason. That ballet-dancer in Leningrad who stayed in London or Paris or somewhere [Rudolph Nureyev]. Did he want for anything here? *Anything?* He had everything he wanted. But he was greedy: he had to make a name for himself, to lap up the "hurrahs" of the Western press and fancy audiences, and make a million for himself. That's the psychology of the "haves" for you. If you find a man willing to sell his Motherland, you can bet he's a rich type, some intellectual or bureaucrat, someone high up in the Party or in a university. He's already got too much compared with everyone else—far too much. But it only makes him want more. That's what's keeping us from Communism more than anything else. But the real Russian worker hasn't got that kind of selfishness. And we want a society that doesn't have it either.

'Sometimes I think the workers will build Communism in spite of the Party, not because of it. Too many of our grand leaders have too many vices, and the worst one is living in luxury while others have nothing. There's no excuse for it. Lenin never lived like that.

'Ask anyone in Russia, you'll never hear a word against Lenin. He walked around in shoes with holes in the soles; they had to force him to heat his flat. Or Dzershinsky—he ate potatoes with his soldiers, and not one bite more than the common ration. They lived for the people—and *like* the people. If only we had our Lenin back again, things would be fine. Lenin was a learned man, an intellectual and a gentleman, but he had the honesty and simplicity and soul of the worker.'

Something in Nadezhda's conversation seemed odd. She had all the political instincts of a Russian worker, and she looked for all the world like any Russian working woman; she could have been driving a bus or bulldozer as easily as a taxi. Yet she seemed far too intelligent, knowledgeable and articulate. Surely she'd been educated somewhere, or had spent part of her life in political work. Perhaps she had once had an office job and dropped back to physical work, as a certain number of Muscovites I know have.

'You've had some higher education, haven't you Nadezhda?' I asked her. 'Why is it you're working as a driver?'

'Educated?' She tried to suppress a smile. 'Wrong there, my boy. This old woman's never been educated in her life, never got further than eight classes [of elementary school]. I've just always read, that's how I pick up things. Always loved books since I was a girl—probably too much for my own good. Actually, I know I could have gone to university if I'd applied. But I preferred the kind of people and life I was born into. No, everything I know I got from talking to people and reading books.' She hunted for something between the seats, found it and handed it to me—a worn copy of *The Count of Monte Cristo*, with an old newspaper for a dust jacket. 'I've always read anything and everything I could get my hands on, every minute I could get my hands free. Suckled my babies with a book in one hand.'

'All right, I take it back: you were never educated. What's your background then? Are you what they call genuine working class?'

'I should hope so! My father was a metal worker in the old Gujon works [one of Russia's oldest metallurgical plants, now called the 'Hammer and Sickle']. You know about men like him—they were the core of the Revolution. He joined the demonstrations and went on strike in 1905, fought at the barricades in 1917, lived a life of terrible hardship and pure struggle for the working class. Then he died in 1937—still a young man. I had my eighth birthday the very day after he died.'

'What did he die of?' I asked. That year, 1937, was the climax of Stalin's purges, for which it is often used as shorthand: any death here in 1937 immediately raises the question of whether it was murder by the N.K.V.D.

'Tuberculosis. He breathed that rusty factory air all his young life, and never got over it. Never had proper ventilation in the factory or a proper doctor until after the Revolution. That's capitalism for you.'

'And your mother?'

'The poorest of the poor. She scrubbed floors and swept

streets. Learnt to read when she was thirty-five—after her own children did. She was a good woman, even though she could never tear herself away from the Church. Crossed herself a hundred times a day—never really understood what the Revolution was about.'

She was silent for a moment, then began again much more quietly, in a different tone altogether.

'That's another advantage of Communism. The state took an interest in me—me, a poor nothing. What could my parents do for me? They did well to keep five children alive. But the state *cared*. Instead of keeping me down because I was poor, it educated me. I went to school, instead of polishing shoes, like I'd have done under capitalism.'

'Just a minute, you're going too far. There is compulsory, free education until fifteen or sixteen almost everywhere in Western Europe. And free universities with grants and so on. Nobody has to polish shoes.'

'Really? Free? Until sixteen? I'm surprised; maybe you're even ahead of us in that. But don't forget, it was our example that made the capitalist give concessions. The capitalists are afraid people will follow our Soviet example and stuff them in the rubbish bin of history—that's why they make concessions over there. And besides, it's more than just school. For example, I spent more than one summer in holiday camps as a child; once, I even had a few weeks on the Black Sea— although my parents didn't have enough money of their own to send me for a bus-ride to the other side of the town. That's socialism: the system works for *us*. And when I'm too old to work, I'll have my pension—I won't be an old hag who nobody wants. I'll have done my work and our state will look after me. But a foreigner can never really understand, I suppose.

'I don't know, maybe Moscow looks poor to you. But we've

had hardships a foreigner can't even picture. We started with tsarist Russia, which was poor and miserable and backward. How did people live in old Moscow? You know Gorky's *The Lower Depths*. People lived like that—like animals. Then came the imperialist war against the Germans [the First World War] and all its waste and destruction. Then the Revolution and three years of terrible Civil War. Four years. All that killing and hunger and chaos and misery—what little we'd had before 1917 was in ruins.

'But finally, in the 1920s, Lenin led us to victory and we started *building*. From nothing we went to almost nothing with tremendous agony and effort. That's the way it is when you're poor and on your own. No one helped us; the capitalist countries all hated us and did everything they could to destroy us. America didn't even recognize us. After all, the English and the French and the Americans and Japanese had all sent their armies here to try and restore capitalism during the Civil War.

'So we were alone, pitifully weak and surrounded by the whole hostile capitalist world, determined to crush our workers' state. But we didn't cry and we didn't give up. Slowly, painfully, we built ourselves up. How? By investing. Where did the investment come from? From going sleepless and cold and hungry—*from us*. From our own bodies, not French banks. But we gave our bodies willingly; people sacrifice, after all, to build their own home. That's what we were doing under socialism, and don't think the working class didn't understand it. And if the Russian worker was then too uneducated to use slide-rules and operate cranes, he was always very good at using his strong back—with nothing in his stomach—to solve the problems of building a dam.

'To make things worse, there were arguments among ourselves; Trotskyites and Bukharinites, damaging our socialist construction. We overcame that. We had to waste huge sums on the army and defence. We overcame that, too. Slowly we built up. After fifteen years of sacrifice, we were beginning to live. Things were easier at last in the 1930s: under Stalin, we were starting to live a normal life again, to see some food and clothing in the shops again. They were hard years, but we had the joy of building—seeing our own Russia get bigger and better and stronger day by day.

'And then, once more, it came crashing down on us: *war*. The Nazis smashed whatever they could and left us in ruins. Why? What did Hitler want of us? We had to start all over again. I remember how terrible it was to see our buildings and factories, the things we'd built with our sweat and blood, being bombed into rubble in 1941.'

'Weren't you evacuated during the war? Lots of civilians I know were sent to the Urals.'

'I stayed in Moscow. I was sixteen; I'd almost finished school. Every able-bodied man went to the front and everyone else went to the factories. I was in a plant making artillery shells and rockets, and there were plenty of fourteen-year-olds working side by side with me.

'I wish you had seen those days, you'd understand us better now. I worked twenty hours straight through, two shifts, and came home to an unheated room when it was thirty degrees [centigrade] below freezing. There was almost nothing to eat: bread, and if you were lucky, potatoes—in their jackets. We went to bed like *this*' (she pointed to her greasy jacket) 'and tried to snatch a few hours' sleep during the bombardments. In the morning, we went to work hungry, picking our way through the rubble and the dead. And there were plenty who were worse off than me. The war took our men, not only our wealth. The best men died, the real men, the Communists. And my brother—my only one.'

Suddenly she turned towards me and stared at my face. 'But you're not *German*, are you? Maybe you're actually German.'

'No, I'm not German.'

She relaxed again and leant over the wheel. 'I'm sorry, then, excuse me. I'm a bit nasty about that.'

'About what?'

'Understand me, *synok*: I don't hate the Germans. I never believed all that propaganda during the war about all Germans being vicious beasts. There's some good in every nation—every people have their national character, their good and bad. The French are a bit cynical and dirty, but know how to live. The Americans are naive and fooled by the capitalists and their government—but they're big-hearted and open-natured like us.

'The Germans are orderly: industrious, disciplined, very accurate and clean and I admire them for that. I know some lads who served in Germany in the occupation army after the war. They could hardly believe how hard the Germans worked. Their cities were levelled, just like ours, but they cleaned up the rubble and were building new factories and blocks of flats ten times faster than we were. On the other hand, Germans are sentimental and savage. A German can stroke a cat with tears in his eyes, and kill a man the next minute. What did they want from my brother, after all? Why did they come here to destroy us?'

The car windows were steamed and frosted. Nadezhda stopped for a red light at an intersection beyond the university where three students, who had apparently walked home from town, were tramping towards the hostel.

'The Russians? Well, frankly, the Russian people are very special. Take the war for example. We were slow and stupid and backward compared to the Germans, but they never could have beaten us. When it matters, Russians win over everything. With their sweat, with their blood. Something happens to us when we're faced with hardship — sometimes our endurance amazes even me. In the army too. Our army is tough, with real discipline — no comforts and pampering like yours. With us it's all iron. Harsh like the winter. Peter the Great modelled the first Russian army on the German pattern, you know.

'True, a lot depended on help from the West. I first learnt to drive on an American lorry — a Studebaker two-and-a-half. It was a perfect beauty; how those people make machines! And I remember beef from American tins: for plenty of people, it was the only meat in months. We haven't forgotten that. Some people say we couldn't have won the war without lend-lease, but I don't believe it. The point is, we'd have done it somehow, just like we're going to build Communism somehow — despite everything. Because *that's* the Russian people. We've been sort of chosen by history to do the impossible.'

We had arrived at the address. Nadezhda pulled over to the kerb, and turned her big frame towards me, one arm over the back of the seat.

'I'll tell you the most important thing. Communism *is* going to be built, I know it is. If the world doesn't blow itself up, it will be Communist. You and me and everyone together. Mankind is progressing, it's becoming civilized and rational, and it's *got* to come to that, because it's a law of nature. With all our horrible mistakes, we are learning. About decency and justice — which means Communism.

'Communism isn't a fairy tale, like God. For centuries people talked about God — my mother most of all. And there wasn't one; there was never any such thing as God; no one has a scrap of proof. But you can *see* Communism being built. It isn't a matter of faith or fairy tales, but of work. Look at our university. Look at Moscow, building itself up. Look at our steel mills.'

'Look at *our* steel mills.'

'Ah, son, that's just the point. It's the system that counts. Can't you see that? You have capitalism there, so that your steel mills, even if they are ahead of ours, mean profits and greed. It's the law of capitalism, the rule of whoever can grab most. But the law of socialism is sharing; our building means progress for everyone and for civilization. It's not just the factories that count, but who owns them and what is done with them and how people feel about them. Our factories are *ours*, so we are building Communism, not selfishness.

'How can I explain this to someone from a bourgeois country. Do you have brothers?'

'Two sisters.'

'Well then, you know how you feel when you do something for them: better than when it's something for yourself. Multiply that by millions of times and you have Communism. Everybody *wants* to be good to their neighbours; everybody likes themselves better when they are. It's human nature to be good as well as selfish, and it's the good side that has to be encouraged — not the grasping side, as in capitalism. That's where the system comes in. Communism brings out the best in people, the family feeling, the generosity and solidarity.

'And Communism is only fair. It's the logical extension of everything civilized and decent in society. People have to work together, not exploit each other; not have a thousand workers no better than slaves for one capitalist who owns a factory. All for one and one for all. It's no one's fault that he's born smaller, weaker or less gifted than another. The strong must help the weak, and *both* will benefit. I'm driving you in this taxi, doing you a service, and I get pleasure out of it because I know I'm needed. You're a student, you're cleverer than me — that means you show me the way in scholarly things, and I listen to you.

'But I can't really explain it well. You ought to read Stalin's *Short Course* [of the history of the Communist Party] where he talks about the inevitability of Communism. Stalin could always set out social ideas very clearly, that was one of his best qualities. A lot of nonsense has been talked about Stalin since 1956, and it's made a lot of people, the working people, very sad. It was an outrage, the way they trampled on his memory after he died. Of course he made mistakes: he could be a cruel man and very suspicious, and some innocent people paid dearly for that. Towards the end of his life, he was a sick man, and some of his lieutenants got out of hand. But there's more to Stalin than that. He was a genuine leader of the working class. Remember: Lenin made him head of the Party, and Lenin *was* the Party. Lenin made it, it was his creation. And Lenin was right, as always: only a Stalin, with his iron will and iron hands, could carry us through those years of the first five-year plans and then the war. Stalin was fearless, merciless to his enemies — and we had to crush our enemies to keep our workers' state alive. Stalin said in 1931 that we were a hundred years behind and had to make up that gap in a decade or be crushed. Which is what we did; and *we* crushed our enemies, besides. In all the main things — in building socialism and building the country — Stalin was absolutely right. We all suffered, but he was good for Russia. He followed Lenin's line and continued Lenin's work, and the working people will tell you the country was better off — we felt safer and more sure of where we were going — under his direction. As for me, I'm very glad the leadership's started remembering that now.

'Anyway, the *Short Course* made the coming of Communism very clear. You can't find that book in the shops any more because of that terrible anti-Stalin campaign under Khrushchev. But most people have it in their homes because it's the only thing that makes the theoretical side of Marxism–Leninism perfectly clear. Stalin explained why the whole world is moving towards Communism. Everywhere in nature, the old gives way to the new—because it is more rational. It is progressive and inevitable. It's the logical progression of society. So Communism will develop *naturally* from capitalism; it *must*.

'But the point is, it's going to take a long time, very long. Not twenty or thirty years, like the Party hacks now hint. Those blasted propagandists, they've got to keep writing things, keep inventing nonsense to earn their huge salaries and make themselves look good. Instead of doing some honest work to actually help bring Communism closer, they sit at their desks and blab about it. You see, to have Communism you must have much more than material wealth. You have to remake men's minds. To have Communism, you must have honesty and morality above all. Pure, selfless, *honest* people.'

'And what about your friends? Do they feel the same way about the coming of Communism? Or are you the rare exception?'

'How can I answer that? Most of my friends, good working people, say, "To hell with Communism, there'll never be any Communism." They've heard too much about it from propagandists who don't care about Communism. They've heard too much criticism of Stalin and other devoted men who cared and fought for it. So they appear cynical. But in their *hearts* they want it. And are willing to sacrifice for it. They're just afraid to admit they believe in it. It seems too far away now. We're too poor and too busy supporting everybody else in the world, from Czechs to black Africans.'

'How poor? Do you have enough to eat?'

'Of course I do, what a question! And not only enough. We have fish and cheese, and sometimes meat—all sorts of things.'

'How much do you earn?'

'Over a hundred' [roubles per month].

'And your husband?'

'A hundred and twenty, hundred and thirty.'

'So together you have almost two hundred and fifty roubles for two people?'

'For four—we have a boy and a girl, you see. The boy's almost grown up, but he wants to go on to higher education. The girl's still in school, she's only fourteen. It's really the children who need the money; they should have pretty things when they're young. But wait, there's more than two hundred and fifty roubles a month. To be perfectly frank, I make some extra on the quiet. You know: tips, extra passengers, fiddling the meter—one thing and another. It all adds up.'

'Illegal?'

'Of course it's illegal. I'd be in prison in a second if they caught me—which they won't. If you've lived here for three years you know the kind of thing I mean. It's just a little fiddling, nothing everybody else doesn't do. You've seen it everywhere: shop assistants, drivers, waiters—anybody who handles cash or goods takes some small change from the state cash-box for his own pocket. I'm not defending it, mind you, but there's no point in denying it either: petty cheating is pretty widespread.'

'Yes, I know. How much does it add to your pay?'

'Three or four roubles a shift, sometimes more. Let's say sixty or seventy roubles a month.'

'Its crazy. Why do you do it?'

'Why? Are you asking seriously? I do it to live.'

'You mean you can't live on your own salary?'

'Of course I can. But not so nicely. With potatoes and kasha instead of the meat and cheese.'

'I don't understand. You talk about the evils of capitalism and the terrible effects of resentment and greed. You sing the praises of Communism, tell me how much you want it, and how directly it depends on people being entirely honest. And then you go about your old way, cheating every day.'

'Maybe you can't understand. The cheating's wrong, I know that. I hate it and I'd gladly stop it—I *want* to stop. But it would make no sense now. I cheat because everyone else does. The Party high-ups live like kings—on the people's money. Factory directors take a share of their plant's profits. Foremen take wage "kick-backs", workers smuggle out what raw materials they can under their coats, shop assistants water the wine. And we drivers fiddle the meter. That's the way it is. You know the proverb, *s volchami zhit', po-vol'chi vit.* [When in Rome, do as the Romans do; literally: when you live with wolves, howl like a wolf.] Cheating's the thing to do. The boss of my taxi park has made a fortune selling petrol and spare parts, and all the shift supervisors take their cuts too. Spare tyres on the black market, batteries and things. Why should I be a martyr? I would if it would help, but it wouldn't change a single thing.'

'And still you believe in Communism and the selfless man?'

'Of course I believe in Communism—if they threw me in prison tomorrow for cheating, I'd still believe in Communism. I know what I'm doing is wrong and must be stopped. And if we had Communism I'd stop it at once and for all—immediately, gladly. If *everyone* agreed to stop it—if someone

N

ordered, "No more, this is the end, things have changed" — I'd be the first to stop. In one second. I long for that day. But meanwhile, it makes no sense.'

'But if that's true, it will never make sense.'

'Of course it will. You've got to understand the *essence* of things. Take Marx, for example—he was no fool. Marx said, "Existence determines consciousness." Get the idea? I'm a product of my surroundings, and for the time being, everyone around me cheats. But change my environment and of course you change me along with it. Or take Gorky's *Vassa Zheleznova* —you've read it?'

'No.'

'You must. Vassa is the widow of a river-boat owner. She poisoned him. A miserable bitch, greedy and grasping, typical bourgeois. At the end of the book, she has an argument with her daughter-in-law, fine young Jewess-revolutionary. She says, "Oh, you don't really know me. I'm bad because *they're* all bad, everyone around me is sick with greed. But I can be good too. If I didn't *have* to be bad, I could be as good as anyone. I can love and be kind, if only I had the chance." And that's the same with me, see what I mean? That woman said just exactly what I feel.'

'And you see no contradiction here? To have Communism, everyone must be good. But to be good, there must be Communism. What comes first, chicken or egg?'

'Of course there's a contradiction. That's the law of nature, the dialectic. All life is made of contradictions. But they are always resolved in the end. This contradiction will be resolved too, and Communism *will* be reached. I know it will. It's just a question of time and hard work.'

'So you really feel that a whole society can be selfless and good?'

'And you don't? But it's happening here, can't you see?

Can't you *see* us moving in that direction? Just think of what old Moscow was like. Think how far we've come already, and against what odds. And if some things look poor and run-down to you, remember, we're going forward. It's just a matter of time. The Russian worker will do it.'

She looked at her watch. It was almost one-thirty.

'*Synok*, I have to move on. Got to make my norm, you know; fulfil and over-fulfil the plan.'

'How much do I owe you?'

She switched on the little bulb over the meter. Together with the fare, it illuminated a stern notice that passengers must pay strictly according to the figure indicated on the meter: tips are (theoretically) forbidden, and extra charges by the drivers for personal profit are (theoretically) to be reported.

'A rouble-twelve,' answered Nadya.

I gave her a rouble and fifty kopecks.

'Oh no,' she protested, 'there's your change. Take it! I won't take a tip from you, never.'

'Don't be silly. Do you want to be the first taxi-driver in Moscow who refused a tip?'

'That's exactly what I'm going to be. I couldn't take anything from you. Not because of what I told you—don't get me wrong. I'm not going to stop cheating because I confessed to a Westerner. But because I enjoyed talking to you. I love talking. It was a pleasure to drive you.'

She shoved the change into my pocket and put out her hand. Her fingers were calloused and oily, and her grip uncomfortably hard. One day, I would like to draw a full portrait of a woman of her type: they stand for something I can feel, but not quite explain. One associates them with various physical details—a coarse, drab, woollen kerchief, steel false teeth, a way of carrying money in a jacket pocket, notes of all denominations rolled together into a crumpled ball, like so much waste paper—but it is much more than that. Nadya was far from an ordinary Russian working woman: on the contrary, she was exceptionally intelligent, articulate and thoughtful—even for Moscow taxi-drivers, among whom one sometimes meets extraordinary purveyors of folk wisdom. Still, there was much about her—fatalism and optimism about the salvation of the human race, weariness and astonishing endurance, down-to-earth concern about bread and potatoes, and a cosmic *Weltanschauung* that includes the age-old Russian sense of mission to save the world—much that is hard to picture in anyone but a Russian worker.

'*Do svidaniya*, son. All the best to you and your people. I hope you like Moscow. I hope you find a Russian girl to marry—they make the best wives. But don't take her away: if she's a good girl, the kind you should marry, she'll never be happy anywhere but in Russia. You come and settle here, it's not a bad life—for you educated types, that is. Not a bad life at all.'

She winked, took a last cigarette for the road, and drove off into the storm, which almost at once enveloped her old green Volga in a dense flurry of snow.

6 THE INTELLIGENTSIA

I WOULD like to attempt now a portrait of a small and in some ways entirely unrepresentative minority: the genuinely educated liberals, whose political instincts and cultural interests would make them at home in most intellectual circles in the West. These 'European' Russians speak of themselves as 'the one per cent'. Perhaps there is an element of snobbery in this; certainly there is pessimism. They may comprise two or three per cent, perhaps as much as five or six. But Soviet propagandists are correct when they describe them as ideological expatriates in their own country: a handful, who are politically, culturally and in some ways spiritually alienated from the vast majority of Russian people.

And this is the tragedy, one of the hundred tragedies, of Russian history. The Russian intelligentsia has always been a tiny minority—a thin layer of essentially Western-oriented culture on an essentially superstitious, anti-intellectual peasant mass. It has included brilliant, consummately worldly men; often, in the nineteenth and early twentieth centuries, in the avant-garde of many branches of science and, of course, art. But they were dazzling exceptions, as remarkable for their divergence from the general level of Russian life as for their achievements.

Tsarist Russia lacked a thriving middle class, traditional source and support of a healthy intelligentsia; more important, it lacked the experience of enlightenment, reformation and renaissance—the whole complex of legal, social,

political, cultural and philosophical growth that gave
Europe its distinctive civilization and humanist traditions.
Russia's backwardness compared to the West could be
measured in many ways at the turn of the century; one of
the most important was the relative sparseness of the intelligentsia, its political weakness and detachment from the
mainstream of national life. By contrast with every major
European country, it was still a tiny minority in 1917 — and,
being more Western than Russian in outlook, was still
estranged from the great peasant mass, its attitudes and way
of life.

Then came the October Revolution — and the death or
emigration of a great part of that minority. Many who remained were killed or fled during the devastating Civil War.
Stalin's psychopathic purges in the 1930s decimated the
meagre ranks once again; and the Second World War took
yet another toll. And this leaves out of account the fearful
pressures to conform exerted on the handful who survived
the cataclysms of fifty years of Soviet rule.

Tens of millions of Russians, of course, have been educated
since 1917, but their education has been Soviet. Aside from
the direct and obvious political indoctrination (an outsider
will find it difficult to comprehend the narrowness of the
humanities as taught in Soviet institutions, and the mass of
propaganda directed at every student in every field), there is
the question of the nature and quality of education. A full
course of study in a Soviet technical institution does not
'educate' a youth of Russian peasant background. (Nearly
fifty per cent of Russians still live in the country, and most
of the others are but one generation removed from this
profoundly rural and isolated way of life.) Russian intellectuals themselves speak of the 'Soviet intelligentsia' as distinct
from intelligentsia in the traditional sense: they mean

engineers, even doctors and lawyers, who have acquired the technical skills of their professions but not the instincts of cultural and political enlightenment—people with a literate veneer over their essentially peasant cast of mind. The men who operate the machinery of the Soviet dictatorship are educated in this sense; they lack not mechanical skills, but intellectual curiosity, open-mindedness, tolerance, a willingness to permit scepticism, dissent and confusion about the great questions of individual and national life without dispatching the offenders to labour colonies.

Westerners who have not lived in Russia must take it on faith that much less has changed in the philosophical and emotional foundations of the 'Russian mentality' than has remained the same. 'Russia is a village,' a young Moscow historian told me recently. 'Moscow is the façade; we have always needed façades. But the truth of this country is still in the village; everything comes from the Russian village and the spirit of the village permeates everything. And that spirit is still what we call "dark". You cannot understand Russia unless you know about this darkness: the fatalism, obscurantism and profound religiosity that made our people bow in genuine reverence to an unbenevolent tsar.'

In terms of mental attitudes, very little has changed in fifty years—and little could have been expected to change even under the most enlightened educational policy. The development of a genuine intelligentsia that draws its inspiration and support from its own civilization and, in turn, plays a significant role in its own national life, is always a slow process of organic growth. Under ideal circumstances, it can be expected to take centuries. Russia's circumstances have not been ideal. Politically and culturally, the great mass of Russian people are still backward by comparison with European countries. And the genuine intelligentsia—the people I want to decribe here — are still a minute fraction of the population.

In Western news stories, it is almost always this minority that is described and quoted — understandably, because it is they who make the news, and who share a common language with the European correspondents in Moscow. Naturally, the most striking news is not about the collective farmers, factory workers, clerks and tram drivers, but the Sinyavskys, Ginzburgs, Yevtushenkos and Solzhenitsyns, as well as the brave groups, mere handfuls, who wait outside the law courts while protestors and dissidents are being tried. But in this respect the Western press is often seriously, if unintentionally, misleading. A casual Western reader might imagine that Russia is populated principally by angry young poets and novelists and their idealistic young followers. This, of course, is far from the truth in relatively cosmopolitan Moscow and Leningrad, and nonsense with respect to Russia as a whole.

The people to whom foreigners usually gravitate in Moscow, and with whom they spend most of their time, are politically and sociologically interesting precisely because they are estranged from many of the main currents of Russian life; because, *mutatis mutandis*, their instincts, responses and cultural attitudes coincide closely with those of most educated Europeans; because through them one can imagine what one's own reactions to the Soviet system might be.

A last word of introduction to this collective portrait. I often use 'intellectual' and 'member of the intelligentsia' synonymously, although strictly they are not always interchangeable. Moreover, both terms imply too narrow a definition of the people I want to portray. It is not so much their work, or even their education, that makes these people compatible with each other and with foreigners. It is their temperament: a set of attitudes, a state of mind. A mechanic who services a friend's car, and who has almost no formal education or travel-acquired worldliness, is nevertheless one of the most broad-minded Muscovites I know. His patriotism and cultural interests, like my friends', are universal rather than national; he has a sense of commitment to justice as traditionally understood, rather than to the ideological and military triumphs of his Motherland. And this more than anything is what distinguishes the 'one per cent'.

However, there is a strong correlation between education and attitudes: the more intellectual one's profession, the more likely one is to be independent of the crude and narrow type of Russian patriotism. And, conversely, the less education a Russian has had, the more likely he is to be mired in the deep parochialism and political illiberalism that the hard climate, geography and history of his country has nourished. Thus, I use 'intellectual' and 'member of the intelligentsia' as a kind of shorthand to represent the genus of people in Russia who are most like 'you and me' — the readers of books, the middle-class liberals.

* * *

Late one autumn evening, a young writer from Voronezh now living with his mistress in Moscow took me to visit an older writer who has published several successful novels, but is better known by the intellectual community for his poetry and satirical sketches that are circulated from hand to hand in blurred, heavily-thumbed typescript. The flat was in a sprawling new development of squat blocks, already crumbling and decaying, although the last units had been completed only the previous winter. We walked up four dark flights of stairs (one lift had broken down and was marked OUT OF ORDER; the other did not work either; it was after midnight, when the current is turned off to conserve electricity) with the whispers and over-the-shoulder glances that are reflex actions—although probably quite futile—when visiting a member of the 'underground'. Our host and his wife received us happily, although we came unexpectedly; my own presence, as a foreigner, was not disturbing because I had met them several times before—on Sunday outings for picnics and mushroom-gathering—and we had close friends in common. In other words, I could be trusted. I would not inhibit the almost vibrant openness and candour of Russians of this type when they gather with their close friends, shut off and safe from 'them'.

We pushed past the jumble of clothes hanging in the hall and into the smoky bed-sitting-room. It was a replica of dozens I'd seen, all inhabited by the inner circle of Moscow intellectuals. The room was furnished with an eclectic assortment of cheap pieces and seemed even more cramped because of the icons, old prints and artefacts of tsarist Russia that were propped between tables, chairs, the studio couch and the walls. A substantial collection of books, largely yellowed, pre-revolutionary Russian volumes and prohibited titles in Western languages, spilt from the bookcases into untidy piles on the floor. Empty bottles were everywhere, together with an accumulation of dirty dishes containing both raw and left-over food (including a carton of thirty eggs, still rather a find, which the young bulldog trampled over and broke, to everyone's merriment). Two other friends were there, a Chekovian, blond-bearded artist, and a balding doctor with an English tweed jacket and a supply of Gitanes; and in the kitchen, two young graduate students without a room of their own were, we imagined, making love.

The music was from a dented tape-recorder: Bob Dylan, Ella Fitzgerald, Nina Simone, The Who and others performing year-old pop songs alternated with Bach organ preludes. The dancing was a ragged free for all, punctuated by panting, yelps and laughter. We drank the vodka and cognac we had brought, together with what remained of the host's vodka and wine. While some couples were telling funny stories and flirting, others were engaged in a serious, perceptive discussion of English youth's fascination with Indian mysticism.

It is difficult to convey the informality and intimacy of these gatherings in Moscow to someone who hasn't experienced them — or who has experienced the opposite atmosphere on Moscow's streets. No one feels a need to appear witty or profound, clever or well-informed; the only compulsions are to be oneself, and to participate (or not) according to one's mood. It is no less true for being a commonplace that what distinguishes Russian social relationships is a quality of naturalness, artlessness and 'sincerity', an ambiance in which *falsh* (phoneyness, insincerity) is rare, because friends, and even recent acquaintances, feel supremely at ease with one another. Among the intelligentsia, this quality, combined with intellectual interests, produces a more authentically Bohemian atmosphere than I have seen anywhere in Western Europe.

It was very late when someone turned the conversation to Czechoslovakia. ('Yes, yes, it's fine to be living it up here — but in Prague, people are facing our tanks ... ') To say there was a tense silence would be too dramatic; these people have learned to live with the barbarism (as they call it) of their government, and are no longer surprised enough by it to be dramatic. Still, all conversation dissolved for a moment, just when a tape had run out. We drained our glasses. The doctor mentioned an observation of Lenin; one of the few, he pointed out, that is conveniently ignored in the stupendous daily outpouring of Leniniana. Russia, said Lenin, is politically a profoundly backward country which the Revolution, with one stroke, made progressive. But if a socialist revolution is achieved in a European country, it is quite possible that Russia will take up its traditional backward position again.

Then, as so often in the weeks following the August 'events', the conversation shifted from bitterness over the invasion to the cup of bitterness — Russia's political environment — from which it flowed.

The host: 'This country is so desperately backward politically, so reactionary and "dark", there isn't a real chance of a change. We go from brutality to brutality — because brutality *breeds* brutality. We haven't yet even reached a take-off point for democratic government.'

My friend from Voronezh: 'Politically, this is a medieval country. We are living in the Middle Ages, ruled by medieval tyrants with modern methods but medieval minds. The Politburo hunts witches and burns heretics at the stake — because the Russian people are still ready to believe in witches and heretics.'

The host again: 'Yes, there *has* been some democratization and liberalization in the last fifteen years, but it's ludicrously exaggerated by Western commentators. One thing every thoughtful person here will tell you, whether he hates the dictatorship or works for it: there will be no genuine liberalism, no substantive changes, in my lifetime.'

*   *   *

These are the kind of comments I hear regularly from this breed of people. Pessimism about Russia's political future is their dominant mood, and it is far-reaching, almost to the point of despair. 'Not in my lifetime' has become a kind of catch-phrase, graphic and dramatic—and self-pitying— enough to represent the vast political, historical and, above all, psychological chasm that separates Russia from Europe and 'normality'. Few Russians expect this normality— meaning, minimally, a reasonable measure of personal and intellectual freedom, and reasonable restraints on the state guaranteed by reasonable respect for the rule of law—in this century. Something is very wrong with Russia, they feel. She has a congenital illness which makes her leaders produce cures worse than the disease.

It is, of course, the dictatorship that has bred this pessimism, and the dictatorship's most recent adventures: neo-Stalinism at home, and the invasion of Czechoslovakia abroad. The invasion—which smothered the hope that Russia might be 'liberalized' by way of influences from East Europe—was a particularly bitter and humiliating blow. So severe, in fact, was the intellectuals' disapproval, that the immediate re-sponse of several of my closest friends was a surge of rejoicing —an instinctive expression of the theory, 'the worse, the better'. The miscalculations on which the use of force were based, according to this reasoning, were so absurd and damaging to Russia's long-term interests and prestige that they would demonstrate the stupidity, if not the moral bankruptcy, of the Politburo to one and all, and might hasten their replacement. But the overall reaction was grief and gloom.

However, as I have said, the invasion itself appalled the intellectuals less than the apathy, acceptance and, worst of all, the approval of the action by the majority of their countrymen. To have invaded Czechoslovakia was a brutal mistake—but every government, whether dictatorship or democracy, is capable of brutal mistakes. Every government, moreover, conceals or justifies its mistakes with its own propaganda line. But Soviet propaganda is unique in the monopoly of the means of communication, and in the absurdity and enormity of its lies. And the vast majority of Russians believe those lies.

A discussion of the issues raised by the invasion will run something like this:

Vitya: 'The most frightening thing is most people here believe what they're told—*whatever* they're told. Every other article ends, "The Czech people love the Soviet Army." Fantastic! No one with the faintest idea about the world would look at it twice, but our people swallow it whole!'

Maya: 'Besides, they want to believe agitprop. Because they're chauvinists: Russia's the Motherland, what's good for Russia is good for the world. And they're jealous. They don't want the Czechs to do better than we do. Mother Russia must be top dog in the socialist world. These people are very happy to see Eastern Europe under our heel. If we're under the orders of the Politburo, all the more reason *they* should be.'

Sasha: 'Before Dubcek started his reforms, all our press painted him in the usual way for satellite leaders: a loyal son of the working class, respected and loved by all progressive people everywhere, for his inspired, selfless leadership of the Czechoslovak nation on the road to socialism. Now, of course, he's a horse of an entirely different colour. And soon, if they decide to get rid of him, they'll make him a secret bourgeois sympathizer who only worked his way up the Party hierarchy to betray socialist Czechoslovakia to the West German Fascists at the appropriate moment. And our people will believe it! After a relatively short barrage of propaganda, just a few weeks.'

Natasha: 'Supposedly educated, rational people are fooled, too. I know an economics professor who taught Dubcek while he was studying in Moscow. Until August, he was telling everyone how brilliant Dubcek was, how he knew that young man would go on to great things. Now he's saying he always suspected Dubcek had to be watched, he somehow sensed bourgeois tendencies in him. And this professor is perfectly sincere! It's double-think. Orwell was a genius.'

* * *

Moreover, the attitudes generated during the Czechoslovakian 'events' are, according to the intellectuals, but the latest manifestation of a traditional Russian weakness. It is not so much the reaction to this or that event as the general level of political consciousness that makes my friends despair. They feel the popular Russian political mind is no less medieval than the Politburo's — is, in fact, as much the cause of the dictatorship as the effect. Here is a representative sample of the intellectuals' reflections on the country's basic political characteristics.

'Russians can be the kindest and most generous people in the world, and in personal relationships the most democratic and egalitarian. But they can't live without a tsar.'

'Most people, meaning *the* people, simply can't conceive of political democracy. They understand quantitative changes perfectly well: more or less suffering, a tighter or looser squeeze, a harsher or more benevolent leader. But only within the system, with someone up above giving or taking back. The idea they might decide for themselves is simply beyond their comprehension.'

'Take censorship, for example. It's by far the most important and efficient part—the dominant factor—of all our literary world and work. You can't have a label for a vitamin bottle or a toothpaste box printed without the censor's stamp—not to speak, of course, of a single word in any publication whatsoever. The control is *total*. Yet nobody mentions the censorship. If the staffs of the censorship offices were ordered to march in some parade, carrying a banner saying, "Soviet Censorship is the Most Democratic in the World!" people would see nothing peculiar in it. They'd hardly notice, of course, but some small part of them would drink it in. Double-think again. The very notion is absurd. But people can't understand this—if the censorship is Soviet, they really believe it's the most democratic in the world.'

'Fifty American psychiatrists and psychologists did an analysis of Khrushchev for Kennedy, just before the 1961 Vienna meeting. They concluded Khrushchev was a rational, strongly motivated man with a high degree of childhood gratification. But it would be better if Kennedy didn't discuss things like democracy, freedom and individualism with Khrushchev because he simply had no understanding of these concepts. They meant nothing to him because he never knew anything about them. Exactly! Khrushchev wasn't a bad type. (And actually, in retrospect, people have come to like him a lot more despite his crudeness; we now remember there can be worse.) But the point is, Khrushchev was a fairly typical Russian muzhik: quick and clever, but with no idea in the world that people might decide things without a Marxist–Leninist church, stuffed with icons of Lenin, telling them how to think and what to do.'

'The fascist American presidential candidate Wallace was quoted in a newspaper here not long ago. He compared Russians to fleas under a glass: if you keep them there long enough, they stop jumping, even when you remove the glass. Much as I detest Wallace, that's a rather fair description of the Russian people. We're *tamed*, we don't *think* of jumping. And the ironic proof of it is that such a quotation could appear in a Soviet newspaper. The intention was to show how stupid, slanderous and dangerous the Americans are — and that's actually how it was taken. Not one person in a hundred stopped to think that he can't travel, can't read this author or that, can't take a step without seeing an article or poster about Lenin — that Wallace was right.'

Wallace's quote was mentioned on another occasion in connection with a recent poem by Yevtushenko that hinted at the same thought:

> He who was conceived in a cage shall yearn for it.
> And with horror I understood that I love
> That cage behind whose wire I have been shut away.
> And the animal farm — my Motherland …
>
> It's true: there have been changes on the animal farm:
> They used to simply strangle people in sacks;
> Now the killing's done by modern methods —
> With electric current. After all, it's cleaner!

'What's missing in the political consciousness of the Russian people is everything democratizing and liberalizing in the last seven hundred years of Western history, from Magna Carta, the French Revolution, and down to the hippie movement. In certain ways, this makes Russia a better place to live. Life is more easy-going and in some ways

o

honest here. But politically, it's been disastrous. While Europe became adult with its renaissances and reformations, we stayed slaves—like retarded children—under the Tartar yoke. The result is hopeless political backwardness; we simply never grew up.'

'The strangle-hold of the Tartars produced the strangle-hold of the tsars—which gave way to the strangle-hold of the Communists. Perfectly logical. Passed with mother's milk from generation to generation. And if there were another revolution tomorrow, the next regime would settle down soon enough to something similar.'

'Last week, my friends and I spent an evening speculating. What would happen if a referendum were held on the desired form of government? A genuine referendum, under U.N. auspices, so people were sure it wasn't a trick to test their loyalty. At first, we felt ninety per cent would vote against Soviet rule. But as we kept talking, we realized it would be the other way round: at least seventy-five per cent would want what they have now. They think things are all right here. Not perfect, of course; there are complaints about this and that. But, in principle, Soviet rule is the best in the world. And *that's* the great tragedy, not Soviet rule itself.'

'Czechoslovakia is ready for democratic socialism; we are not. Everyone who's thought about it understands that dictatorship is the natural form of government here. A thousand years of Russian history has prepared us for it. Go and look at Red Square; whenever the mausoleum is open, people will stand for hours in the pouring rain, in sleet, in terrible cold, in blizzards, to see Lenin. They don't know anything about Leninism, really. But psychologically and emotionally, they must see the Great Father. He will bless them, purify them, tell them everything's all right.'

'Tsarism fell apart when Russia was actually near her

strongest point. There were seven million people in its army — the largest in the world. Industry and education were in an upsurge, and most of the terrible muddle of the bureaucracy's handling of the war had finally been worked out. It had an enormous autocratic apparat. But it fell because of rising hopes, demands and expectations — because, despite the improvements, the government couldn't keep up with the people's demands. Well, Communism will no doubt fall for the same reason some day — although that day is not now in sight. Communism is an anachronism, socially, economically, politically — in almost every way. It's terribly out of date, ultra-conservative, rigid, backward, *afraid*. One day people's hopes will soar, Communism will fall, and we'll all rejoice. Wrongly. Because what will replace it? Something more or less the same, more or less in keeping with the environment and attitudes here. In other words, more darkness.'

'The most meaningful single sentence about Russia is still the opening to Trotsky's *Russian Revolution*: "The fundamental and most stable feature of Russian history is the slow tempo of her development, with the economic backwardness, primitiveness of social forms and low level of culture resulting from it." Of course Russia has changed since then — but in keeping with what Trotsky wrote: in keeping with Russia's essential inertia. The revolution shifted the locus of power and ownership of property, but it didn't change the underlying characteristics of Russia and Russians.'

*   *   *

The intellectuals' judgment, if accurate, is much more disheartening than my own, before I came to Russia. If the dictatorship were responsible for the country's condition, there would be suffering — but hope. One could look forward, as in Nazi-occupied Europe, to the expulsion of the tyrants and the return to normal life. But 'normal' in Russia is in fact some form of autocracy. Not necessarily cruel or totalitarian, but powerful, jealous and suspicious. Not without periods of surging social development (as in the reign of Alexander II, the period between 1906 and 1917, and in the 1920s), but always retreating, after the adventure, to the safety of orthodoxy.

Thus it is not the dictatorship that saddens the intellectuals, but something far more powerful and lasting: the attitudes bred during the last thousand or so years of Russian history. A politically backward people that is suited to dictatorship must be educated—and this, of necessity, will be a slow process, particularly when the principal political effect of Communism is to preserve backwardness. (Little hope, incidentally, is placed on the younger generation in the Politburo and Central Committee. The well-dressed men who must soon replace the relatively elderly ruling coalition will be less rigid about jazz, narrow trousers and perhaps the latest Western dances, but not the essentials of free art and free government. They are considered to be thoroughly cynical careerists, lacking all ideological commitment, but devoted to winning and keeping power for themselves.)

This is not to imply that the intellectuals feel Russia can never change, or that the tiny protest 'movement' kindled by the writers' trials is not a salutary development. On the contrary, the protests, however insignificant in numbers and however impotent vis-à-vis the power-structure, are considered by most of my friends to be the beginning of something important: the first step on a long road to political democracy.

'You must remember', said a brilliant young mathematician, 'that fifteen years ago, when Stalin died, we started with nothing. Political life in this country was completely and totally dead. People were too terrified even to think of protesting about anything then. Now, with some people at least, there's been a psychological breakthrough.'

There are even grounds for optimism in the conduct of the writers' trials themselves. 'No matter how bad they were, they were still trials,' said the mathematician's friend. 'The defendants were allowed to plead innocent. In the old days, they would have disappeared one midnight, and their friends would have been too frightened even to ask what happened to them. These new trials were blatant judicial crimes, but not murder. And they are not kept entirely secret. The government makes efforts to hush up the trials, but they're only half-hearted. Now at least there are channels of information through foreign sources and *samizdat* [the underground cottage-industry 'publishing' system by which banned manuscripts are laboriously re-typed in several carbons and distributed among friends]. The dark deeds are still performed, but unlike the Stalin era, anyone who takes the trouble to find out about them can. And there's no misguided sentimentality about the ends justifying the means for the sake of socialism.'

In this sense, the position of the intelligentsia has improved markedly since the Khrushchev thaw, and continues to improve. My friends are far better informed about what happens in Russia and the rest of the world than they were even five years ago. There is a far sharper awareness that something is essentially wrong with the Soviet body politic, and far more information about how other societies work. 'It's a kind of concession on the part of the authorities,' said a girl in my hostel. 'They let you know things and leave you alone—if you keep your mouth shut about what you know.'

This is gratifying progress, and when they are in an optimistic mood, Russian intellectuals recognize it as such, and are grateful. More important, they are optimistic about the breaking of the psychological barrier that enabled even a handful of activists to protest and most of the genuine intelligentsia to support them—not vocally, but in spirit. My best friend put it like this: 'We are no longer robots, and "they" understand this. We don't have a chance against them, but at least we're not snivelling, submissive lackeys, and they know it. Yes, it was sad on August 21st—but twelve years ago, when our tanks smashed into Budapest, the fear and conformism and apathy in Moscow were far worse.'

But the intellectuals feel that this progress in their own condition is minute compared to the backwardness of the country as a whole. 'We've gone a centimetre,' said this same friend in another mood, 'and we're still light years behind.' The K.G.B.'s grip on the country remains firm, has even tightened, and political life as we would understand it is as unthinkable as ever.

In 1959, the hey-day of Khrushchev's reforms, the intellectuals had hopes for steady, if slow, progress towards normality. Now, by contrast, they talk about the huge, underlying obstacles to progress rooted in Russia's backwardness and tortured history.

*　　*　　*

Is this pessimism justified? To some extent, it says more about the intellectuals' state of mind than about the state of Russia. For, like their counterparts everywhere, Russian intellectuals are inclined to exaggerate the shortcomings of their own country and social system, and ignore its virtues and accomplishments. It is not as clever or smart to bemoan the Establishment in Russia as in most Western countries (probably because it is a more serious business here), but the same tendency to be critical of one's own exists here as in left-wing circles everywhere in the world.

Beyond this, Russian intellectuals are demoralized by the special difficulties of Soviet life. Corruption is endemic here; only the saintly take no part in it. This means that hardly any of the intellectuals can maintain normal personal or professional integrity. Like everyone else with a bit of money, they use it to bid for the spoils of the underground, private-enterprise world hidden beneath the socialist system. They buy items of Western clothing, sunglasses and gramophone records on the black market, bribe officials for reservations in resort hotels, cultivate a network of acquaintances and contacts among shop and restaurant managers for access to the country's trickle of luxuries. They are always on the watch for something pretty to buy in a private transaction, for ever manoeuvring for position in the struggle to beat the system and spend a pleasant hour here or acquire a 'deficit' article there.

Not that my friends spend most of their time talking about and acquiring things for conspicuous consumption. On the contrary, they are distinctly less motivated by the acquisitive instinct and the desire to impress than their European counterparts of the same standing; and the casual attention — to put it delicately — they pay to keeping their flats tidy testifies vividly to this. (As does the way they spend their money: literally the last rouble of the month will go without a second thought on food and drink for one lavish evening, for an underground Skira book on Dali that costs a fort-night's salary, or for a bouquet of chrysanthemums at a peasant market — at a rouble a bloom.) They quite clearly carry on the Russian intelligentsia's traditional indifference to 'success' measured in terms of one's career and worldly possessions. Nevertheless, they are not ascetics, and when they do want something worldly, they are forced, paradoxically, to spend much more time and energy acquiring it than their more materialistic European and North American counterparts.

Take, for a very minor example, tape for tape-recorders. The quality of domestic brands is very poor. One must find a Western spool somewhere on the black market or through a friend of a friend, and pay extremely dearly for it. Or take a present for a sweetheart: it is extremely difficult to find anything at all fashionable in the shops. What few attractive articles of Soviet and imported manufacture appear on public sale are snapped up almost instantly. This means the black market again. And to penetrate into a crowded restaurant without freezing for an hour or two in a queue outside the door means being in league with the director through a system of mutual favours: he supplies a table, and you, perhaps, a pass to the House of Journalists where he can see a private screening of a Western film, or the name of a friend who can help him secure a pair of shock absorbers for his car. And similarly with trips to holiday camps and artist colonies, reservations in resort hotels, recommendations from Party and job supervisors for a tourist visa to Bulgaria or Romania. One can live without this manoeuvring, but only a grey existence. Almost all the luxuries of Russian life require something underhand in the acquisition. And while the intellectuals hardly think of themselves as criminals, they are in fact pushed outside the law, and over the years this saps their nervous energy.

Moreover, the good things of intellectual as well as material life lie outside the system, and must be acquired and enjoyed *à couvert*, if not always altogether illegally. Russian intellectuals, in fact, have developed a negative guide to what is worth reading, watching and listening to. If the work is produced or published by a Soviet institution (and does not concern a totally apolitical subject), it is probably too distorted and dishonest to be excited about. It may be read for the 'good parts' (i.e. the honest points or pages the author was able to get past the publisher and censor); it can be valued for its oblique implications, between-the-lines meanings and minor revelations (as Ehrenburg's memoirs were valued, even though they revealed but a small part of what Ehrenburg knew and distorted much by omission). But it cannot be a fully honest or worthwhile book. If, on the other hand, the work is prohibited (in a state with a total monopoly of the means of communication, non-publication often equals prohibition), it presumably contains something honest or important, and is eagerly seized upon. Similarly, a book, play or film criticized for political slackness by an orthodox organ such as *Pravda* commands immediate attention.

These being the criteria for judgment, intellectuals spend most of their time with non-Soviet materials and sources. 'The radio' has come to mean, Western short-wave broadcasts; Moscow radio is almost totally ignored. Books on both social and artistic subjects are predominantly Western or Russian manuscripts rejected or not submitted for publication. A surprising amount of unauthorized literature, from Deutscher to Mikhailov, Djilas to Genet, circulates underground, together with satirical poems and songs of young Russian ballad-singers.

It is not a criminal offence *per se* to possess most of this literature. Much of it—fiction, say, by Robbe-Grillet, J. P. Donleavy and most of Françoise Sagan; the most important works of Camus and Kafka; the sociology of Raymond Aron and most of C. Wright Mills; the works of most major contemporary Western historians—is not available through normal, public sources simply because it was considered not worth the expense of translating and publishing by the cultural officials empowered to make these decisions. (Because of their extremely sensitive function, these cultural officials are certain to be extremely reliable—that is, narrow-minded and dogmatic—Party mandarins whose personal tastes complement their official duty to keep the country free of 'poisonous' literature.) A huge body of both fiction and non-fiction, including the works of the most modish and respected authors in Western and even Eastern Europe, is rejected because of its sexual, political or ideological liberalism. (A list of authors not published in Russia should be published some day. It is sufficient to say here that the only book by James Joyce to be translated is *The Dubliners* and that Proust has been out of print since the 1930s. The Soviet 'index' includes works ranging from *Ulysses*, the writings of Doris Lessing since she left the Communist Party, the more experimental plays of Ionesco, the seamier books of authors like John Braine, down to the thrillers of Ian Fleming and Len Deighton. And a vast number of authors are on the index for more overtly political reasons.) But 'un-Soviet' does not necessarily mean 'anti-Soviet', and a person who obtains copies of these works in Western languages is not subject to prosecution. There is nothing dangerous in prominently displaying, say, *A Portrait of the Artist as a Young Man* on one's bookshelf, even though it is considered unfit for translation into Russian. Even *Lolita* can be kept in one's home, although with greater diffidence. I once saw a copy of it bound inside an old Soviet history textbook.

(Russian intellectuals, incidentally, have developed an extremely keen sixth sense about what will be considered 'un-Soviet' and why; but my own instincts are still weak. A young Estonian writer who had seen *Elvira Madigan* during a trip to Yugoslavia told me why it could never be shown in Russia. I, too, felt it couldn't: it was too 'anarchistic' and too 'pessimistic', and it made too much of the power of love and complexities and weaknesses of human nature. In short, it provoked too many thoughts about human motivation that had nothing whatever to do with the class struggle, materialism, the whole Marxist explanation of the psyche and society. But I had missed, said my Estonian friend, one of the film's most dangerous flaws: the discredit it cast on the officer class and the obligations of patriotism and military service. 'The Soviet Army and Soviet officer corps are absolutely sacrosanct, and, funnily enough, this often extends to other armies so that our people won't get "queer" ideas. So when a Swedish officer deserts, our censors think carefully about what effect that might have on people's respect for military authority in general. That's one of the reasons why an anti-war military film like *The Bridge Over the River Kwai* can't be shown here, even though it has nothing directly to do with anything Soviet. It's all tied up with the reason why we can't have the full story of student protests in Paris, even though they are protesting against the bourgeois government. The very idea of protest against authority is dangerous.'

A good part of the underground literature, however, is of a more overtly political nature and is correspondingly more incriminating. Freud, Trotsky and Orwell, for example, are highly popular among young intellectuals, and their books are carefully concealed. Orwell is particularly admired; they wonder how he, who never lived under Communism, perceived its essence and nuances so brilliantly. *Animal Farm* is a great favourite, excitedly read and passed secretly from hand to hand. 'The most perceptive thing about this book', said a friend recently, 'is that those poor animals on the farm were good-hearted, hard-working beasts but — precisely like ninety

per cent of the Russian people—too simple to understand
how they were being manipulated. "But surely you don't
want the Joneses back?" the pigs threatened. The animals had
forgotten what the Joneses were like; most of them never
knew. Still, brought up on propaganda, they bleated back the
horror of the Joneses. The parallel to the Russian people is
almost perfect. The horror of the moment is counter-revolution in Czechoslovakia—people bleat back automatically
about it, but have no idea whatever of what's happening
there.'

It is a favourite story in Moscow that customs officers used
to permit tourists to bring in *Animal Farm*, under the impression it was a book about animal husbandry. Last year,
however, customs inspection was severely tightened, and
officers now search meticulously for just such literature, as
well as for 'anti-Soviet' manuscripts leaving the country.

Freud is not officially prohibited, but presents an obvious
challenge to Marxist–Leninist dogma about the nature of
man; and since he has not been published since the early
1920s, non-psychiatrists can read him only in old Russian
and foreign editions, circulated underground. Orwell, of
course, is much more dangerous; and many people will not
take a book by Trotsky into their homes.

It would be wrong to over-emphasize or romanticize the
dangers of simply owning literature like this, or taking part
in the underground 'lending library' system. One young
man I know, whose room is a small library of Western
sociology and contains many books extremely unflattering
to the Soviet system, dismisses my fears for him with a shrug
of resignation rather than bravado. He likes to repeat the
old Russian proverb, 'If you're afraid of wolves, don't walk in
the woods.' His parents are worried about him, however, and
he must often soothe them, telling them he knows what he is

doing, and assuring them times have changed. 'It's the generation gap,' he says. 'They don't even like to have a biography of Goering in the flat because they're still living psychologically in the Stalin times. And my mother hates me going out with foreign birds at the university. She keeps on telling me to get myself a nice Russian girl. It's hard for them to understand that these things by themselves can no longer get you sent to a camp—provided you toe the line in other ways.'

Nevertheless, the dangers are real and the tensions palpable. Some books—like the unauthorized transcripts of the writers' trials and the new Solzhenitsyn novels—can be used in evidence in criminal proceedings against the owners. Mimeographed material of any kind is particularly dangerous, for there are severe laws prohibiting unauthorized reproduction by duplicating machines of so much as a single page. And even though most of the underground literature circulates fairly freely—the newspaper wrappers and plain brown covers are more for discretion than secrecy—the whole system of underground literature and underground information inevitably induces a certain attitude of mind. The daily tensions of living an 'anti-Soviet' intellectual life, of whispering, smuggling and hiding things under overcoats, are wearying and depressing over the years.

*　　*　　*

Even more depressing, however, is the necessity for prostituting professional integrity. Great compromises must be made to earn a living and maintain a respectable position in Soviet society. One young poet I know has managed not to make these compromises by withdrawing almost totally from the 'real' world. Supported by his mistress and his mother, he spends his time writing poetry for himself and his friends. He has no job and never shows his work to editors, not only because it stands no chance of being published, but also because the very act of submitting his poetry to editors of a state publishing house would be a 'sell-out'. But he is the only person I know in this situation. Russia is still too poor to support a mass 'drop-out' movement — and not to work is to subject oneself to real danger of prosecution and exile as a 'parasite'. Almost all intellectuals, therefore, earn their livings working for the system they despise.

The surrealist sculptor who will never be able to exhibit his work illustrates children's books, tailoring his drawings to the editor's instructions and producing sketches — children awed by belching factory chimneys, for example — that he himself can barely tolerate.

The passionate young Gorky scholar who, like literary scholars everywhere, loves his subject and devotes his life to research about it, writes simple-minded and sometimes vicious half-truths for the popular press. He is vastly knowledgable about the complexity of Gorky as a man and writer, especially about one of the most intriguing questions in recent Russian literary history: Gorky's ambivalent — and changing — attitude towards Soviet rule. Yet he is forced, in his published articles, to ignore his own research entirely or distort it beyond recognition, making of Gorky a fierce, loyal fighter for socialist-realism, Bolshevism and Leninism — a dogmatic hack in the *Pravda* pattern.

This scholar has unearthed Gorky's political writings in the years following the October Revolution, in which Gorky, enraged and anguished by the lies, cruelties and naked terror of Lenin and the Bolsheviks, brands them as pitiless, amoral tricksters. But this research, of course, must be suppressed, together with anything else that might challenge the official view of Gorky, the function of Soviet literature, or the infallibility of Lenin and the Party.

It is precisely Russian writers who must be ignored or distorted most, because they pose the most dangerous questions to the Soviet dogma about the nature of man and society. And the more interesting the writer, the more important his comments on the Russian experience, the greater the pressure to lie about him. The works of the most perceptive writers, or details which do not fit in into the propagandists' portrait of the lives of popular writers—Gorky, Mayakovsky, Pasternak, Solzhenitsyn, Babel, Rosanov, Zamyatin, Zoshchenko, Mandelshtam—are suppressed. And even this is not enough: critics and scholars must not only keep silent about what they know, but also join the conspiracy to falsify these writers' biographies and intentions. This year, for example, the centennial of Gorky's birth, is hardly a time of celebration for the Gorky scholar, for he must now lie more than usual.

These are the kinds of pressures exerted on virtually everyone involved in creative, scholarly or critical work in the arts and humanities. I know several intelligent, highly sensitive men who produce nearly pure propaganda for relatively handsome fees, in order to give themselves as much time as possible for their own underground work. 'If I really had to think about it,' said one, 'it would make me sick.' Almost everyone I know lies in his work as a matter of course.

The 'prostitution', as these men themselves describe their own work, stops well short of total degradation. Most intellectuals try to find work as far removed from politics as possible: editing a journal of ancient history, for example, is preferable to working on contemporary history because of the obligatory half-truths and evasions the latter entails. The natural sciences are preferred to the humanities and social sciences for the same reason: Marxism–Leninism makes no claim on the behaviour pattern of atoms. In writing, the pure adventure story is preferred to any story that involves a factory, sociology or politics in any way. In research, the obscure writer or thinker is preferred as a subject to the well-known one.

In everything, the light-weight, peripheral project is preferred; it is less likely to attract attention, and hence there is a greater chance of honesty. For example, no one would dream of writing an honest book about contemporary Belgium. But a young Leningrad historian I know is writing about a late nineteenth-century Belgian historian, and hopes to publish a valuable treatise. The important points are always made indirectly: through allegory, allusion, metaphor and implied comparison—as much as can be got past the censor. Anyone criticizing, say, the cultural revolution in China is also, for readers who are attuned to the symbolism and implied comparison, commenting on the domestic Soviet situation.

A young draughtsman I know recently completed a novel based on his two years at the construction site of the famous Bratsk Dam in southern Siberia—largest in the world, subject of an immense flood of propaganda. The novel described actual working life, which was very different from the propagandists' picture: cheating, bribery and incredible waste; bitter feuding, drunkenness and labour-camp conditions as well as occasional heroic work and genuine exaltation. 'But of course I can't submit the manuscript like this; the very *last* thing our censors will pass is an account of how it actually was.' Now he must spend several months adding Party heroes and stock building-Communism triumphs, eliminating unmentionable 'slanderous' episodes. He does not despair about this, for 'doctoring' of manuscripts is taken for granted; before writing, in fact, he considered whether it would be better to do an honest first draft and manipulate later, or write to the demands of censorship from the start. 'My job is to retain *some* truth in the book, more than anything published so far on the Bratsk Dam. Since that's all I can hope for, it's important—and will be quite satisfying—if I'm able to manage just that.'

Several of my friends deliberately work less well than they can, or refuse promotions—which carry with them the need for greater responsibility (and balder lying) and, often, membership in the Communist Party. In these ways—by compromising only as much as necessary to earn a living—they preserve their personal honour.

Moreover, Russians have developed a powerful immunity to guilt about this, just as to the deluge of propaganda. The art critic who writes regular articles attacking 'formalism' (any deviation from socialist-realism) hangs abstract paintings exclusively in his own flat, and his best friends are young painters who experiment in the prohibited styles he publicly reviles. People do not blame each other for making these compromises; nor do they blame themselves. 'Our situation', said the art critic, 'makes us all prostitute ourselves to a greater or lesser extent. The question is, what is a man like in his private life? Is he loyal? Can he be trusted never to betray his friends for the sake of his own advancement?'

Despite this compensatory tolerance among the intelligentsia, however, the restrictions on the development of their talents, not to speak of their enforced dishonesty, are necessarily demoralizing in the long run.

* * *

Beyond this, there is the pessimism caused by political

P

isolation and weakness, and this was again seriously aggra-
vated last year by the wave of neo-Stalinism. Intellectuals
bitterly resented the writers' trials and invasion of Czechoslovakia—and were depressed by the knowledge that their
resentment, if publicly expressed, would change nothing, but
only provoke reprisals on themselves. In other words, they
were impotent and shown to be impotent—with dire effects
on their self-esteem.

'The morale of the Russian intelligentsia is now as low as
it's ever been,' said a young anthropologist whose father is
well-placed in the Party. 'Liberals are beginning to despise
themselves for their weakness. It's a well-established Freu-
dian principle, after all: if you oppress people long and hard
enough, they begin to take out their hatred not on their
oppressors, but themselves. Koestler, too—the expert—
writes very perceptively about the psychological pressure of
persecution and defeat leading to self-hate.'

* * *

Despite the certainty of reprisals, my friends feel guilty about
doing virtually nothing in defence of their convictions. They
recognize that part, at least, of the responsibility for Russia's
condition is their own. Everywhere else in the world, young
intellectuals are shouting, marching, participating in or
bringing down governments. But they themselves are lazy
and passive; given to dreaming, in the tradition of the
Russian intelligentsia—but not to self-sacrifice. They are
busy feathering their nests—manoeuvring for better flats,
obtaining assignments and commissions (although not the
highest-paying ones that would require them to join the
Party), absorbing themselves in their intellectual and artistic
pursuits and in their friends and love affairs.

'It would seem we have nothing to lose but our chains,' said my friend, the writer from Voronezh, sadly. 'But despite Marx, this was never true of the workers — or of us. Workers are afraid to lose their jobs and food, no matter how gruelling and miserable. And we, the intelligentsia, are afraid to lose the little half-comfortable niches we've carved out for ourselves. It's pitiful, you know: instead of fighting the good fight (which only *we* can win from inside Russia; no foreign influences can ever win our war), we content ourselves with the few bones thrown our way, and grumbling about our masters.'

'There is a deep longing to *do* something at last,' said my instructor friend at the institute. 'Of course, doing something means going to a [labour] camp. But still, everyone's haunted by the feeling he should be doing more. We know what's wrong, and we'll sit around complaining about it in our comfortable little flats. The only way Russia will change is if people like us work and sacrifice for change. *But the Russian intelligentsia is not made for action.* We're lazy, perhaps cowardly. And selfish! It all adds up to self-disgust. We probably deserve our own condition.'

Yet together with this longing to do something, there are great inhibitions, much more internalized — and therefore more powerful — than the obvious ones provided by the K.G.B. These people feel in their bones what most of the Russian intelligentsia have always felt — that the practice of politics, like the making of money, is inherently, inevitably, dishonourable and corrupting. Their attitude is neatly summed up in a little-known comment by Gorky, discovered and often quoted by the Gorky scholar I mentioned above: 'One should rise above politics ... Politics are always repulsive, for they are inevitably surrounded by lies, slander and violence ...' (This although Gorky himself was among the most political of Russian writers.)

Oddly enough, this aversion to politics extends to 'good' politics as well: to the protest movement inspired by the Sinyavsky-Daniel trial. Even the noble cause of Ginzburg and subsequent protesters, although deeply admired, failed to move most Russian intellectuals emotionally. For Ginzburg, after all, was principally a political activist – not a novelist or poet dedicating his life to pure art. (Many young Russians, even while supporting Ginzburg, Litvinov and the others, questioned what made them take their brave actions. Were their motives 'pure', or mixed with an element of glory-seeking?)

This, as much as anything, explains why all but a handful of young Russian intellectuals take no active part in the protest movement. 'Take me,' said the Voronezh writer, 'I'm a sad but fairly typical example. I'd rather write a good book, an honest book, than take part in any active protest. That's where my bent lies. And there are many of us who, even while knowing the injustice of everything, would rather even *read* an honest book than get our hands dirty in some political action. That's what our instincts tell us – to withdraw. To seek solace and purity in art and talk and drink. And that's the tragedy of the Russian intelligentsia.'

The 'tragedy', and remorse about it, seemed to manifest themselves more frequently during the last year or two. I shall not soon forget the sentencing of Ginzburg and his co-defendants last winter, and of Litvinov and his co-defendants less than a year later. I spent both evenings in the company of friends – young men and women who sympathized wholly with the convicted protesters, but had not been willing even to risk going to the law court to demonstrate their solidarity with them, for they knew K.G.B. agents were there, photographing everyone in the small crowds. There was much drinking on those evenings — much more than usual — and deep despondency about what had happened. But it was not only the fate of the courageous protesters my friends were lamenting; it was also their own impotence and weak will. 'We didn't even have the guts to go and see the martyrs and show we're with them. All right, it's dangerous. It wouldn't have changed anything. *But how do you think it makes us feel?* What do we deserve if we're not willing to make sacrifices?'

*   *   *

However, this mood of dejection is not my friends' normal state. The joys of Russian life are as intense as the sorrows, and people naturally gravitate towards the former. There is enough money for periodic splurges of prodigious eating and drinking; enough intellectual sustenance (the underground material spiced by its freshness and quasi-illegality) for absorbing talk; and more free time, in spite, or because of the relatively low material incentives, than in the West. As I have said, there is as much social freedom as political restriction.

And there are movements in taste and fashion. The latest started three or four years ago, and has been gaining momentum since: an intense interest in pre-revolutionary, and especially peasant, Russia. Old books, icons, artefacts, peasant embroidery and prints, even photographs of the Romanovs decorate the flats of almost all the intellectuals. (The icons and antique samovars are increasingly valued as investments, but many peasant artefacts, such as old felt boots, are hung on walls solely for their decorative properties; they give intimacy and 'colour' to otherwise stark, standardized flats.) Old church architecture and music are particularly admired — for their aesthetic and symbolic, not religious, value. Visits are made to the working churches of Moscow and Leningrad, to enjoy the rich — and novel — sights and sounds of the services. Week-end trips are made to the countryside to explore crumbling old churches and admire what remains of the old wooden architecture. Holidays are spent in primitive little villages deep in the hinterland (the far bank of the Volga is a favourite area) instead of in the traditional smart resorts on the Black and Baltic Seas. Peasant blouses and kerchiefs with traditional patterns and embroidery are the latest thing. Films set in Old Russia are newly popular, and books about the life of the peasantry and gentry under the tsars are read assiduously.

Why this strong interest in Old Russia? To some extent, it is simply the latest fad, like art nouveau in the West. 'You know how it is,' was Edik's answer. 'Always something new — and the best new thing, of course, is re-discovering the old things. A girl wears an old gold cross around her neck here, and it's actually a new and exciting fashion idea. Actually, Old Russia *was* more colourful in many ways than what we have now. Everything these days is cheap, standardized and prefabricated. In the old days, even the poorest peasant did wood carvings on the windows of his cottage — and this was symbolic of a more human scale of life.'

But this vogue is more than a change in fashion. It also expresses the intelligentsia's profound boredom with Soviet taste and propaganda. In 'Mother *Rus*', they are seeking something that they feel is missing from their lives. Brought up in an orgy of ritual, pseudo-scientific sermonizing about class struggle, dialectical materialism and the vanguard of the world proletariat, the younger generation feels it has lost contact with its roots. 'Old Russia,' said one of my fellow students, 'the *real* Old Russia, was outlawed for decades. It was obscured and almost destroyed by an attempt to fit our background and history into Marxist–Leninist slogans. So we grew up nearly rootless in our own country, almost like immigrants. People now want to know where they really came from. Besides, it's delightful: there's no propaganda in a peasant tunic, a wooden cupola, a birch tree.'

It is paradoxical that the intelligentsia's search for something genuine and meaningful to replace the political jargon has taken them back into the past. For, as I've said, it is to Russia's traditional political and cultural backwardness that they attribute her congenital apathy, and the inevitability of dictatorial rule. Despite the apparent contradiction, however, it is certainly true that most people who yearn for radical changes in the present system are Slavophiles by inclination. If this phenomenon appears strange, perhaps it has a parallel in certain young radical intellectuals of the West who look back fondly—and perhaps mistakenly—to earlier centuries in their countries' histories, when the 'establishment' was less ubiquitous and manipulating, and life in general seemed far freer. Certainly the parallel with the rediscovery of folk music in the West is unmistakable. In this country too—here, perhaps, more than elsewhere—students and young intellectuals with suitably untrimmed hair love to cram themselves into a room and, to the accompaniment of three or four guitars, sing the old Civil War, labour camp, and peasant songs that have been rediscovered recently and now enjoy a huge vogue.

Temperamentally, too, my friends resemble leftish intellectuals in Europe—except that they are far more anti-Communist (in the sense of anti-Communist Party) than their Western counterparts. This does not mean that they are anti-Soviet in the voluble, emotional fashion that American intellectuals tend to be anti-American. In fact, they rarely talk politics, even in private; it is too painful—and besides, what new can be said about it? About intrigues in the Kremlin and policy-making at the highest level, they know almost nothing; all this—the stuff of political talk in the West—is *terra incognita*. And as for the fundamental characteristics of Soviet public life—the dictatorship and its total power; the cynicism, corruption and ruthlessness of the apparat—all this is too obvious for comment. Political jokes and anecdotes abound, but they are principally variations on old themes, and not very profound comments on personalities. Weeks pass—days and nights of overwhelming lethargy alternate with bursts of intense work and reckless sprees, in the Russian manner—without so much as a comment about the dictatorship or political situation.

This is not to say politics are never discussed at all. Occasionally, there is rather idle speculation about in-fighting at the top—about, for example, which Politburo members favoured the invasion of Czechoslovakia, and which opposed it. The guesses are remarkably similar to those made on Western short-wave news analyses, probably because the information comes from the same sources. One evening, recently, I was present at a lengthy discussion of who in the Politburo will eventually pay (with his political life) for the blunder of Czechoslovakia. It is a cardinal rule of Soviet political life that the Party never errs; the Party, as the apostle of genuine Marxism–Leninism, possesses divine, revealed political wisdom, and is therefore infallible. If mistakes have been made, they are the fault of fallible individuals or factions. Thus the Party played no role in Stalin's 'excesses'; this was the work of Stalin himself. Under Khrushchev, it was Malenkov, Molotov and others who made grievous errors; under Brezhnev-Kosygin, Khrushchev was responsible for the failures of his years. Never mind that these men were Party leaders who spoke and acted for the unanimous membership at the time of the errors, and who were clothed in that very same infallibility. The Party itself was, as always, blameless and wholly virtuous; the Party *cannot* err. These being the rules of the game, most people that evening guessed that Brezhnev would eventually be named as the sinner in the Czechoslovak affair. It was felt—or hoped—that the damage to Soviet prestige and to the Soviet position in the world Communist movement was too great not to have a scapegoat for the great blunder, when it is finally admitted.

But perhaps this was wishful thinking. For Brezhnev is despised by most members of the intelligentsia. They consider him not only empty and soulless, but coarse, ignorant and crude—representative, therefore, of the personal qualities of the apparat that runs the machinery of the dictatorship. Many anecdotes, limericks and jokes about him circulate among students and young intellectuals, the most popular of which is the nickname *brovenosets v potyemkakh* (eyebrow-carrier in the darkness), a play on words with *bronenosets Potyemkin* (Battleship *Potyemkin*). It is also said, with symbolic as well as descriptive meaning, that he wears Stalin's moustache on his eyebrows.

Kosygin, on the other hand, is tolerated, if not admired. Much is made of the fact that, by contrast with Brezhnev, 'he is at least educated'—a trained economist, a rational, fairly worldly man who understands that Russia must somehow be made more liberal and civilized, if only in order to compete economically. Kosygin is believed to appreciate the crippling effects of Russia's autocracy and backwardness and to have opposed all the crucial 'hard-line' decisions of recent years—the intensification of censorship, writers' trials, support of Arab nationalism, invasion of Czechoslovakia. Nevertheless, he lacks the courage and integrity to resign because, like all the present leaders, he is deeply compromised by his fondness for power and life-long association with the Party and its Stalinist past. Like virtually every major Soviet leader he is Stalin's former accomplice as well as his heir, with all this implies.

*　　*　　*

However, persistent interest in Kremlinology and other purely political matters is rare among the intelligentsia. Usually, friends exchange the latest political *anekdot* or rumour at some point during their conversation, then quickly return to more private, and satisfying, themes. This is the limit of their political discussion; serious, detailed analysis of policies, personalities and options does not make good dinner-party talk. And for many intellectuals, the characteristic pattern is a long period of silence on political matters, broken by rare outbursts of anguish, not over day-to-day Kremlin policies, but the very notion of the Kremlin itself.

Just the other evening, for example, I was a guest at a splendid, typically Russian party in a novelist's stuffy, log-cabin studio-cum-flat. The eating, drinking, dancing and story-telling went on until nearly four in the morning and — since it was fiercely cold and public transport had, of course, stopped — most couples were making preparations to sleep somewhere in the flat. Then a recently-married graduate student, who had never said a word to me about politics during all the months I had known him, took me aside to unburden himself. He had consumed about half a litre of brandy, and was stuttering badly.

'Everyone's having a grand time, yes — but don't let that fool you. Inside, we're all sick, full of hate and disgust. We hate those bastards at the top, those Brezhnevs, those

Suslovs. Hate them with all our might. And hate ourselves too. A handful of martyrs are brave enough to protest openly—and we don't even lift a finger for them, we have parties like this to try to *forget* them. They're our heroes, the Don Quixotes of Russia. Ninety per cent of our people are happy to see them squashed. And we stand by while they're sent to their camps. That's what's inside us, behind the merry façade: pain and disgust and guilt and hate. Inside all of us, every moment of every day. I drink to the real heroes of this country, the people in the camps—but that's all I do about it: drink.'

It may be months before this young man—who is ordinarily cheerful, energetic, and devoted to his work—has another outburst like this one.

A late arrival at this gathering, incidentally, was a rather well-known young French writer visiting Moscow at the invitation of the Union of Writers. (He came because that evening a French translator, an old friend of the host, had him in tow.) Soon after he arrived at the party, the French writer too was pleasantly tight, and between his attempts to dance, made a series of toasts to Marxism–Leninism and the building of Communism. He spent most of the evening trying to explain to anyone who would listen that he was not really a Stalinist, but a quasi-Trotskyist; he was 'against' the bureaucratic distortions of the 1930s, but felt the Soviet people had nevertheless built socialism and were building Communism, and this was still the hope of Europe, because Europe otherwise had no hope, etc., etc. My friends were puzzled by the man's earnest monologues. Nothing could have been more out of place in that room. Was he joking, talking about building Communism? Of the two dozen people present, the Frenchman was the only one who knew none of the facts of Soviet life—and was also, logically

enough, the only Communist. Our host and his friends, however, merely shook their heads and refilled his glass while
he lauded the collectivization of agriculture and five-year
plans. It was a display of hospitality unusual even for
Russians.

*   *   *

Episodes like this remind one, paradoxically, that Marx's
original social concern, that which prompted all the later
writings known as Marxism, was the problem of alienation.
For Russian intellectuals suffer from an extreme form of
that affliction. They are far more alienated than their
Western counterparts—even, from everything one has read,
more than their pre-revolutionary predecessors described by
Dostoevsky and others. Virtually everything 'Soviet', from
fashion to new ballets, repels them; they have withdrawn
into an inner world where only their *own* work and careers,
their *own* families and friends, their *private* material and
intellectual pursuits matter. 'If there is a single rule that
dominates our lives,' the Chekovian doctor put it, 'it's this:
live and let live—*and let alone!* We have had enough of
glorious theories, triumphs of socialism, the victory of
Communism. We simply can take no more—even Russians
have a breaking point. We've become the most apolitical—
no, *anti*-political—people in the world.'

It is the politicization—it is often called 'contamination'
—of every aspect of public life that repels them more than
anything, and to escape it, they spin psychological as well as
physical cocoons around themselves. They have developed
an instinctive, ceaseless caution in protecting their inner
world—not only from the K.G.B., but from the great mass
of workers and peasants, 'the people', as well. For they sense
a strong popular hostility to themselves, their ideas and

their complaints about the system. The literary radicals who cry out for freedom of expression are not the heroes of the Russian masses — quite the contrary; they are 'dirty double-dealers' who live well, yet slander the Motherland.

'Workers themselves grumble, of course,' said my mathematician friend. 'But like soldiers in the army do. In fact, they are proud of the Soviet Union and intensely patriotic. It's our country, they feel, *our* socialist state, our dictatorship of the proletariat. Even our bad things — our shortages, sacrifices and propaganda. Our Mother Russia, in other words. And when they hear the likes of us, with our education and privileges, complaining there's something terribly wrong with the Motherland, they can be very unpleasant. If I'm waiting with a friend in a bus queue, I'm very careful about what I say in criticism of holy Russia.'

However, these habits and attitudes have been gestating for some considerable time. The intelligentsia's 'anti-politicism', for example, had long been developing when I first arrived. What is new — a product of Czechoslovakia, neo-Stalinism and the most recent and perhaps final disillusionment with Soviet rule last year — is the beginning of irreverence towards Lenin. This year, for the first time that my friends can remember, mild jokes are circulating about the formerly sacrosanct architect of socialist society.

Beyond this is the loss of faith in socialism itself. Much of the Russian intelligentsia has been socialist for a century. Even during the worst of the Stalin years, it was felt that Soviet rule, whatever its perversions, was worth defending, because socialism was morally, socially, historically and (potentially) economically more progressive and ennobling than capitalism. Private ownership of the means of production was essentially evil; a just and humane society could not be built on that basis. Socialism provided at least the foundation—the only foundation—for a genuinely civilized society.

Now this belief, the cornerstone of Marxism–Leninism, has been abandoned. 'By itself, socialism is meaningless—no, call it worthless,' said the novelist with the bulldog. 'Divorced from the other aspects of society, private or public ownership of the means of production is neither good nor bad. In fact, no general theory of society holds water. The only question is, what *works*? What makes life better or worse for a larger or smaller number of people in a country? Socialism itself can't make any difference in the quality of life. In Russia, certainly, it's caused as much harm as good —and if you include agriculture, far more harm than good.

'The intelligentsia is beginning to understand this—and it is potentially a big step. People are suddenly realizing that no ideology or sweeping theory is of any importance at all.'

'Then what is important?'

'It sounds banal. Self-improvement. Individual effort. Study and thought for one's own moral development. The classical, liberal virtues. Being honest and loyal and kind to the ten people closest to me rather than professing my good intentions to world history or social movements. And for the country as a whole, tinkering with the economic and social system in small daily ways and stopping to *measure* what works. Measuring real wages instead of mouthing Marxist slogans. Measuring real freedom and well-being instead of talking about class struggles and "socialist" freedoms. In other words, *pragmatism*. And an end to Marxism and all other "isms".'

'We used to assume socialism by itself would produce a better society and better human beings,' said my best friend. 'But this obviously isn't true. Socialism alone doesn't make good men, good art, good buildings, good anything. And certainly not goodwill. And so we've realized a man's principal duty is not to perfect society or the world, but himself. Making his own work, his own understanding, his own personal relationships good or virtuous in the sense those words have had throughout civilized history. Of course, these have always been the most important things in every society, but we Russians are rediscovering this after decades of obsession with social forces and progressive movements.'

This approach sounds thoughtful and reasonable enough. True, it is somehow old-fashioned and not left-wing enough to be fashionable among the radical young Western intelligentsia; but it would certainly be understood in any intellectual circle in the West. Indeed, there is no problem of any kind in communicating with the Russian intelligentsia: no cultural gap, no misunderstanding about the meaning of words and the dilemmas of the human condition. But it must be remembered that these are the 'one per cent'. And when one reads in the foreign press of Russians protesting and appealing in ways that parallel the Western liberal tradition, one must not be misled. These are the language and aspirations of a tiny minority.

Of course, they have influence beyond their numbers, and this influence will grow. But for the moment, it is still far removed from the general level of Soviet life and from the places where decisions are made and power wielded. And one of the more consistent phenomena of Russian history has been the rulers' ability to make use of the Western-oriented intellectuals, but keep them isolated and under control — to prevent their ideas about government and culture from penetrating to the sources of political power, thereby preserving the autocratic, religious essence of Russian and now Soviet government.

7 PAST AND FUTURE

THERE is something about Russia that makes most of us foreigners who live here spend most of our idle hours discussing the country's ills, proposing remedies and speculating about prospects for recovery. In a sense, this is patronizing. However, it also demonstrates Russia's unique ability to stimulate foreigners' interest, even love. Perhaps because of the universality of its great literature and art, perhaps because of its size, strength and a particular kind of purity, Russia represents the human condition and struggle of the human spirit more vividly than our own countries. We are fascinated by what is here; we want to be part of the struggle. We personally—often involuntarily—identify with this people's difficulties and fate. And this is not patronizing, but a testimony to Russia's greatness.

What can I say by way of summary? Russia's political system is more crude than people not living here imagine. Westerners, particularly—those who visit briefly—do not really believe the extent of the K.G.B.'s mastery over people's lives and their viciousness towards those they consider to have challenged that mastery. Western tourists cling to a sanguine confidence that not even the K.G.B. could really be so unreasonable. They assume Russia is moving steadily towards freedom, democracy and liberal common sense; that governmental affairs will return to normal in the near future; that things will be as they should. This, however, says more about Western political instincts than Russia's political history or reality. The great mass of Russian people simply do not have the same liberal political values and interests as the great mass of West Europeans. And the movement known as neo-Stalinism—although it is almost certain to be temporary—illustrates the difficulties purely technical obstacles present to Russia's democratization in this century.

Nor can Westerners appreciate the quantity and quasi-religious tone of the political propaganda. The preaching, chanting and twenty-four-hour broadcasting of Marxist–Leninist slogans and jargon is as frighteningly manipulatory as anyone can imagine: it is the Party force-feeding newspeak and double-think to helpless masses, hypnotizing them to love the Party. It is truly Orwellian.

Yet, somehow, all the political control and propaganda, the gargantuan efforts to reshape reality to fit Marxist–Leninist slogans and the Politburo's whims—all this matters less than one would imagine. Soviet rule is considerably worse—more repressive and obscurantist, more backward—than I had expected, yet it is also less relevant to daily Russian life.

Perhaps it has always been like this. Perhaps it is another example of the infinite capacity of Russians to endure, or of the essentially apolitical mind of most Russians. No state tries harder to make its people 'active fighters in the ranks of our Party's universal–historical struggle'; and no people has a greater natural resistance to the kind of mobilization and regimentation. In a vague way, most of them believe what they are taught. They are strong Russian patriots and happy with strong leadership. But they are politically passive, undeveloped, uninterested. A woman is shopping for a lemon in a food store; her husband and young son are enjoying an ice cream—they do not even hear the radio urging them to march to Communism. The joys and sorrows of Russian life, the feeling of contact with the mysteries of the

Q

soul and infinitude of nature — and the petty bargaining over a used woollen sweater or a second-hand pair of shoes — these continue, and they occupy most people's attention, almost to the exclusion of what Party and state leaders plan inside the Kremlin. This is, when one thinks of it, a natural enough state of affairs: surely life could not be lived as described in the prose of *Pravda*.

This, I think, is what explains the non-reaction of most Russians to the news of the invasion of Czechoslovakia on August 21st. It was a manifestation of this country's lack of interest in foreign affairs as a whole. Certainly this was the most dramatic demonstration of it since I've lived here; but the phenomenon itself is repeated daily in the near total obliviousness to the kind of political events that normally interest Europeans. Here, where almost everyone is deeply preoccupied by the routine concerns and triumphs of his daily life, the Cuba crises, Berlin crises, even the China crises, seem to be taking place in another world. They are dimly perceived through a heavy veil of official interpretation; they are remote events and ordinary Russians have scant knowledge of them, can exert no possible influence over them, and therefore, quite logically, feel virtually no interest in them.

Political meetings are held everywhere, of course: the workers of this factory protesting against American aggression in Vietnam; the workers of that plant damning Israeli imperialism in the Middle East. But these are staged on orders from higher authority by the factory Party committees, and every moment of the ritual procedure is planned in advance, according to that day's editorials. The workers themselves are so bored that they often do not bother to inquire about the theme of the meeting. 'It might as well be a protest against the Crusades,' explained an engineer. 'The workers come because they're ordered. They will raise their hands for the unanimous "yes" vote when ordered, or for the *Pravda* photographer. But they're thinking of the half-hour they've had to waste in the battle of the shops and queues on their way home. They simply couldn't care less about foreign affairs.'

This state of mind is a reflection, I believe, of Russia's enduring isolation: the isolation once imposed by vast distances, cruel climate and difficulties of transport, and now by a suspicious, jealous and somewhat xenophobic dictatorship — rulers, that is to say, with a distinct inferiority complex vis-à-vis the West. One is always conscious here of being cut off from the rest of the world, with all the welcome and unwelcome consequences that implies. More than this, however, the lack of interest in foreign affairs is a reflection of the lack of interest in politics of any kind, domestic or foreign. It is difficult to goad most Russians into speculation even about something as crucial to them as who thinks what inside the Politburo and who will replace whom there. And this too is logical enough. The stuff of politics everywhere is controversy, dissent and conflict, and when these elements are removed — together with all information except a ritual 'line' — all interest disappears with it. 'Disappears', however, might not be the correct word, since (except for brief intervals) Russian politics has for centuries lacked the open give-and-take that stimulates popular interest. Political instincts and awareness, therefore, never had an opportunity to develop to anything near the level considered normal and healthy in most parts of Europe.

This is not to say that nothing political affects the Russian people. When Senator Robert Kennedy was shot last spring, there was an immediate and strong concern. People avidly read reports about the event. And this interest, I am assured, was mild compared to the spontaneous outpouring of grief over President John Kennedy's assassination. On that day, according to my friends, all Russia was stunned and horrified, and Moscow was no less grief-stricken than the capitals of Western Europe. But it takes precisely this kind of event, something with which they personally can identify, to move the Russian people.

All the circumstances of life here combine to dull the political senses. Officially, public life in Russia is more saturated with politics than anywhere I've seen; yet private life is the most apolitical. Surely there is a natural law in operation here. In any case, it was entirely characteristic that few Russians were in a position to know, or took the trouble to learn about, the importance of the invasion of Czechoslovakia to the future of that country, to Russia itself, to socialism or world politics.

*　　*　　*

And this too is what makes so many Western textbooks about Russia misleading. The chapters about the dictatorship and its methods of control are more or less accurate — but far less relevant than a Western reader would imagine. The Kremlinology may be perceptive and even clairvoyant, but Russians themselves are far less interested in these things than the Kremlinologists, political scientists and Soviet specialists in Western universities. Political oppression is indeed an ugly fact of life, but only a small part of the whole. Winter's oppression plays a much greater role in daily Russian life than the dictatorship — and Russians have learned to live even with this, although now, as I write, we have already endured an eternity of paralysing cold, and the end is nowhere in sight.

One day, you meet your first professional agitator, and

she turns out to be an extremely attractive blonde girl with a fondness for love with a 'collective' of men. She performs her duties as an agitator because a certain number of volunteers were 'requested' from her office and she, being the last to be hired, was saddled for several weeks with the job. After the encounter with her, the whole system of agitprop can never again seem as repulsive as it did on paper. On another evening, an older woman describes the built-in microphones in the new hotel where she works (the much-advertised Russiya, opposite the Kremlin), and no one at the party that evening is in any way surprised or shocked. The woman describes the elaborate 'bugging' system matter-of-factly, after which we immediately return to our toasting, drinking and dancing. Her information might have been frightening elsewhere; here it is taken for granted. Besides, everyone has long understood he must never say anything sensitive in an Intourist hotel; it has become habit, and therefore not onerous, to unburden oneself only in a secure private place. And when a former K.G.B. agent (who was recently sacked without a pension for drinking) humbly approaches my friends for a small loan, they are generous with him, even though they despise what he represented. For he too was caught up in the system, had his thirst and family to support, and wasn't really to blame. Somehow, perhaps because of everything else in the Russian character and in Russian life, these things are less sinister in context than they would appear in news stories or textbooks. And in any case, they are all part of the environment, which is shaped by ancient forces we are powerless to change. The important thing is to work one's way round them, shut oneself off from them, and bring a bottle of brandy or a bar or two of imported chocolate to that evening's party—where we will eat and talk and dance.

* * *

What does this mean in terms of Russia's future? Neo-Stalinism; the uncomplicated pleasures of daily life and intense human relationships; the pessimism of the intelligentsia which is combined with a deep love for their country; all this, and much of what I see around me here, seems to suggest something simple, yet profound: that Russia remains primarily *Russian*. This is not the place to plunge into the great debate about the extent to which Soviet society is Communist as opposed to Russian: and I have nothing to add to the huge body of literature that, with impeccable reasoning and exhaustive research, has been written to prove both sides of this question.

But during my years here, the country seems to have become more and more Russian, less and less Communist. I cannot defend this impression with creditable academic arguments and evidence. Perhaps it is caused not by changes in the country, but changes in me: the longer I am here, the deeper I am taken into 'real' Russian life—farther and farther from the official surface.

But it does seem to be supported by the broadest changes affecting the Soviet Union. As the trauma produced by the October Revolution and the cataclysms that followed it subsides, Russian society, albeit with a new economic and political system, seems to be settling back into many of the general patterns developed during the ten or twelve centuries of Russian civilization before 1917. And as international Communism breaks down into separate—and sometimes hostile—national parts, this tendency to return to traditional Russian patterns will probably accelerate. The fact is, of course, that the Soviet Union is now in no sense a revolutionary society, but one of the most conservative in the world—about as conservative, give or take a little, as tsarist Russia was.

The Communist Party promised to build a new world, and now announces the metamorphosis is well started, perhaps half complete. (This dream of building a shining new world, free of all despair and darkness, is itself characteristically Russian: the product of the intolerable misery and despair of Russian life.) But the longer I am here, the more often I turn to the classical Russian novelists—for, as I have said, it is they who best describe the important qualities of contemporary Russian people and life. And the more I look at the operation of Soviet government, the more clearly I understand it is primarily the wording that has changed, and not the important qualities of style, attitudes and the relationship of the governing to the governed. Sometimes I despair that the Revolution has changed Russia's inner essence so little. Sometimes I rejoice. More and more I am coming to understand that neither despair nor rejoicing are justified. For it was inevitable that Russia remain Russian. And the generations of Westerners who did not understand this, and who became passionate supporters or foes of the Revolution, were often grappling with illusory issues, far removed from the sober reality of daily Russian life.

APPENDIX 1

Pravda's front page on August 21st, 1968, is entirely representative of the Soviet recipe for news and the daily diet of information. Like every page of every newspaper, it conforms wholly to Lenin's famous dictum, 'A newspaper is not only a collective propagandist and collective agitator, but also a collective organizer.' It is free of outright propaganda, but every sentence is meant less to inform than to instil Communist ideals, love for the Motherland and, above all, gratitude to the Party — infallible because it is guided by Marxist-Leninist teachings — for being the hope of mankind.

Here is a verbatim translation, with several minor abridgements, of page one for August 21st. The Tass announcement, as I have mentioned, was in the left-hand corner. Opposite it, in the most prominent right-hand-corner position, was a somewhat larger photo-story. The photographs — of a crew operating a sophisticated construction machine and a dedicated and optimistic bulldozer-driver on his machine, were described in the extensive captions:

> The scope of construction in our country is unparalleled. The photographs we publish today testify to this once again.
>
> In the Daghestan A.S.S.R., [Autonomous Soviet Socialist Republic] on the Sulak River, the Chirkeiskaya Dam, with a capacity of a million kilowatts, is under construction. Its first generating units will be supplying energy for industry during the current five-year plan.

In the photograph above: assembly of mobile casings for a transport tunnel inside the dam.

In the lands east of the Volga, the fate of the harvest often depends on nature's whims. To overcome them, an irrigation system is being constructed here, which includes a ninety-kilometre canal called the Great Irgiz and the Greater and Lesser Uzeni. Three hundred and sixty thousand hectares of earth will receive life-giving moisture. The clamour of excavators, scrapers and bulldozers carries deep into the steppe. Work on the construction of the canal is being carried out by mechanical columns of the Saratovcanalwatbuild Trust. In their ranks are workers who completed irrigation systems in Kazakhstan and Siberia. In the photograph below: bulldozer-driver Vladimir Shustov. He has been awarded the title, 'Best Skilled Worker at the Construction Site.'

Photo R. Dik (Tass) and Yu. Nabatov.

The extreme left-hand column was devoted to a three-section article under the general headline, 'Preparing for the Leninist Anniversary' — the one hundredth anniversary of Lenin's birth in April, 1970, twenty months from the date of the article.

THE FIRST SUCCESS

Vilnius, 20th. (*Pravda* correspondent A. Rudzinskas.) The Vilnius experimental factory of synthetic materials is one of the Lithuanian capital's youngest enterprises: it is only two and a half years old. The factory's product — linoleum — is in great demand at new construction sites. But has much of this material already been manufactured?

'The conveyor lines have already delivered up a million square metres,' says the factory's director, A. Bertulis. 'Thus the planned volume of production has not only been achieved, but surpassed by ten per cent.'

This difficult achievement is the collective's first success in the competition for a worthy commemoration of the hundredth anniversary of the birth of V. I. Lenin.

The factory continues to expand. At the end of this year, the opening of an experimental automated department is planned. In the first quarter of next year, it is planned to put a granulator into operation.

AN EXHIBITION IN CHARDZHOU

An exhibition entitled 'V. I. Lenin and Technical Progress' opened on August 20th in the Chardzhou Central Municipal Library named after N. K. Krupskaya.

Collections of articles, brochures and magazines about technical progress in the U.S.S.R. and the Leninist plan for the scientific-technical rearming of industry are displayed on the stands. Here too the Leninist words are cited: 'He prevails who has the most advanced technology, organization, discipline, and the best machines.'

Among the literature in Russian and Turkmen, principal attention is devoted to the programme of the C.P.S.U., materials taken from the Twenty-third Congress of the Party, and a collection entitled, 'V. I. Lenin On the Development of Heavy Industry and the Electrification of the Country.' (Tass)

FIFTY HALLS

Lvov, 20th. (Tass) The staff of the Lvov branch of the V. I. Lenin Central Museum is helping collective farms, enterprises and educational institutions of the western regions of the Ukraine to organize Leninist halls and rooms.

In the cities, regional centres and villages of Lvov, and Ternopolsky, Volinsky, Ivano-Frankovsky and Zakarpatsky regions, fifty Leninist halls and Leninist rooms have been opened since the start of preparations for the hundredth anniversary of the birth of the great leader.

The foreign news was printed under the traditional heading, 'The World Today, Foreign Information.' It included a short report, date-lined New York, about demonstrations by Uruguayan workers and students protesting against the abrogation of constitutional guarantees and repressive measures taken against striking workers; and another, date-lined Damascus, about a projected reform of local government in Syria described as resembling the soviet pattern. There was also a longer report from Hanoi on a series of successful offences in South Vietnam by the National Liberation Front, after several weeks of relative lull in the fighting. The N.L.F. was reported to have used heavy artillery and tanks in its attacks, all of which were highly successful: fifty Americans were killed in one battle and at least eighty-five in another. The Americans were said — on the basis of North Vietnamese releases — to have suffered very heavy losses in material as well as men. A supplementary dispatch from Saigon reported successful N.L.F. attacks against thirteen cities and American military bases in the Mekong Delta, together with simultaneous attacks against American bases to the north, south and east of Saigon.

The other first-page foreign news (there were, as is

customary, more items on an inside page) consisted of three articles:

A GLORIOUS DATE

Helsinki, 20th. (Tass) In connection with the forth-coming celebrations on the occasion of the fiftieth anniversary of the Communist Party of Finland, a press conference was held today in the C.C. [Central Committee] of the C.P.F. [Communist Party of Finland.]

The General Secretary of the Party, Ville Pessi, the Chairman, Aarne Saarinen, and Chairman of the Organizational Committee arranging the anniversary celebrations, Anna-Lisa Huvonen, told Finnish and foreign journalists about the forthcoming festivities, which will take place on August 23rd–25th, and answered questions.

In connection with the anniversary, an exhibition devoted to the history of the C.P.F. will open in the Finnish capital's House of Culture. On August 24th, a seminar will start work on the subject 'C.P.F.-Revolution-Youth'. The principal report at the jubilee plenum of the C.C. C.P.F., which is also scheduled for August 24th, will be given by the General Secretary of the Party, Ville Pessi.

As announced at the press conference, representatives of fourteen fraternal parties, among them representatives from the U.S.S.R. and other socialist countries of Europe, have been invited to the anniversary of the C.P.F.

On the occasion of the C.P.F.'s jubilee, a brochure by Antta Huvonen, 'Fifty Years of the Communist Party of Finland', has been published, as well as an anniversary issue of *Communists*, the Party's theoretical magazine.

THEY WILL NOT STOP

Amman, 20th. (Tass) Israeli aggressors yesterday twice violated the cease-fire agreement. At dawn, the little village of Al-Manshia, in the northern part of the Jordan River valley, was subjected to rifle and machine-gun fire, and an artillery barrage. At 6 p.m., fire was again directed against Al-Manshia, as well as the settlement of Khirbet Chekhba. The aggressors were subjected to return fire.

As announced by a representative of the Jordanian military command, the Jordanian forces suffered no losses during the exchange of fire, which lasted ninety minutes. On the Israeli side, a supply depot was set on fire, one vehicle was destroyed, and nine Israeli soldiers killed.

Today the Israeli aggressors resumed their provocation in early morning. At 3.30 a.m. local time, they opened fire in the Beisan valley, and several minutes later in the Jordan River valley. In both cases, Jordanian forces returned their fire.

EARLS COURT AT THE CENTRE OF ATTENTION

London, 20th. (Tass) The Soviet trade-and-industrial exhibition in London is approaching its end; however, the number of visitors is not decreasing, but increasing day by day. Among the thousands of English people entering the exhibition halls of Earls Court, not a few are paying their second and even third visit. The demand for Soviet literature is growing and the auditorium in which films about the life of the Soviet people are shown is constantly full.

As before, the space pavilion is the centre of attention.

Englishmen come here with their entire families and, having settled themselves comfortably on the benches arranged around the pavilion, gaze at length at the many sputniks soaring under the cupola, and form long queues in order to glance into the port-hole of the space-ship of the world's first cosmonaut, Yu. A. Gagarin.

The visitors' book at the display of medical equipment is full of rapturous comments by medical experts. Today, one of its principal exhibits—an artificial lung—was sent to one of the London clinics for demonstration.

V. Hunt observes that he would very much like to have taken Herbert Wells—who could not perceive what Russia's future would be, and did not forsee her perspectives—to the exhibition.

'It takes my breath away when I compare all these achievements with the illiterate, poverty-stricken and famished Russia of 1917,' writes Queenie Knight, one of the exhibition's visitors.

The remainder of the page was devoted to domestic news. There was a brief notice about the opening in Moscow of the Seventh Congress of the World Energy Conference. ' ... The session was opened by the Chairman of the Soviet National Committee of the W.E.C., the U.S.S.R. Minister of Energy and Electrification, P. S. Neporozhny. In the name of the Praesidium of the Supreme Soviet of the U.S.S.R. and the Soviet government, the congress's delegates and guests were greeted by the vice-chairman of the Praesidium of the U.S.S.R. Supreme Soviet, Ya. E. Kalnberzin. I. T. Novikov, Vice-Chairman of the U.S.S.R. Council of Ministers and other U.S.S.R. Ministers are taking part in the work of the congress ... '

And three more articles completed the page:

COMBINE OPERATORS POINT THE WAY

From the Campaign for the Harvest

The left-bank Volga steppe stretched out over hundreds of kilometres. Sixteen of the most important corn-growing districts of Saratovsky region are situated here. At this time, the sounds of the harvest never cease on the boundless steppe.

It was last winter that the Maxim Gorky collective farm of Dergachevsky district inaugurated its campaign for improving the quality of its produce and for growing top-quality corn. Based on the example of Saratov's leading factories, the agricultural experts worked out a system of procedures to eliminate defects in the collective's work.

'The first commandment of every combine operator, every collective farmer,' recounts the Chairman of the collective, N. Melnikov, and the Secretary of the part-com [Party committee], R. Barzhanov, 'has become the maxim: check the quality of your own work yourself, before handing it in to the brigade leader or control supervisor. If you see a defect somewhere — correct it.'

The combine operators correctly evaluated the value of this system; they saw it as an important reserve for increasing the efficiency of their work.

Together with the farm's managers, we tour its fields. Around us are golden ribbons of wheat windrows, unharvested cornfields, ricks of straw. On the steppe road, we met brigade leader Alexander Putienko.

'In our brigade,' he says, 'there are over 3,500 hectares.

Room enough to turn round in. We were the first on the farm to introduce the system of procedures for eliminating defective work. And during the pre-planting cultivation of the fields during the sowing, during the harvesting, we made no mistakes and received no criticism.'

There are no laggard combine operators. Every one over-fulfils his assignment. Leonid Mitrofanov mowed 436 hectares and produced 9,373 hundredweight of corn from his harvesting combine's bunkers. Other operators are also doing excellent work.

The job is being tackled with equal enthusiasm in other brigades. The farm has already fulfilled the state's order, has dispatched 10,000 tons of corn to the Motherland's granaries, and is now selling surplus corn, above the plan figure. For the high quality of its wheat alone, the enterprise will receive more than 300,000 extra roubles this year.

This skilful management and a precise work schedule lead to a highly productive and efficient use of machinery on other farms as well. Dergachevsky district is successfully completing the wheat harvest. Fifty-eight thousand tons of wheat have been poured into the country's granaries, and not less than 260,000 tons will be sold — twice the figure in the plan.

Special attention in the region is being given to the fight against losses. On the region's collective and state farms, all combines, as a general rule, have been hermetically sealed. Other channels for the loss of corn have also been eliminated. Mown corn is gathered at reduced speeds. The tempo of the harvest grows more intense. The stream of maize into the elevators has also been increased. The toilers of the fields are striving not only to fulfil, but to over-fulfil the plan for corn sale. Already more than 2,330 thousand tons of Saratovsky corn have been delivered into state granaries.

I. SHIRSHIN
(Part-time *Pravda* correspondent)
Saratovsky region.

A POWERFUL CONVERTER

Karaganda, 20th. (Part-time *Pravda* correspondent I. Kazantsev) Assembly of a converter with the capacity of two hundred and fifty tons was completed a few days ago at the metallurgical factory in Temir-Tau.

The oxygen-converting complex was the factory's new project for this year. The unit's fitting out was completed in record time.

THE BIRTH OF RELIABLE MACHINES
Reportage

At the Novocherkass electric-locomotive plant, an interesting event has taken place: one of the leading departments has adopted a system of computer-controlled management. This makes possible up-to-date planning and daily control over the progress of production, as well as helping improve the quality of the product. Today we will describe what the department's personnel are doing to improve the reliability of the locomotives.

First a large vibrating platform. The side of an undercarriage, seven metres long, is fastened to it on supports; the mechanism is almost too thick to get one's arms around. One would have supposed the metal giant could hardly be moved at all. Yet it is trembling like an aspen leaf.

What is the purpose of all this? When an electric locomotive is in operation, many of its mechanisms and

R

couplings vibrate. In order to determine whether a locomotive's parts will stand up under these stresses, they are
tested under the same conditions in which they will have
to work in the field.

The side of the massive under-carriage has been
given a specific task: to swing back and forth thirty
million times; if it stands up to this, it goes into production, if not, the design must be changed, or a different
sort of alloy chosen.

We move on to other platforms. At the test point for
electrical machinery, one sees row upon row of panels.
On one of them, twenty-five magnetic switches are in-
stalled.

'We've already switched them on a million times,'
V. Parshin, the test point's supervisor, explains. 'This
is twice the safety margin. Yet we're going on with the
tests. We'd like to know how much these switches can
take.'

Nearby is a laboratory simulating climatic conditions, where insulating structures and electronic machinery are undergoing their tests. The lab operator,
V. Dirin, explains that the temperatures here can vary
from minus sixty to plus one hundred and fifty degrees
centigrade. He opens the thermostat, removes a coil
with new insulation from the oven, and places it in the
cooling chamber, where a Siberian frost is maintained.
Then he approaches the heat-and-humidity chamber.

'And here we have tropical conditions: a temperature
of forty-seven degrees centigrade and humidity of
ninety-six per cent,' explains Dirin, carrying in a heavy
engine manifold from the refrigerated section.

'It was in the cold for three hours, and stood up to it.
Now we'll see what it does under heat.'

Two-thirds of all the equipment of electric locomotives now undergo this kind of testing. This year, two more laboratories are being prepared for service: one for testing the breaking point of auxiliary equipment, another for testing the electrical equipment's resistance to vibration.

The factory went over to the new system of planning and economic incentives at the beginning of the year. The first months demonstrated that the forecasted volume of production has been achieved, as well as the planned nomenclature. Profit has exceeded the figure set in the plan, expenditure of the wages fund is lower than the norm, and productivity of labour in the shops is increasing.

But all possibilities are not yet exhausted. There remain the tasks of improving the regularity of production and the quality of the products, and speeding up the design and development of new locomotive models.

In the second half of the year, the plant will turn out a sample group of new electric locomotives that work on both a.c. and d.c. Next year they will go into mass production.

The vehicles of the next five-year plans are already on the designers' drawing boards.

One is an a.c. traction unit with eight thousand five hundred horsepower. It consists of three sections: electric locomotive, diesel and a self-powered tipping carriage. This unit is designed for use in strip mining, where deep quarries are involved, in the extraction of coal and ore. The locomotive will be supplied from mains. But where local conditions do not permit installation of mains power, the diesel generator unit will go into action.

The work of the thousands of men building electric

locomotives is going forward with great intensity. In the various departments, new methods of improving the reliability of locomotives and of implementing all the new ideas introduced into the life of the enterprise by the economic reform are being worked out.

Almost every day, *Pravda* runs its leading article in special bold print and a special place—the two columns on the extreme left of the front page. It was missing from this issue, but—aside from pointed allusions to the topical issue of Czechoslovakia—the leading article of the day before was typical of the instruction and exhortation printed daily under the two Lenin medals.

THE FRONT OF THE IMPLACABLE STRUGGLE

The present international situation is characterized not only by economic competition between the two diametrically opposed social systems, but also by a sharp intensification of the ideological struggle between capitalism and socialism. The revolutionary, progressive forces of our time have mounted an historic offensive. However, imperialism does not want to give up the field. Having suffered serious shocks and experienced grave reversals in both domestic and foreign policy, reactionary imperialist circles, and above all the imperialists of the U.S.A., are using all and every means possible to retard revolutionary progress.

Together with adventurers in the military sphere, the imperialists are pouring more and more effort into their subversive political and ideological struggle against the socialist countries, the Communist movement and the democratic cause as a whole. As the declaration of the April plenum of the C.C. C.P.S.U. [Central Committee

of the Communist Party of the Soviet Union] empha-
sizes: 'The whole huge apparatus of anti-Communist
propaganda is now concentrated on the goals of weaken-
ing the unity of the socialist countries and the international Communist movement, disuniting the progressive
forces of our time, and attempting to undermine socialist
society from within.'

Bourgeois propaganda is making desperate efforts to
discredit Marxist–Leninist ideology and disparage the
social and political systems of the socialist countries.
In so doing, our ideological enemies count principally
on revisionist and nationalist elements.

At the present moment, the ideological struggle is the
fiercest front of the class war. In ideological matters,
there is not and cannot be peaceful coexistence, just as
there cannot be class peace between the proletariat and
bourgeoisie. The Bratislava Declaration of Communist
and workers' parties of the socialist countries points the
way in this matter. It declares that fidelity to Marxist–
Leninism, the inculcation of the spirit of socialist ideas
and proletarian internationalism among the masses, an
uncompromising struggle against bourgeois ideology
and anti-socialist forces — these are the measures needed
for success in strengthening socialism's position and
defeating the imperialist plots.

The Communist Party of the Soviet Union and other
fraternal Communist and workers' parties understand
their tasks: intensifying vigilance, taking active measures
against every manifestation of bourgeois ideology, exposing its lies and hypocrisy, strengthening the solidarity
and unity of action of the forces of socialism and the
world workers' and national-liberation movement.
Communists well remember V. I. Lenin's instructions:

'Our task is to overcome all resistance on the part of the capitalists; not only military and political but ideological resistance as well, which is the most profound and powerful.'

The apologists of the bourgeois order are willing to cloak themselves in any pseudo-socialist disguises, employ any propagandistic techniques, to bring about socialism's 'erosion', to weaken and undermine it from within and achieve, in the end, the restoration of capitalism in socialist countries. However, it was not for this that the brotherly countries rid themselves of capitalism—not in order to permit a return to the old order of oppression and exploitation. Unwaveringly and for all time, they have tied their fate with socialism and Communism, and will not allow themselves to be pushed from this path.

Recognizing their great responsibility for the future of socialism, the Communist and workers' parties of the socialist countries are building up their forces for a general offensive against bourgeois ideology. They have given notice—and this was confirmed at the Bratislava Conference—that no one will ever be allowed to drive a wedge between the socialist states or undermine the foundations of the socialist system. The fraternal parties consider it their duty to defeat the imperialist schemes at their very inception, and to strengthen the unity of the socialist community and of all revolutionary forces.

The fate of socialism in other countries, and of the common course of socialism and Communism on earth, cannot and never will be a matter of indifference to Marxist–Leninists. Our Party has always considered and now considers it a matter of utmost importance to secure international solidarity of the fraternal socialist countries and Marxist–Leninist parties, and to organize a single political front in the struggle against imperialism.

Long experience, accumulated by our Party and other Marxist–Leninist parties, demonstrates that in a society building socialism and Communism, steady growth of the Communist Party's role as the working class's militant avant-garde is the guiding force of the new society. The fraternal parties will resolutely and decisively counter with their unbreakable solidarity and powerful vigilance any attempt by imperialism, as well as all other anti-Communist forces, to weaken the leading role of the working class and its Communist avant-garde.

Our Party — founded and fostered by V. I. Lenin, deeply faithful to the ideas of Marxism–Leninism — considers its most vital task to be exposing imperialism's inhuman ideology and aggressive plots, and strengthening its ideological endeavours in all fields. The July plenum of the C.C. C.P.S.U. emphasized the need to continue strengthening the unity of Party and people by all possible means, developing and expanding ideological work in all ways, and intensifying the propaganda of Marxism–Leninism's teachings.

On the ideological front, as on all others, strength is on the side of socialism, not imperialism. 'Socialism and the Communist and workers' movement,' said the general secretary of the C.C. C.P.S.U., L. I. Brezhnev, at the national congress of teachers, 'continue to be on the offensive, winning more and more strata of workers from under the influence of bourgeois ideas. Life itself and objective reality are our allies in the ideological struggle. The entire course of world events unmasks imperialism and strengthens trust in the immortal ideas of scientific socialism.'

The balance of forces in the world continues to shift in favour of socialism. And however cleverly capitalism's ideologists try to do their work, that obsolete social system is doomed. The Marxist–Leninist parties, armed with revolutionary theory, are confidently leading the working masses towards new victories in the fight for peace, democracy, national independence and socialism.

APPENDIX 2

There is always one major propaganda campaign in progress in the Soviet Union. Immediately after one anniversary has been celebrated, the apparat switches to the next theme, as if propagandists abhor a vacuum. It is like a series of continual Christmas celebrations for the Russian people, except that they are given not gifts, but exhortations to work harder, produce more, and join 'socialist competitions' for greater efficiency as a worthy way of marking the forthcoming glorious date. Marx's birthday, Engel's birthday, the anniversary of the publication of *Capital*, the anniversary of the founding of the Bolshevik party ... the propagandists can pick their dates at will, to achieve the most effective timing of the campaigns.

The most recent campaign was in honour of the fiftieth anniversary of the October Revolution. It began almost two years before the event, and by October 1966, the *forty-ninth* anniversary of the Revolution, people were so weary of that group of slogans and exhortations that they could barely read a newspaper.

The campaign in progress at the moment is in honour of the hundredth anniversary of Lenin's birth; it was inaugurated about six months ago, and will run with ever-increasing intensity for fifteen more months, until April 1970. It is impossible to describe its proportions; to reproduce the tone of awe and reverence affected each time — be it the hundredth time that afternoon — Lenin's name is pronounced on the radio; or to convey the extent to which Leniniana saturates the press. But the document below may serve to suggest what these campaigns are like, as well as how they come about. It is a resolution of the Central Committee of the Communist Party, adopted on August 9th, just under a fortnight before the invasion of Czechoslovakia. It establishes guide-lines for propaganda and agitation in every Party committee and every public organization of every kind—there are no private organizations in Russia—for the next twenty months.

CONCERNING THE PREPARATIONS FOR THE HUNDREDTH ANNIVERSARY OF THE BIRTH OF VLADIMIR ILYICH LENIN

In April 1970, the Communist Party, Soviet people and the workers of all countries will commemorate the hundredth anniversary of the birth of Vladimir Ilyich Lenin.

All contemporary history is indissolubly linked with the name of Lenin. Lenin brilliantly continued the revolutionary doctrine of Marx and Engels, was the founder of the Communist Party of the Soviet Union, leader of the greatest social revolution and architect of the first socialist state in the world. Lenin's ideas have exerted and continue to exert an extremely profound influence on the entire course of world development.

The name of Vladimir Ilyich Lenin is immortal, as are his ideas and the deeds he accomplished. He devoted his entire life to the noble cause of serving the proletariat, the working masses, and the revolutionary rebuilding of the world. Lenin voiced the aspirations and hopes of the working class and working people, and answered the fundamental questions that life urgently posed. Under Lenin's leadership, our Party led the working class and all working people in the struggle for the overthrow of the exploiting system, for a better life, for socialism.

The most outstanding revolutionary achievements of the twentieth century are linked with Leninism — the Great October Socialist Revolution, which marked the beginning of a new era in the history of mankind; the formation of the world socialist system; and the mighty liberating battles and victories won by the working class and working people under capitalism. The name of Lenin has become a symbol of proletarian revolutions, of socialism and progress, a symbol of the Communist transformation of the world.

In the struggle for the victory of Communism, we continuously derive strength and inspiration from Lenin's ideas. The Communist Party, Soviet people and workers of all countries express feelings of boundless love and respect for Ilyich, and cherish their finest thoughts and aspirations for him.

Lenin has gone down in history as the brilliant theorist of the proletarian revolution and the socialist transformation of society. He organically combined the wisdom of a philosopher with experience of the people's life, a brilliant knowledge of Marxist theory with an understanding of the crucial requirements of the worker's movement. Standing at the frontier between two historical eras, Lenin creatively developed and enriched Marx's doctrine on the basis of new historical experience and a study of the struggle waged by the international working class and the people's national-liberation movement. Leninism is the Marxism of a new historical era, an era of imperialism and proletarian revolutions, of mankind's transition from capitalism to socialism and of the construction of Communist society. Leninism is the eternally living source of revolutionary thought and revolutionary action.

The works of Vladimir Ilyich have further enriched and made concrete all components of Marxism — philosophy, political economy, scientific Communism.

Lenin's teachings on imperialism as the final stage of capitalism, on the new type of Party, on socialist revolution, the dictatorship of the proletariat in its various forms, socialist democracy, the alliance of the working class with the peasantry and all the working people on national and agrarian questions, on ways to construct socialist society — all this Leninist ideological wealth is a reliable weapon for our Party and the world revolutionary liberation movement.

Lenin uncompromisingly defended the positions of dialectical and historical materialism, provided profound philosophical generalizations about the latest scientific discoveries, and enriched social thought with new conclusions that have been brilliantly confirmed in social practice and in the successes of contemporary science. The priceless pages of Lenin's works are still relevant today. Leninism is the theoretical basis for resolving the most complex questions of the revolutionary struggle and the construction of a new society.

Lenin considered theory not as dogma, but as a guide for action. It is precisely in the creative development of Marxism that the enduring, effective force of V. I. Lenin's ideas lies. Lenin's attitude towards theory combined revolutionary creativity and fidelity to the principles of Marxism — the bond of theory with life and revolutionary practice.

Lenin's thinking was always focused on the interests of the workers.

Lenin consistently upheld the purity of Marxism and waged an implacable struggle against revisionist and dogmatic distortions of revolutionary theory. Historical experience has shown that any deviation from the principles of Marxist–Leninist doctrine, from its international essence, and any attempt to substitute bourgeois–liberal or pseudo-revolutionary cant for scientific theory invariably comes into irreconcilable conflict with the historical goals of the international working class and with the fundamental interests of socialism.

The ideas of Marxism–Leninism live and triumph in the mighty transformations accomplished by the Soviet people under the leadership of the Leninist Party. The ideas of Marxism–Leninism live and triumph in the achievements of the peoples of the socialist countries and in the successes of the world Communist movement, the international working class and the forces of national liberation. Revolutionary theory is constantly enriched by the theoretical work of the C.P.S.U. and the fraternal parties, by the collective thought of the world Communist movement.

Lenin has gone down in history as the greatest leader of the proletarian revolution, as the creator and leader of the Bolshevik Party — the vanguard of the working class, a new type of Party, the Party of socialist revolution and the dictatorship of the proletariat, the Party of the construction of socialism and Communism, the highest form of social-political organization. His life and work are inseparable from the struggle of the working class and the Communist Party. He saw clearly that the victory of the socialist revolution and the construction of socialism and Communism were impossible without a revolutionary Marxist Party.

Life has confirmed Lenin's idea that only a party guided by advanced theory, a party capable of ensuring correct political leadership, can play the role of an advanced fighter. Lenin taught the Party, proceeding from actual conditions, to take the initiative boldly, to use flexible and varied tactics and to make use of the various forms and methods of class struggle. The Party and Lenin elaborated a programme of democratic and socialist revolutionary transformations, and politically organized the working class and toiling masses for the assault on autocracy and capitalism. The Great October Socialist Revolution and the world-historic gains of socialism constitute Leninism's greatest strategic and tactical victory.

Lenin revealed the Communist Party's leading role in all its aspects, not only in winning power but also in building socialism and Communism. He defined the Party's great goals and historic mission over a long period. 'In rearing a workers' party,' Vladimir Ilyich pointed out, 'Marxism is rearing a vanguard of the proletariat that is capable of taking power and leading all people to socialism, of directing and organizing a new system and of acting as teacher, guide and leader of all working and exploited people in organizing their societal life without the bourgeoisie and against the bourgeoisie.'

The Communist Party, which unites in its ranks the finest representatives of the working class, peasantry and intelligentsia, acts as the guiding political force of socialist society. In solving the complex new tasks that arise in the course of building Communism, our Party relies on the theory of Marx, Engels and Lenin and the rich experience of the Soviet Union, fraternal socialist countries and world Communist and workers' movement. The Communist Party develops and enriches the substance of Marxism–Leninism, the science of building socialism and Communism. Profound analysis of the objective processes of society's socio-economic and spiritual life and a comprehensive account of the alignment of class forces and of the concrete features of each historical period constitute the fundamental basis of the development of Marxism–Leninism and the elaboration of the Communist Party's domestic and foreign policy.

Lenin attributed immense and decisive importance to the

unity of the Party's views and actions, to the strengthening of conscious discipline and solidarity among its ranks, and to the development of inner-Party democracy and creative activeness among Party members. He developed and refined norms and principles of Party life which have enabled our Party to achieve outstanding successes. The strength and invincibility of our Party lie in solid, deep ties with the working class and all working people, and in constant, critical self-scrutiny.

The documents of the Twenty-Third Congress of the C.P.S.U. indicate the most important requirements of further strengthening Party ranks; developing inner-Party democracy and strengthening Party discipline; raising the primary Party organizations' capacity for militancy; improving the work of selecting, placing and training personnel and checking the execution of Party decisions; and taking a scientific approach to Party work. In carrying out the decisions of the Twenty-Third Congress of the C.P.S.U., Party organizations have substantially intensified their work and increased the activeness of Communists.

Lenin has gone into history as the founder and leader of the world's first socialist state, a state of workers and peasants. Lenin developed the Marxist doctrine of the state and revealed in comprehensive detail the historical significance of the Republic of the soviets — a new type of state, incomparably higher and more democratic than any bourgeois–parliamentary republic. He emphasized that the working people, united by the soviets, can and must administer all affairs of state. In the continuous strengthening of the Soviets and the socialist state, Lenin saw the chief and essential condition that will guarantee full protection of the interests of the working class and of all working people, as well as the transformation of societal life to socialist principles.

Mankind, V. I. Lenin pointed out, cannot advance without moving in the direction of socialism. Socialism is both the fulfilment of the objective requirements of social development and the expression of the interests of the working class and broadest popular masses. Only a socialist organization of society can turn the development of the economy, science and culture to the people's benefit, elevate the working people to free labour and creativity, and provide scope for comprehensive development of human talents and capabilities. Socialism means rapid and uninterrupted progress in all spheres of social life and human activity.

Lenin emphasized that only large-scale industry, founded on the basis of the latest scientific and technical developments, can serve as the material base of socialism. Only highly developed production is capable of easing the labour of workers and peasants and creating an abundance of material benefits. As V. I. Lenin pointed out, the only kind of construction that deserves to be called socialist is one pursued under a large-scale overall plan, while seeking to make co-ordinated use of the values of economic technology and management.

On V. I. Lenin's initiative and under his direct leadership, the GOELRO [State Commission for the Electrification of Russia] plan was elaborated — the first uniform national-economic plan, whose fulfilment was the most important stage in creating the material and technical base of socialist society. The country's industrialization, which was launched with the first five-year plans, represented the Soviet people's gigantic battle for socialism. It created a solid foundation for the development of all branches of the national economy and for a dramatic improvement in the people's well-being, ensured our homeland's defence capability and advanced the country to the frontiers of scientific and technical progress. Half a century of experience with socialism has confirmed the correctness of Lenin's policy of creating large-scale socialist industry.

In order to put an end to the peasantry's age-old backwardness and to create a solid economic foundation for socialism in the countryside, it was necessary to bring about extremely profound socialist transformations in agriculture on the basis of Lenin's co-operative plan. V. I. Lenin frequently said that small farms will never extricate themselves from poverty, and that the foundation for Communism in farming can be ensured only by effecting a vast technical evolution.

The voluntary mass unification of the peasants into collective farms, the liquidation of the kulaks — the last exploiting class — and the organization of state farms signified a radical social change in the life of the peasantry, and led to the creation of modern, large-scale agricultural production which has changed the whole structure of rural life. Collectivization has led the countryside on to the socialist path of development and consolidated the alliance of the working class and the peasantry. Half a century of experience with socialism has confirmed the correctness of the Party's Leninist policy of the socialist transformation of agriculture.

V. I. Lenin said that socialism is the people's living creative activity, when the workers themselves build a new life and, through their own experience, solve the extremely difficult problems of socialist organization. Here lies socialism's real democratic spirit. Socialism elevates millions of workers and peasants to active social-political lives, opens up full opportunities for them to participate in administering society's affairs and provides material and political guarantees of the workers' rights and freedoms.

Improvement and further development of socialist statehood and democracy take place in the course of building

s

Communism. The agencies of people's rule—the soviets—and the public organizations—the soviet trade unions, the Leninist Komsomol, and co-operatives and other organizations—occupy an important place in the life of Soviet society and development of the masses' political and production activeness. Our party considers its task as doing everything possible to further increase the activities and initiative of the soviets and trade unions, Komsomol and other public organizations. The guiding role of the Communist Party as the exponent of the interests of the working class and popular masses is an essential political condition for consolidating and developing socialist democracy.

For the working people, freedom is above all freedom from exploitation, from social, political and national oppression, from backwardness and ignorance. Lenin taught that the question of freedom should be considered only from its concrete—historical standpoint: Freedom to do what? The interests of socialism and of the people demand that the gains of socialist democracy be protected from imperialism's intrigues and from anti-social, anti-socialist elements. Further development of socialist democracy and of freedom of the individual requires instillation in every member of society of uncompromising resistance against all encroachments on the principles and norms of the socialist community.

It is extremely important for strengthening socialism and for the people's welfare that every member of society correctly understand his responsibility for our common cause and his civic duty to the socialist homeland. Freedom is inconceivable unless every member of society has a sense of responsibility to society. Lenin emphasized that it is impossible to live in society, yet be free from it.

The construction of socialism, Vladimir Ilyich pointed out, is impossible without an entire historical span in the masses' cultural development. The October Revolution and Soviet rule created the conditions for the education and conscious constructive creativity of workers and peasants. The cultural revolution in our country gave the Soviet people education and enlightenment and a flowering of science and scholarship; it created a people's intelligentsia, affirmed socialist ideology in all spheres of society's spiritual life and preserved and increased the values of world culture. Inspired by the ideas of the socialist revolution, literature and the arts have become an integral part of the overall proletarian cause and the nation-wide struggle for the victory of Communism. Half a century of experience with socialism has confirmed the correctness of the Party's Leninist policy in the area of cultural development.

Lenin's genius provided a theoretical and practical solution to the nationalities question. V. I. Lenin emphasized the necessity of an alliance among the liberated nations — an alliance based on complete trust and a clear awareness of fraternal unity in the struggle for the victory of socialism and Communism. The consolidation of the indestructible brotherhood of the peoples of the U.S.S.R., the flourishing of the economies and cultures of our Motherland's socialist republics and their solid unity convincingly confirm the correctness of Lenin's doctrine and the Party's policy in resolving the nationalities question and the triumph of the ideas of proletarian internationalism.

The birth of the Soviet Armed Forces and their heroic history are indissolubly linked with the name of V. I. Lenin. To him belongs the historical credit for laying the foundation of the proletarian revolution's military programme and for the defence doctrine of the socialist homeland. Throughout the Soviet state's history, our armed forces have honourably borne their combat banner in struggles against our enemies, defended the freedom and independence of the socialist homeland and saved the peoples of the world from Fascist enslavement. The Soviet people and their armed forces will always remember Lenin's behest — to exercise vigilance and always be on guard against imperialistic intrigues.

The Party and the Soviet people, following Lenin's behests and overcoming immense difficulties and the violent resistance of remnants of the exploiting classes, transformed our country, in an extremely short period, into a mighty socialist power, based on the indissoluble alliance of the working class and the peasantry and on fraternal friendship among all peoples of the U.S.S.R.

The Party upheld the general policy of building socialism in the struggles against Trotskyism, 'left' and right opportunism, national deviationists and other anti-Leninist groups that attempted to push the Party from the correct path indicated by Lenin.

The complete and decisive victory of socialism in the U.S.S.R., and the transition to the construction of Communism, are the real embodiment of Lenin's ideas, the triumph of the Communist Party's policy. Socialism demonstrated to the whole world its great transforming force and its incontestable superiority over capitalism. The Soviet people's victory in the Great Patriotic War [Second World War], the rout of Fascism — the most evil enemy of progress and civilization — convincingly confirmed the Soviet state's invincibility and the multi-racial Soviet people's fidelity to the ideas of Marxism–Leninism.

The results of half a century of Soviet development provide irrefutable evidence of the correctness and pertinence of Marxist–Leninist doctrine and the correctness of the path our people are following under the Communist Party's leadership.

Lenin has gone into history as the acknowledged leader of the world proletariat and the international Communist movement. On the basis of generalizing the experience of three Russian revolutions and the struggle of the international working class, he made an immense contribution to working out the strategy and tactics of the Communist movement. V. I. Lenin fought tirelessly to strengthen the proletariat's unity. He saw in the unity of the working class the most important condition for reaching the desired goal.

Lenin raised high the banner of internationalism, and instilled in Communists and all working people the spirit of international solidarity. 'Capital', Lenin explained, 'is an international force. To defeat it, an international alliance of workers, an international working class fraternity is needed.

'We are opponents of national enmity, national discord and national isolation. We are internationalists.'

The Communist International, created on Lenin's initiative, played a crucial role in rallying revolutionary forces. With characteristic revolutionary passion, V. I. Lenin fought against opportunism, adventurism and nationalism in the international workers' movement and warned Communist Parties of the danger posed by these 'isms' to the future of revolution and socialism.

The course of history fully confirms Lenin's analysis of world development and the characteristics of imperialism's reactionary essence, as well as his evaluation of the Great October Socialist Revolution as the turning point in mankind's development—as the beginning of the world Communist revolution.

Under the militant banner of Marxism–Leninism, the international Communist movement has travelled a truly heroic path—from a handful of revolutionary fighters, to a mighty army uniting tens of millions of Communists in its ranks. The Marxist–Leninist Communist and Workers' Parties, which exist in almost all countries, are marching in the vanguard of the revolutionary movement and are making their contribution to the common store of Marxism–Leninism.

The Communist Parties, working class and working people have achieved outstanding victories in the struggle against imperialism for liberation from capitalist class oppression and for destruction of the disgraceful system of colonial enslavement. The advancement of the international working class and the world socialist system to the centre of the present era, and the successes of the national-liberation revolutions, signify the world-historic victories of Marxism–Leninism. Lenin's prediction has come true. No matter how much the members of the imperialist bourgeoisie rave or how malicious they are, the victory of the new socialist system is irreversible.

Imperialist reaction, in attempting to cope with economic and political upheavals and to escape from the blind alley of insoluble social contradictions, has increasingly embarked on a path of military adventures and provocations. Imperialism threatens to destroy the lives of millions of people and the fruits of civilization and culture. American imperialism, which has posed the chief threat to peace and the security of the peoples, is intensifying its criminal actions in various areas of the world. The forces of reaction are making inroads on the people's independence and freedom. As in the past, the imperialist bourgeoisie is resorting more and more frequently to the methods of Fascist dictatorship. In these conditions, the Leninist call for unification of all revolutionary, progressive forces in the struggle against the imperialist bandit policy and for the cause of democracy, socialism and peace rings out with special force.

In today's world, an extremely sharp struggle is being

waged between two ideologies, socialist and bourgeois — a struggle that reflects the irreconcilability of the class positions of the proletariat and bourgeoisie, of socialism and capitalism. V. I. Lenin emphasized that 'our task is to overcome all capitalist resistance, not only military and political but also ideological resistance, which is the most profound and powerful'. The imperialist bourgeoisie counts principally on nationalist, revisionist and leftist elements, and attempts to weaken class consciousness, weaken the ideological-political unity of the peoples of the socialist countries and disunite the workers.

Neither neutralism nor compromises can or do exist in the struggle against bourgeois ideology: class principles cannot be reconciled; they are victorious in struggle. Unmasking bourgeois ideology is the revolutionary duty of Marxist–Leninists.

Under the banner of Marxism–Leninism, the workers of the entire world have rallied in the struggle against imperialism, against the imperialist policy of military adventures and international provocations and for peace, democracy and socialism and the peoples' national independence and freedom. The doctrine of Marx, Engels and Lenin is omnipotent because it is true.

Lenin has gone into history as an ardent fighter for the freedom and happiness of the working people. He fought selflessly for socialism's victory. 'This is a great cause,' Lenin wrote, 'and one does not regret devoting one's entire life to such a cause.' His whole life was indeed devoted to the cause of the working class and working people, the cause of revolution and of Communism. Ilyich was uncompromising towards enemies, principled in policy and flexible in his approach to concrete problems. An indissoluble bond with the masses, sensitivity to and consideration for the people, modesty, exacting standards towards himself and others—this is the enduring image of our leader and teacher.

Nothing is more lofty and noble than to follow Lenin and to struggle selflessly for the cause to which he devoted his life. The workers, peasants, intelligentsia, the entire multi-national Soviet people are faithful to Leninism; they live, work and triumph with Lenin's name. With politically conscious labour and constructive creativity, the masses demonstrate their fidelity to Leninism and the cause of Communism. All the achievements of Soviet people serve as living embodiment of the grandeur of Vladimir Ilyich Lenin's ideas and thoughts. Throughout its glorious history our Party has followed Lenin's general line of Communist construction. The Party Programme and the decisions of the Twenty-Third C.P.S.U. Congress define our future tasks of creating the material and technical base of Communism, perfecting social relations and educating Soviet people in the spirit of high political consciousness.

V. I. Lenin attributed enormous importance to youth's Communist upbringing and active participation in the revolutionary struggle and the construction of a new society. He emphasized the importance of developing in youth a revolutionary world view, assimilating the extremely rich experience of older generations and knowing how to turn Communism into guidance for practical work. Ilyich said that the vast and noble—but also difficult—task of struggling for socialism falls upon youth. V. I. Lenin wrote that the edifice of socialist society, whose foundation we have laid, will be built with even more ardour by our children. It is to our boys and girls that the ardent Leninist appeal is addressed: 'Intensify your work in this direction, young comrades, in order to begin organizing a bright new life with fresh young strength.'

In embarking on adult life, young people, under the

Party's guidance, travel the road of their fathers, maintain revolutionary traditions and multiply our society's material and spiritual resources. The Communist Party and the Soviet people are proud of the heroic fifty-year history of the Leninist Komsomol and the glorious deeds of our youth, who have demonstrated selfless devotion to the ideas of Communism at all stages of the revolutionary struggle and socialist construction. Under the Party's guidance, the Leninist Komsomol became an important school of public life, political tempering and Communist upbringing for generations of youth.

Under the Party's guidance, the Soviet people have achieved great successes in all phases of Communist construction. With immense enthusiasm, our people are implementing the political, economic and organizational measures worked out by the Twenty-Third Party Congress and Central Committee plenary sessions, designed to increase the effectiveness of social production, raise the material and cultural level of the workers' lives and further strengthen the moral-political unity of Soviet society. Economic development has been characterized by an accelerated rate of industrial production. The agricultural situation is improving. The people's standard of living is increasing. All this inspires the Soviet people to cope successfully with important new tasks.

The Party will continue, firmly and unswervingly, on its Leninist course.

To follow Lenin's course and to fight for Lenin's behests means:

— to do everything necessary for building Communism and, through selfless work, to multiply the material and spiritual resources of the socialist Motherland;

— to create the material and technical base for Communism,

to achieve both steady growth in industrial and agricultural production and an upsurge in the people's living standards and culture, to perfect methods of managing the national economy, to increase the productivity of labour, to fight persistently for accelerating scientific and technical progress and to instil respect for the working man;

— to consolidate further the moral-political unity of the working class, peasantry and people's intelligentsia and brotherhood and friendship among the peoples of our country—the guarantee of all our victories;

— to strengthen the Soviet state, to develop socialist democracy, to enhance the role and responsibility of the soviets and public organizations in all aspects of our life, to draw the working people more and more fully into the practical affairs of administering the state and to educate the new man—the active fighter for Communism;

— to constantly strengthen the ranks of the Communist Party, to keep guard over the unity of Party and people, to live up to the strict Leninist norms of Party and state life, to be high-principled, be efficient in work, to be modest and sensitive, implacable towards anti-social acts and resolutely uncover and eliminate shortcomings.

— to guard the purity of Marxist–Leninist theory, to enrich it creatively in accordance with the concrete historical conditions of social development, and to wage a principled, uncompromising struggle against all manifestations of bourgeois ideology—to demonstrate constant concern for increasing the Soviet Motherland's defence power, to maintain people and army in a state of constant preparedness for repelling the imperialists' aggression and to defend the socialist homeland;

— to sacredly fulfil our international duty, to strengthen international proletarian solidarity in the fight against imperialism and reaction, to do everything possible to support the proletariat's revolutionary struggle, oppose capitalist slavery and oppression and support the national-liberation movement, and to strengthen the might of the socialist system and solidarity of the international Communist and workers' movement.

Our Party, the working class and the Soviet people were the first to embark on the path of socialism and Communism. The Soviet people recognize their lofty historical responsibility and are devoting all their strength to the triumph of the ideas of Marxism–Leninism.

The Central Committee of the C.P.S.U. resolves:

That the Central Committees of Union-republic Communist Parties, the territorial, provincial, city and district Party Committees, the primary Party organizations, the Chief Political Administration of the Soviet army and navy and the politorgans of military units and military institutes shall launch political and organizational work on a broad scale to prepare for the centennial of V. I. Lenin's birth, and regard this work as a cause of the Party and the entire people.

That Party organizations, together with the agencies of the soviets, public organizations and the political bodies of the Soviet army and navy, shall work out concrete plans in preparation for the centennial of V. I. Lenin's birth by republic, territory, province, region, city and district governmental bodies, by individual enterprises, state and collective farms, and by military units and ships.

The C.C. of the C.P.S.U. considers that the best way to observe the hundredth anniversary of V. I. Lenin's birth is to centre attention on implementing the vast plans for economic and cultural construction that face the Soviet people. Efforts should be directed chiefly towards resolving urgent economic, social-political and ideological tasks set forth in the decisions of the Twenty-Third Congress of the C.P.S.U.

The C.C. of the C.P.S.U. notes with satisfaction the initiative of many work forces in industry and transport and on construction projects and collective and state farms; and as an expression of the masses' infinite love for Lenin, and vigour in their struggle to fulfil his behest, socialist competition has developed widely to give a fitting welcome to the great date marking the centennial of the birth of our leader and teacher, and to fulfil successfully the five-year plan for development of the national economy.

Making use of the experience of the preparations for the fiftieth anniversary of the Great October Socialist Revolution, propaganda and mass-political work shall be launched among all sections of the population. The principal content of political work should be a comprehensive demonstration of the struggle by the Party and entire Soviet people to make Lenin's great behests a reality; to provide deep understanding of both the importance of Marxism–Leninism to revolutionary transformations and V. I. Lenin's historic role as a great thinker, revolutionary, founder of the Communist Party and of the world's first workers' and peasants' socialist movement; and to explain the importance of Marxist–Leninist doctrine to the construction of socialism and Communism in the country and to the development and strengthening of the socialist system and the world revolutionary movement.

Political work shall be directed towards educating the Soviet people in a spirit of fidelity to Lenin's precepts and Communist conviction, and of implacable hostility towards capitalism and bourgeois ideology, towards further developing the Soviet people's civic and productive activities, towards instilling patriotism and internationalism, and towards doing everything possible to strengthen our homeland's economic and defence power.

The C.C. of the C.P.S.U. considers that an extremely important task in connection with the preparations for this famous date is creative work in further developing the theory of Marxism–Leninism—our party's mighty ideological weapon in the struggle for the victory of Communism.

The Institute of Marxism–Leninism and the Academy of Social Sciences under the C.C. of the C.P.S.U., the humanities institutes of the U.S.S.R. Academy of Sciences and the social sciences departments of the higher educational institutions shall concentrate their efforts on working out important questions of Marxist–Leninist theory—the economic problems of Communist construction, the development and strengthening of socialist democracy and Communist upbringing—and on theoretical generalization of the processes of the revolutionary liberation movement and of all world development.

Intensive study and propaganda of the ideas of Marx, Engels and Lenin constitute the basis of the Party organizations' ideological work in the Communist indoctrination of working people. In preparing for the centennial of V. I. Lenin's birth, the Party organizations must intensify their work in the Marxist–Leninist education of all Communists and in seeing that the broad masses of Communists and non-Party people devote profound study to revolutionary theory.

The Central Council of Trade Unions shall be instructed to work out measures for the trade unions' participation in the preparations for the centennial of V. I. Lenin's birth— measures designed to develop both the initiative of the broad masses in socialist competitions and the Communist labour movement, raise the productivity of labour and intensify the work of organizing the workers' labour, daily life and recreation.

The Komsomol Central Committee shall be instructed to work out a plan for the Komsomol organizations' activities in connection with the preparations for the centennial of V. I. Lenin's birth, paying special attention to educating Komsomol members and Soviet young people in a spirit of loyalty to Leninism and selfless struggle for the great ideals of the Communist Party. It is the Komsomol's noble task to inculcate in young people the will, readiness and ability to live and struggle in the Leninist way. Youth and the Komsomol organizations will continue to be called upon to carry out Ilyich's precepts — to study, study and study again, to master profoundly and creatively Marxist–Leninist theory and the latest scientific, technical and cultural achievements, and discipline one's will and character in conscious, disciplined labour.

The editors of *Pravda*, *Izvestiya*, *Ekonomicheskaya Gazeta* [*Economic Gazette*], *Selskaya Zhizn* [*Country Life*], *Soyetskaya Rossia* [*Soviet Russia*], *Trud* [*Labour*], *Komsomolskaya Pravda* [*Komsomol Pravda*], and *Krasnaya Zvezda* [*Red Star*], the editors of the magazines *Kommunist*, *Partiinaya Zhizn* [*Party Life*], *Politcheskoye Samoobrazovaniye* [*Political Self-Education*], *Agitator* and of Tass and the editors of national and local newspapers and magazines shall work out plans for the publication of materials devoted to the centennial of V. I. Lenin's birth. Lenin's life and revolutionary activities in many various spheres, the theoretical wealth of Lenin's ideas, and the struggle waged by the C.P.S.U. and entire Communist movement to implement the ideas of Marxism–Leninism must be fully and completely described.

The U.S.S.R. Council of Ministers' State Radio and

Television Committee shall provide for diverse ways of reporting the preparations for the centennial of V. I. Lenin's birth, shall give a vivid and profound portrayal of Ilyich, his life, revolutionary activity and the wealth of his theoretical legacy, and shall narrate the struggles waged by the Party and people to implement Marxist–Leninist ideas.

In connection with the preparations for the Lenin jubilee, the U.S.S.R. Ministry of Culture shall make preparations for competitions to select the best dramatic and musical productions and thematic concert programmes; for holding festivities under Lenin's motto: 'Art Is for the People' in Moscow, Leningrad and the Union-republic capitals; for art festivals in individual cities linked with V. I. Lenin's life and activities, and for the organization of exhibitions of fine art.

The U.S.S.R. Council of Ministers' Cinematography Committee shall arrange that feature and documentary films about V. I. Lenin and films reflecting the creativity of Marxism–Leninism are made, and that the best feature, documentary and popular-science films on V. I. Lenin are widely shown.

It will be recommended to the Boards of the U.S.S.R. Writers' Union, the U.S.S.R. Artists' Union, the U.S.S.R. Composers' Union, the U.S.S.R. Film Workers' Union, the U.S.S.R. Journalists' Union, the Novosti Press Agency and the U.S.S.R. Architects' Union that they work out plans for the participation of these creative unions in the preparations for the centennial of V. I. Lenin's birth.

*   *   *

The Central Committee of the C.P.S.U. calls on workers, collective farmers, the intelligentsia and Soviet soldiers to observe the centennial of Vladimir Ilyich Lenin's birth with new victories in the struggle to implement the plans for Communist construction as outlined by the programme of the C.P.S.U., the decisions of the Twenty-Third Party Congress and the documents adopted in connection with the celebration of the fiftieth anniversary of October.

Our party and our people, tempered in revolutionary battle and in the struggle to build a new society, are filled with unshakable determination to steadfastly fulfil the great behests of their leader and teacher, Vladimir Ilyich Lenin.

We will continue to work and live in the Leninist way, creating a beautiful monument to Vladimir Ilyich — the edifice of Communism, a great and worthy embodiment of his immortal ideas. Let us rally our ranks ever more closely! More tenacity, selflessness, discipline and organization! More creative initiative in all sectors of Communist construction! Raise even higher the revolutionary Marxist–Leninist banner of the struggle for Communism!